MOLIÈRE was the stage name of Jean Baptiste Poquelin, the son of a wealthy merchant upholsterer. He was born in Paris in 1622. At the age of twenty-one he resigned the office at Court purchased for him by his father and threw in his lot with a company of actors to found the so-styled 'Illustre Théâtre'. The nucleus of the company was drawn from one family, the Béjarts. Armande, the youngest daughter, was to become his wife.

Failing to establish themselves in Paris, the company took to the provinces for twelve years. When they returned to the capital it was with Molière as their leader and a number of the farces he had devised as their stock in trade. Invited to perform before Louis XIV, Molière secured the King's staunch patronage. In 1659 *Les Précieuses ridicules* achieved a great success, which was confirmed by *L'École des femmes* three years later. With *Tartuffe*, however, Molière encountered trouble; it outraged contemporary religious opinion and was forbidden public performance for several years. *Don Juan* also had a controversial history. *Le Misanthrope*, first played in 1666, is generally considered to be the peak of Molière's achievement. Among the plays that followed were *l'Avare*, *Le Médecin malgré lui*, *Les Femmes savantes* and *Le Bourgeois Gentilhomme*, one of the comedy-ballets to which Lully contributed the music.

By 1665 the company had become 'la troupe du Roi', playing at the Palais Royal. While taking the part of Argan in *Le Malade imaginaire* on 17 February 1673, Molière was taken ill, and he died the same evening. The troupe survived, however, to become one of the forerunners of the *Comedie-Française*.

JOHN WOOD was born in 1900 and went to Manchester University. After some years in teaching and adult education he spent his working life in educational administration. Enthusiasm for the arts in education led to his involvement with the theatre and particularly, as a producer and translator, with the work of Molière. He also translated Beaumarchais' *The Barber of Seville* and *The Marriage of Figaro* for Penguin Classics.

DAVID COWARD is Emeritus Professor of French and Senior Fellow in the University of Leeds. He has written widely on the literature and culture of France, and has translated tales by Sade and Maupassant, *La Dame aux Camélias* by Dumas *fils* and Albert Cohen's *Belle de Seigneur* (Penguin,

1997), for which he won the Scott-Moncrieff prize for translation. His *History of French Literature: From 'Chanson de Geste' to Cinema* was published in 2002. He is a regular contributor to *The Times Literary Supplement*, the *London Review of Books* and other literary periodicals.

MOLIÈRE

The Miser and Other Plays

The School for Wives
The School for Wives Criticized
Don Juan
The Miser
The Hypochondriac

Translated by JOHN WOOD *and* DAVID COWARD
with an Introduction and Notes by DAVID COWARD

PENGUIN BOOKS

PENGUIN BOOKS

Published by the Penguin Group
Penguin Books Ltd, 80 Strand, London WC2R ORL, England
Penguin Putnam Inc., 375 Hudson Street, New York, New York 10014, USA
Penguin Books Australia Ltd, 250 Camberwell Road, Camberwell, Victoria 3124, Australia
Penguin Books Canada Ltd, 10 Alcorn Avenue, Toronto, Ontario, Canada M4V 3B2
Penguin Books India (P) Ltd, 11 Community Centre, Panchsheel Park, New Delhi – 110 017, India
Penguin Books (NZ) Ltd, Cnr Rosedale and Airborne Roads, Albany, Auckland, New Zealand
Penguin Books (South Africa) (Pty) Ltd, 24 Sturdee Avenue, Rosebank 2196, South Africa

Penguin Books Ltd, Registered Offices: 80 Strand, London WC2R ORL, England

www.penguin.com

Published in Penguin Books 2000
Reprinted 2004
8

Don Juan and *The Miser* translation copyright 1953 by John Woods
The Hypochondriac translation (under the title *The Imaginary Invalid*)
copyright © John Woods, 1959
Introduction and text revisions of the above
copyright © David Coward, 2000
The School for Wives and *The School for Wives Criticized* translation
copyright © David Coward, 2000

Set in 10.5/12 pt Monotype Fournier
Typeset by Rowland Phototypesetting Ltd, Bury St Edmunds, Suffolk
Printed in England by Clays Ltd, St Ives plc

The terms for the amateur or professional performance of these plays
may be obtained from the League of Dramatists, 81 Drayton Gardens,
London SW10 9SD, to whom all applications for permission should be
addressed

CONTENTS

INTRODUCTION

Molière, one of the world's greatest comic playwrights, is a shadowy figure whose physical passage through this life is confirmed by little more than a few receipts and a signature which appears on fifty or so legal documents. No manuscripts of his plays have survived nor is there any extant correspondence. It is said that some time in the nineteenth century a peasant arrived in Paris with a barrowful of Molière's papers which he offered for sale. There were no takers and he was never heard of again. Had there really been such a peasant and such a barrow, there would have been fewer Molières.

For while the Molière of tradition is primarily a public entertainer, scholars and historians, in the absence of firm evidence, have discovered many others lurking in his shadow. Some have suggested that Molière was merely an actor-manager who lent his name to plays written by other hands: Lord Derby, Corneille, even Louis XIV, the Sun-King. He has been identified as the original 'Man in the Iron Mask' who became, by an amazing sequence of events, the forebear of Napoleon. While the eighteenth century thought of him as a comic scourge of men and manners, the Romantics saw a distinctly tragic side to him and played Arnolphe, Alceste and Harpagon as victims of wounded sensibilities. He has been called an embittered satirist, the defender of middle-class values and a champion of the 'golden mean' of moderation in all things. Other admirers, unhappy with Molière simply as a man of sound common sense, have detected in him dark and dangerous philosophical convictions though, since the 1930s, actors and producers have tended to treat him not as a philosopher but as an essentially theatrical animal, a wizard of stagecraft. His comedies have been found to be indebted to literary borrowings so numerous as to turn him into a shameless plagiarist. Even his acute understanding of human psychology has worked against him: the 'great' comedies turn out not to be plays at all but non-dramatic, abstract studies of character unnecessarily complicated by plot and, regrettably, farce.

In his day Molière had many enemies and they did not mince their words. He alienated a section of the Court, the devout party, doctors, the Faculty of Theology, not to mention rival actors and authors, who called him a 'public poisoner', spread slanderous rumours about his private life and tried to silence him. Against them, however, he could count on literary friends like La Fontaine, and Boileau, the arbiter of classical taste, and the protection of Henrietta of England, the Prince de Condé (who let him perform the controversial *Tartuffe* in his house) and, not least, the king. That he survived at all is an indication of his courage, determination and diplomatic adroitness. But it also suggests a steely determination to succeed which seems at odds with the impression of sturdy optimism given by his plays.

Not that the plays have been allowed to speak for themselves, for they have been made to yield hidden meanings. Working on the assumption that Molière did more than draw 'types' and 'characters' from his observation of people and manners, scholars have unearthed specific 'models' and historical 'originals' for Don Juan, Tartuffe and assorted pedants and 'affected ladies'. Or was he an observer of himself? If so, the plays are coded autobiography. Surely the Molière who married a young woman only months before he staged *L'École des femmes* (*The School for Wives*) must inhabit the skin of Arnolphe, who is only prevented from doing the same by a flick of the plot? How close is Argan's hypochondria to his creator's own ill-health? How much of Molière's literary creed is voiced by Dorante in *La Critique de l'École des femmes* (*The School for Wives Criticized*)? How far does *Don Juan* reflect his views on religion?

The few surviving portraits of Molière are unrevealing, and engravings which show him in costume bury him beneath the roles he played. There is evidence to suggest that he was of medium height, heavily round-shouldered and not handsome. Those who knew him best left only rare glimpses of his character. They hint that he was an impatient, ambitious man with expensive tastes, perhaps even something of a domestic tyrant. But they also show him to have been generous and honourable and no bearer of grudges. He was a dutiful son and a good husband. Scarron, the burlesque playwright and novelist, thought him rather 'too serious' for a clown, a view confirmed by La Grange, keeper of the register of Molière's professional activities, who mentions that he was considered rather introspective, even melancholic by disposition. But if Molière seems to fit the classic description of the lugubrious comedian, it is clear that he also possessed considerable personal charm. For while he was far from happy in his relations with women, he earned and kept the loyalty, respect and even affection of the actors he directed.

The historical record is meagre and shows Molière almost exclusively from the outside, in his public and professional life. He was born in Paris in 1622, the first son of Jean Poquelin, a well-to-do tradesman in the rue Saint-Honoré, who in 1631 became one of the suppliers, by royal appointment, of furniture, curtains and carpets to the king's household. His mother died in 1631 and two years later his father remarried. Contact was maintained with his mother's family, however, and his grandfather may have taken the young Jean-Baptiste to see the farces performed by the actors of the Théâtre Italien and the tragedies for which the Hôtel de Bourgogne was famous. He was sent to the Jesuit Collège de Clermont (later the Collège Louis-le-Grand) where his fellow pupils included the sons of the nobility and future free-thinkers like Bernier and Cyrano de Bergerac. Through the father of a school friend, Chapelle, he met the sceptical philosophers Gassendi and La Mothe le Vayer.

In 1637 he became the reversioner of his father's court appointment which, in 1643, he would transfer to his brother, though he remained officially a 'valet de chambre du roi', one of many who held the title. After leaving school, he studied law, possibly at Orléans, but, though he practised for six months, he was not suited to a legal career. He had by then become an honorary member of the Béjart family which was middle class, had literary connections and performed amateur theatricals. In 1642 he informed his father that he proposed to give up law in favour of an acting career, and the following year signed an agreement with Joseph Béjart and his sister Madeleine, to set up a drama company to be called the Illustre Théâtre. While premises were being made ready, they played tragedy at Rouen, where Jean-Baptiste met Pierre and Thomas Corneille.

The new company opened its doors on 1 January 1644 and, helped by a fire which closed the theatre at the Hôtel du Marais, made a promising start. A document dated 28 June of that year reveals that Jean-Baptiste Poquelin had taken the stage-name of 'Molière', which he may have borrowed from any one of thirteen hamlets of that name in France or perhaps from a long-forgotten novelist, Molière d'Essartines. But although the Illustre Théâtre enjoyed the rather distant patronage of Gaston d'Orléans, brother of the late Louis XIII, it was soon in financial trouble and in the summer of 1645 its creditors sent in the bailiffs. Molière was jailed briefly for debt in August and shortly afterwards left for the provinces where the Béjarts followed him.

They joined a company of strolling players, based at Bordeaux, which was financed by the Duke d'Épernon. For the next thirteen years they toured the towns of Languedoc, few of which had fixed theatres, eventually emerging as the best of the dozen companies then performing in the French provinces. Though no strangers to inconvenience and temporary stages made of trestles, they did not live the hand-to-mouth existence of the struggling touring actors described by Scarron in his novel *Le Roman comique* (1657), nor did they have adventures comparable to those imagined by Gautier in *Le Capitaine Fracasse* (1863), which is set in the 1630 and 1640s. They performed in noble houses to the notables of Languedoc and were well rewarded. Nor did they lose touch with developments in Paris: Molière visited the capital at least once, in 1651.

In 1650 the Duke d'Épernon withdrew his support and in 1653 the company acquired a new patron, the dissolute Prince de Conti, who declared Molière to be 'the cleverest actor in France'. By this time, he had emerged as the leader of the group which, in 1655, performed his first play, *L'Étourdi* (*The Blunderer*), at Lyons and, possibly, his second, *Le Dépit amoureux* (*The Lovers' Quarrel*), the following year, by which time Conti had turned religious and disowned them. But their reputation was growing – Madeleine was said to be the best of the touring actresses – and at last they decided they were ready for Paris, where they arrived in 1658.

The Paris stage was at that time dominated by two major companies. The Hôtel de Bourgogne, originally built in 1548 to stage mystery plays, was the home of tragedy, though when faced by competition from Molière its actors responded by adding farce and comedy to their repertoire. After 1670 they reverted to tragedy, and it was in their hands that Racine would score his greatest triumphs. In comparison, the Théâtre du Marais, founded in 1629, had seen better days. Its association with Pierre Corneille in the 1630s and 1640s had made it the rival of the Hôtel de Bourgogne, but in 1660 it was finding difficulty in recruiting and retaining actors and new playwrights. Increasingly it turned to spectacular productions in response to public demand, but closed its doors for good in 1673. A third theatrical presence – if the popular entertainments of the two permanent Paris fairs are discounted – was provided by the Théâtre Italien who performed the improvised farces of the *commedia dell'arte* in Italian.

Between them, they covered a wide range of theatrical forms, from farce to tragedy by way of intricately plotted comedies. The Hôtel de Bourgogne in particular was increasingly associated with the classical taste which was firmly rooted by the time Louis XIV assumed personal rule of his kingdom in 1661. The doctrine, developed by scholars and theorists over more than half a century, required authors in general to be 'plausible', to respect the niceties of the new, more refined social morality, to avoid extravagant and 'unrealistic' characters and situations, and to adapt to a new purity of language. Dramatic authors were further enjoined to obey the rule of the three unities of time, place and action which were designed to end the confusion of wildly proliferating plots. Originality and imagination were not highly regarded, for the route to excellence lay in the imitation of good models. Tragic authors took their subjects from ancient writers; comic playwrights looked to Spanish and Italian sources for their inspiration.

While the dogma of classicism established a set of standards by which literature should be judged, theatre audiences also responded enthusiastically to less formally constrained entertainments. Thus while the classical ideal set its sights on the universal, they welcomed plays which satirized contemporary French manners and topical events. Farce had been superseded in the capital by the sophisticated requirements of preciosity, but it was kept alive by the rumbustious improvisation of the actors of the Théâtre Italien based in Paris. Play-goers were intrigued too by the new interest novelists showed in the analysis of sentiment and took to playwrights who offered a more coherent form of the comedy of character. They warmed to the fashion for spectacle which called for lavish productions involving ingenious sets and a liberal use of stage machinery. To Italian opera, they preferred the home-grown comedy-ballet which added music and dance to plays in the form of free-standing interludes and finales normally unconnected with the characters or plot of the main entertainment. Plays with music and song grew in popularity and in 1669 an Académie d'Opéras was opened, a grand theatre which first staged musical extravaganzas before giving birth in 1673 to French opera. Thus, although classical discipline was in the ascendant, public taste was sufficiently flexible to allow authors considerable freedom for manoeuvre. Molière would seize his opportunities with both hands.

In 1658 he found a new patron in Philippe d'Anjou, the king's only brother, leased a theatre and the ten-strong company opened with a season of tragedy which was judged inferior by the standards set by the actors of the Hôtel de Bourgogne. But in October Molière concluded a royal command performance of Corneille's *Nicomède* with a 'modest entertainment', possibly written by himself, *Le Docteur amoureux* (*The Amorous Doctor*). The king laughed and authorized the company to share the Petit-Bourbon, a theatre then used exclusively by the Italian actors. There Molière persisted with tragedy but varied the repertoire by reviving the farces he had written during his touring days. On 18 November 1659 he staged *Les Précieuses ridicules* (*Such Foolish Affected Ladies*) which brought him acclaim both as an author and as an actor. He was said to have only a modest talent for tragedy, but as the Marquis de Mascarille, in a huge wig crowned with a tiny hat, high-heeled shoes and festooned with ribbons, he enjoyed the first of many personal acting triumphs.

He maintained good relations with his Italian co-tenants and improved his own stage technique by observing the body-language they used when miming to audiences who did not understand Italian. When the theatre he shared with them at the Petit-Bourbon was demolished in 1660, Louis XIV, who continued to be amused by Molière, allowed him to move to the Palais Royal which would serve as his base until his death. As manager of the company, he commissioned tragedies and comedies but also staged plays of his own.

At first he persisted with farce, then tried his hand unsuccessfully at a tragi-comedy in verse, *Don Garcie de Navarre* (1661), before discovering a way of combining farce with the more sophisticated comedy of character and manners which pleased his public. His rising popularity was resented by rival authors who did not hide their feelings, and it brought a venomous reaction from the actors of the Hôtel de Bourgogne who felt threatened by his success. But he also brought protests from the religious zealots with *Sganarelle, ou le Cocu imaginaire* (*Sganarelle, or the Imaginary Cuckold*, 1660) which contained the first of his many attacks on those who claimed to direct consciences but often abused their position for their own ends. The bitterness flared into a 'comic war' in 1663 in the aftermath of *The School for Wives* (1662) which pleased theatre audiences but outraged the moral majority who thought it vulgar, tasteless, badly written and an insult to the 'holy mystery' of marriage. Molière was subjected to abuse that was both professional and personal. He was portrayed as a vulgar showman who puffed his plays shamelessly, licked the boots of aristocratic patrons and packed his first nights with his own supporters. But he was also attacked in his private life. Early in 1662 he married Armande Béjart, Madeleine's sister, who was young enough to be her daughter – and his too, as some said openly.

The furore lasted over a year. Molière, assured of the king's support by the award of a royal pension, fought back with *The School for Wives Criticized* (1663), a witty rebuttal of the writers who had attacked him, and *L'Impromptu de Versailles* (1663), which was his answer to the charges made by rival actors and the attacks made on his private life. But in May 1664, as the din of battle was fading, he staged for the king at Versailles three acts of a new play 'written against the hypocrites', which the zealots immediately denounced as an attack on religion. Though Louis XIV did not take this view, powerful influences ensured that *Tartuffe* was banned. Leading the opposition was the Compagnie du Saint Sacrement, a charitable if sinister organization set up in 1627 for the relief of the poor and the promotion of strict religious observance. It used methods so inquisitorial (errant sons were denounced to their families and hardened sinners publicly shamed) that in 1660 Colbert had effectively outlawed it. The effect was to make its operations more secret than ever; backed by persons as important as the Queen Mother and the Prince de Conti, Molière's former patron, it was a force to be reckoned with. Molière was engulfed in a new and much more dangerous controversy, for the penalties for convicted blasphemers were severe: one pamphlet called for him to be burned at the stake. *Tartuffe* was banned, and, although he read and staged it in private houses and a toned-down version entitled *L'Imposteur* was given one performance in 1667, the affair grumbled on until 1669 when the play as we know it was finally staged.

Meanwhile, Molière's company continued to perform comedies and tragedies by other hands, though his own plays formed the basis of its repertoire. In 1665 his spectacular version of the life and death of Don Juan who defies God, was well received but it was withdrawn after its initial run, the victim not of an official ban but of the discreet pressure of the zealots. Molière was reassured, however, when, in August, the king himself became the patron of the company which was henceforth known as 'la Troupe du Roi'. A month later, *L'Amour médecin* (*Love's the Best Doctor*), a comedy with ballet and music by Lully, delighted the public with the first of Molière's assaults on the doctors. He offended them further by returning to them in 1666 with a farce, *Le Médecin malgré lui* (*The Doctor Despite Himself*). By then, he had considerable experience of the medical profession. His first child (like the two that would follow) had died in infancy and he himself had been kept off the stage for several weeks at the end of 1666 with a neglected chill which was followed by severe complications. He started to cough, lost weight and by 1667, when he was too ill to appear for two months, he had become, as one contemporary observed, 'a walking skeleton'.

Although he carried a heavy responsibility as author, actor and manager of a company which depended on his talents and management skills, he now entered his most productive period. He maintained his output of farces which proved popular with audiences, and he continued his partnership with Lully who composed the music for a number of his comedy-ballets which were as popular at Court as they were with his Paris public. In 1668 he added *L'Avare* (*The Miser*) to the great comedies of obsession which had begun with *The School for Wives*, *Tartuffe* and *The Misanthrope* (1666).

But as he turned fifty he was dealt a series of body blows. In 1672 Madeleine Béjart died, he lost his third child and the king transferred his favour to Lully who acquired the monopoly of musical plays. Undaunted, he staged *Le Malade imaginaire* (*The Hypochondriac*) on 12 February 1673, casting himself as Argan. The glittering first night audience cheered and the play looked set for success. But the effort had drained Molière, who, towards the end of the fourth performance on 17 February, coughed blood, though he remained on stage until the final curtain. La Grange's register records what happened next:

After the play, towards 10 o'clock in the evening, Monsieur de Molière died in his house in the rue de Richelieu, having acted the role of the Hypochondriac while suffering considerably from a cold and an inflammation of the chest which caused him to cough so rackingly that in straining to clear his lungs he burst a vein in his body and did not live above half or three quarters of an hour.

Although Molière had asked for a priest, he died unconfessed and,

as an actor, was at first refused a Christian burial. The Archbishop of
Paris relented, however, and allowed the body to be interred in the
cemetery of his parish, but without ceremony and not during the hours
of daylight. His friends and admirers wrote many tributes. His many
enemies rejoiced. The Palais Royal gave no performances on the following Sunday and Tuesday but opened again on Friday 24 February, with
The Misanthrope. The show went on as, doubtless, Molière would have
wanted.

In the fourteen years since arriving in Paris, Molière had staged over a
hundred plays. Of these, he had written and directed twenty-nine and
also acted in twenty-four. He began with what he knew best, farce,
which had been the mainstay of his provincial successes. He never
abandoned its broad strokes and was not afraid of vulgarity. But for the
more discriminating Paris public he rang some sophisticated changes
on the staple techniques and themes.

In 1659 audiences were accustomed to two quite distinct types of
comedy: farce, unsubtle and often physical, with its traditional comic
valets, pedants and boastful soldiers, and the comedy of intrigue with
its over-complicated, sometimes incomprehensible plots involving disguises, intercepted letters, pirates and magic spells. The first was largely
a French tradition, though the Italian actors had popularized new types,
like the Harlequin, while the second drew heavily on Spanish and Italian
models. During the 1650s farce had disappeared from the Paris stage,
but authors who wished to amuse now began importing it into plays
which, for example, might attach a comic valet to a marquis who had
embarked on an *amour*. The result was usually a poor fit, with the already
wandering plots being unhinged at any moment by an unconnected piece
of burlesque business. Molière would bring these disparate comic strands
together in plays which drew their unity from a more consistent concern
with human behaviour. In his hands, familiar stage types become three-
dimensional: comic valets accumulate other functions, pedants are linked
to wider social and human foibles, tetchy fathers acquire a new depth
of character and young lovers express humane and civilizing values.

Of course, Molière worked within a specific theatrical tradition and,
as an experienced actor, had a memory filled with stock jokes and
audience-proof stratagems. He recycled familiar ploys and stole old
comic routines, like the 'Without a dowry!' which conveys the depth

of his Miser's stinginess. He repeated plots, situations and characters from play to play – the father who wishes to give his daughter to a son-in-law who shares his obsession, the valet or maid who conspire against their master, the stagy denouements which restore sanity – because they worked well in theatrical terms. But even his broadest comedy is always used for a purpose: to highlight the folly of his monomaniacs or to show some social failing in an absurd light.

Like his contemporaries he borrowed liberally from a common pool of sources which were mainly French for farce, and Spanish and Italian for comedy of situation, character and manners. But from the start he also drew on his own observation. *Les Précieuses ridicules* is a social comedy which owed less to tradition than to his knowledge of people and their ways. While he remained loyal to farce and continued to recycle theatrical conventions in his plots, the ratio of borrowing to his own experience increases in favour of the latter. He may have taken up the story of Don Juan because the subject was fashionable. He almost certainly found the subject of avarice in Plautus. But his Don Juan is a much more ambiguous character than any of his predecessors, just as Harpagon has a personal and social dimension lacking in previous misers. Molière may have taken hints and ideas from other writers, but his 'high' comedies – *Tartuffe*, *The Misanthrope*, *The Miser*, *The Would-Be Gentleman*, *Those Learned Ladies* and *The Hypochondriac* – are highly original creations. No two of his *bourgeois* are the same for, although they may be types, they are vividly individualized. There is more to Arnolphe, who is capable of friendship and honourable behaviour, than his blind spot about marriage. Harpagon is not just a tightwad but a man of business highly conscious of his social status, who is torn between his money-box and the regrettable expense to which keeping up appearances commits him. We sense that behind Argan's hypochondria he is a not unkindly man who can no longer tell who among his entourage are honest. This depth of characterization prevents Molière's gallery of eccentrics from being caricatures and raises them to the level of enduring types which audiences still recognize.

As much may be said for his social satire which is expressed through characters whose actions contradict what they say. Béline's mercenary streak ultimately breaks through her show of wifely virtue. Harpagon cannot sustain his hopes of acquiring an image as a respectable man of business when he is forced to choose between his social ambitions and his money. The same technique is used against philosophers who lose their tempers, poets who trade insults like common lackeys and ladies who pride themselves on their taste and discernment but misread people and situations. It is by drawing these self-incriminating characters of *précieuses*, prudes, zealots, philosophers, doctors, lawyers and well-to-do obsessives that Molière attacks what they represent: preciosity, prudery, zealousness, intellectual pretension, professional dishonesty and obsession. Their discomfiture derives from the mismatch between self-image and reality, and it is through the oldest of comic traditions that Molière shows them to be what they are: when their mask falls, Tartuffe and Béline, Arnolphe and the doctors, poets and *précieuses* stand before us to be judged.

And clearly Molière, who several times stated his belief that theatre has a moral vocation, expected audiences to judge them and learn from their example. Exactly what he wanted his public to learn, however, has been the subject of much debate. There is least disagreement about his social attitudes which are quite clear: he reworked the old jibes about the ignorance and self-interest of doctors and lawyers, the knavery of money-lenders like Harpagon and snobbery in general, not only among the middle classes but among upper-class women and fashionable marquises who were uncritical followers of every passing fad. His literary views also seem clear. While the aim of comedy is to correct manners, the greatest rule of all is to amuse and entertain – even if this meant on occasions courting vulgarity and straying from the path of 'regularity' which the theorists had clearly signposted. But his own ethical values are much less clear-cut.

At first sight, the 'raisonneur', usually a middle-aged man, from Cléante of *Tartuffe* onward, seems to put a comprehensive case for moderation and 'le juste milieu'. It is a stance reflected in less rational and more instinctive terms by valets, maids and sometimes wives, who openly mock bourgeois pretension and the follies of monomania. Yet Molière's plots cannot be said to underwrite traditional morality in its entirety, for they require domestics to cheek their masters, and children to defy their parents. They draw attention to the way girls are brought up, for Agnès, who is kept in ignorance, is no better prepared for adulthood than the *précieuses* who are over-educated. Nor is there any support for marriages arranged by parents, for they are regularly overturned in favour of sentiment. Rather than articulating some mathematically balanced 'golden mean', Molière's plays promote an elastic notion of 'natural' behaviour: tolerance, awareness of other people, spontaneity and the rights of exuberant youth. Molière makes no objection in principle to the social structures and moral assumptions of his society, but rather shows that without love they are oppressive. When imposed without regard to human freedoms, marriage, paternal authority and the hierarchy of established values are empty of human warmth.

Similar reservations must be made about Molière's repeated assault on preciosity, a cultural fashion which was hardly new in 1659. Between 1620 and 1640, what was first known as 'honnêteté' had sought to raise the tone of literature by insisting on only the noblest sentiments, defining love as swoon and anguish, and making a virtue of outlandish similes, metaphors and allegory. By the 1650s, when the precious taste for bizarre emotion and contorted language had become decadent and grotesque, its over-refinement had become a butt for satirists. Throughout his career, Molière repeated jokes which were not only familiar to audiences but even amused the new generation of *précieuses* who laughed at Magdelon, Cathos and Mascarille who were as anachronistic as Climène and the Marquis in *The School for Wives Criticized*, and they were still laughing at the foolish antics of Philaminte and Trissotin in *Les Femmes savantes* (*Those Learned Ladies*, 1672), a year before his death.

But while Molière mocked the excesses of preciosity, he was not unsympathetic to its call for the improvement of literature and manners. When he allows his young lovers to express their feelings, he puts undeniably precious terms into their mouths. Nor was he at odds with the misgivings expressed by the *précieuses* about female education and the marriage of convenience. Where he parted company with them, however, was in their wish not simply to change literature but to coerce manners. They were all too easily offended and they actively campaigned against what they affectedly regarded as the vulgarity of theatre, poetry, even of certain words, and to physical love preferred platonic relationships and the union of souls. Molière's target is not their call for the refinement of manners and language as such, but the sour chastity of the prudes, which is as much outside 'nature' as Béline's hypocrisy, Harpagon's avarice or Argan's hypochondria. Just as it is unnatural for children to be made the victims of their fathers, so it is natural that daughters should wish to marry young men not greybeards. Molière's learned ladies are wrong to despise their home-making role in exactly the same way that Alceste, the misanthropist, errs in rejecting all society: it is natural for people to be sociable. Against them, women like Elmire of *Tartuffe* or Henriette of *Those Learned Ladies* stand out. They are intelligent, unimpressed by fashion and modestly self-assertive. What they want is sane and reasonable, and they know how to set about getting it without offending others, endangering families or making the world march in step with them.

But most controversial of all is Molière's attitude to religion. In his lifetime, he was called an enemy of the Church and an atheist. The eighteenth century regarded him as an early kind of anticlerical deist rooting moral values in the belief in a creator-god who was neither catholic nor protestant. Since he had some acquaintance with sceptics like Gassendi, some modern scholars have further suggested that he was sympathetic to the current of free-thought, that intellectual *libertinage* which attempted to reconcile a spirit of rational inquiry with Catholicism. His plays reveal that, while he was not a bookish man, he was aware of the scientific and intellectual debate going on around him. He understood the principles of Descartes's solution to the problem of base and sublime matter, followed the debate about the use of antimony as an emetic and was convinced by Harvey's revolutionary thesis of the circulation of the blood. True, his most enigmatic play, *Don Juan*, features a master who believes in nothing except that two and two make four and a servant who is incapable of defending religion. Yet there is nothing to suggest that Molière shared the atheism of his hero. Don Juan, though he has certain admirable traits – not least, his heroic courage in defying the Statue – is portrayed as a hypocrite who behaves callously to his father, Dona Elvira and everyone he encounters, irrespective of social standing. In this he is no different from Tartuffe who hides behind a façade of religious zeal as a way of serving his own interests.

The modern consensus is that while Molière had little objection to religion in principle (his three children were christened, and on his death-bed he called for a priest), he was probably sceptical in his own beliefs. But in matters of faith, he was as opposed to extremism as he was to any other kind of private or public excess. Indeed, Molière is very even-handed in his approach to religion. He is no more in favour of the laxity of the Jesuits which gave encouragement to Tartuffian directors of conscience, than to the puritanism of the Jansenists which led to intolerance and persecution. Nor does he promote atheism which leads Don Juan to deny all human values. But while Molière invites us to laugh at the gullibility of Orgon in *Tartuffe* or the foolishness of his pedants and learned ladies who talk reason, molecules and 'falling worlds', his message is at times uncompromising. If Don Juan and Tartuffe are stopped in their tracks, it is by means of stagy denouements contrived to please the public, and he leaves us with the uneasy feeling that in real life they would succeed. But whether he is humbling the predators or mocking their prey, Molière never openly attacks religion itself. His targets are the 'impostors' who exploit those foolish enough to be duped by them. Molière attacks the singers, not the song.

He never broke faith with the time-honoured purpose of comedy, which is to correct manners. He had no wish to reform institutional structures in any recognizable modern sense, but aimed at puncturing the pretension and dishonesty of the society in which he lived. His stage is crowded with zealots who do not believe in God, doctors who have a blinkered faith in medicine, lawyers who bend the law, critics who cannot tell good from bad, pedants who use science to acquire honour and reputation, and self-satisfied women whose professed love of litera-ture and ideas is no more than a cover for their endless snobbery. Molière was a moral rather than a philosophical writer, though his morality is not the sum of the exhortations of his raisonneurs to follow custom, discipline desire, and practise honesty because it is not only the best policy but also the safest. His target is rather the generalized mendacity of a society based on hypocrisy, that 'privileged vice' as Don Juan calls it. He challenges intimidation and artifice and encourages us to think clearly, so that we may tell truth from falsehood, honesty from narcissism, self-respect from self-regard, in a word to recognize egoism in others and avoid the promptings of our own baser natures.

He was not, however, a closet pessimist secretly convinced of the vanity of life and the shabbiness of all human endeavour. Had he been so inclined, he would have written tragedies. He judged people and manners sternly, but his plays express his amusement at the follies he castigates. As a moralist, he chose to laugh, and he ensured that audiences laughed with him. In any case, reading moral lessons could not be the principal concern of an actor-manager with a theatre to fill. At a time when thirty performances meant success and playhouses were rowdy, even dangerous places, he could not afford to lecture his public. Nor could he ignore changing tastes. He never forgot that farce was the great laughter-maker, but he civilized it, building it into situations which highlighted personal and social folly. But he was prepared to experiment and did not allow himself to be governed by the rules of classical theatre which are ignored or bent in at least half his plays. He tried out new genres, staging his first comedy-ballet, *Les Fâcheux* (*The Impertinents*), in 1661. He attempted the fashionable 'spectacle play' with *Don Juan*, and 'tragi-comedy and ballet' with *Psyché* (1671). In *Le Bourgeois Gentilhomme* (*The Would-Be Gentleman*, 1670) and *Le Malade imaginaire* (*The Hypochondriac*, 1673) he turned the ballets and interludes into an extension of the plot, devising absurd ceremonies which are comments on the obsessions of Monsieur Jourdain and Argan. Molière blended the various strands of traditional comedy – farce, spectacle, manners, character and situation – into a new kind of integrated comedy of observation. At its heart lies the individualized type, never simple, always three-dimensional, and invariably lightened by an injection of an older, more physical style of comedy: the cuckold as a figure of fun, the misunderstanding which sets characters at cross-purposes, or the carefully orchestrated plan which backfires. He allows Sganarelle to worry about his wages and Argan to speak incessantly of his bodily functions. Farce persists even in his choice of names – lawyer Bonnefoi, who is patently lacking in good faith, or Monsieur Purgon, the doctor, who is always ready to perform an enema.

During his lifetime the public preferred the farces to the 'great' comedies of monomania which are now most admired. Then, his most performed plays were not *The Misanthrope* or *Those Learned Ladies* but *Sganarelle* (1660) and *L'École des maris* (*The School for Husbands*, 1661), which were essentially farces, and his comedy-ballet *Les Fâcheux*. Changing tastes have long since altered the line-up, and the plays which have worn best are those which, behind the fun, raise questions about human nature and the permanent absurdities of social living. If Tartuffe and Harpagon still wear the face of hypocrisy and avarice, the targets of Molière's satire remain familiar. Preciosity still exists as intellectual snobbery, his zealots represent the perennial forces of intolerance, and his doctors and pedants continue to be useful reminders of the limitations of experts.

By giving his archetypes a distinctive personality and by focusing on issues which never lose their topicality, Molière escaped the limitations of the age he lived in. He has travelled effortlessly through space and time. While he was still alive he was performed in England, Holland and Germany, and his plays immediately struck sympathetic chords with spectators unacquainted with the specific social culture of France. Since then they have continued to hold their universal appeal. They are best taken at speed and they rarely leave audiences indifferent. For if Molière the actor wrote fire-proof roles for actors, Molière the director left plenty of space around the dialogue for producers to add stage business of their own. Three and a half centuries on, Molière, the observer of people and manners, remains a magician of the theatre.

CHRONOLOGY

1622   15 January: baptism in the church of Saint-Eustache in Paris of Jean, first of the six children of Jean Poquelin, a well-to-do tradesman, and Marie Cressé. In 1624 a second son, who would die in infancy, is given the same name and the first Jean is known thereafter as Jean-Baptiste.

1631   Jean Poquelin purchases his brother's court appointment as 'tapissier ordinaire de la maison du roi', which meant that he supplied furniture to the Royal Household.

1632   Death of Marie Cressé.

1633   Jean Poquelin remarries.

1636–41   Jean-Baptiste is sent to the Jesuit Collège de Clermont. In 1637 he becomes the reversioner of his father's court appointment. After leaving school he studies law, possibly at Orléans, and is admitted to the Bar in 1641. He practises for six months, and draws close to the Béjart family.

1642   Informs his father that he intends to make a career as an actor.

1643   6 January: transfers his court appointment to his brother.

February: birth of Armande Béjart, sister of Madeleine (b. 1618).

30 June: Jean-Baptiste signs an agreement with Madeleine and her brother Joseph Béjart and nine actors to create a stage company to be known as the Illustre Théâtre.

1644   1 January: the new company, with Gaston d'Orléans as patron, opens its doors and performs mainly tragedy to a mixed reception.

28 June: first recorded signature of Jean-Baptiste Poquelin as 'Molière'.

1645   2 August: the company having been dunned for debt, Molière is briefly jailed.

Autumn: Molière leaves for the provinces where he is joined by the Béjarts. They enter the touring company of actors supported by the Duke d'Épernon and for the next thirteen years tour the south of France.

1650   The Duke d'Épernon ceases to be their patron.

1653   The company is now 'the troupe of His Grace the Prince de Conti'.

1655   Summer: at Lyons, *L'Etourdi* (*The Blunderer*) is the first of Molière's plays to be staged. The Prince de Conti turns to religion and ceases to be his patron.

1656   *Le Dépit amoureux* (*The Lovers' Quarrel*) performed.

1657   Now regarded as the best of the dozen provincial touring companies, Molière and his actors decide to try their fortunes in Paris.

1658   24 October: the company follow a performance of Corneille's tragedy *Nicomède* in the presence of Louis XIV with a farce, *Le Docteur amoureux* (*The Amorous Doctor*) which amuses the king. Molière finds a patron in Philippe d'Anjou who, as the king's younger brother, is known as 'Monsieur'.

        2 November: the 'troupe de Monsieur' receives royal permission to share the theatre of the Petit-Bourbon with the Italian actors. Unable to compete in tragedy with the Hôtel de Bourgogne, Molière stages comedy and farce.

1659   Some of Molière's actors are lured to other troupes and are replaced. He recruits La Grange who, in addition to playing major roles, also keeps an invaluable register of the company's activities.

        18 November: *Les Précieuses ridicules* (*Such Foolish Affected Ladies*) brings Molière success as actor and author.

1660   On the death of his brother, Molière resumes his court appointment. He prosecutes Ribou for publishing *Les Précieuses ridicules* without his consent.

        May: *Sganarelle, ou le Cocu imaginaire* (*Sganarelle, or the Imaginary Cuckold*), a farce.

        October: when the Petit-Bourbon is demolished Louis XIV authorizes the company to move to the Palais Royal.

1661   February: failure of *Don Garcie de Navarre*, a tragi-comedy.

        24 June: *L'École des maris* (*The School for Husbands*), the most frequently performed of Molière's plays during his lifetime.

        August: *Les Fâcheux* (*The Impertinents*), first of the comedy-ballets.

1662   23 January: marries Armande Béjart.

26 December: *L'École des femmes* (*The School for Wives*) which has thirty-one consecutive performances but provokes a controversy that will last for more than a year.

1663   Easter: Molière is awarded a royal pension 'for the fineness of his wit and his excellence as a comic author'.

1 June: *La Critique de l'École des femmes* (*The School for Wives Criticized*).

18 or 19 October: *L'Impromptu de Versailles*.

1664   January: *Le Mariage forcé* (*The Forced Marriage*), a farce with ballet and music by Lully.

19 January: birth of first son, Louis, who dies the following autumn.

May: summoned to provide entertainment at Versailles, Molière stages a comedy-ballet, *La Princesse d'Élide*.

12 May: for the king, Molière performs three acts of a play written 'against the hypocrites': it marks the beginning of the Tartuffe affair which lasts until 1669. The Compagnie du Saint Sacrement uses its influence to have it banned.

1665   15 February: *Don Juan*, with Molière as Sganarelle and La Grange in the title role, is a triumph. But after an initial run, it was never staged again in Molière's lifetime as the result not of a formal ban but of discreet pressures.

4 August: birth of Esprit-Madeleine.

14 August: Louis XIV awards Molière a pension of 6000 livres and becomes the company's new patron.

15 September: *L'Amour médecin* (*Love's the Best Doctor*), first of the farces written against doctors.

1666   4 June: *Le Misanthrope*, twenty-one performances.

6 August: *Le Médecin malgré lui* (*The Doctor Despite Himself*), twenty-six performances. Publication of the first collection of Molière's theatre. His plays are already translated and performed abroad. Continues to be unhappy in his married life. His health begins to suffer. He is unable to appear on stage at the end of the year, and again for two months in 1667.

1667   January–March: as part of the Ballet des Muses, a court entertainment, Molière performs *Mélicerte*, a 'heroic pastoral comedy', and *Le Sicilien*.

5 August: believing he has royal authorization, he performs *L'Imposteur*, a revised version of his play 'against the hypocrites'. It is closed after one performance and, though he writes further in its defence, it is not restaged.

1668   13 January: *Amphitryon*.

18 July: *Georges Dandin*, which is not a success.

9 September: *L'Avare* (*The Miser*), which has a short run. Thereafter, Molière will write no more five-act plays for three years.

Relations with Armande are strained. He rescues his father whose business is in difficulty. His health does not improve and there are rumours that he is dead.

1669   5 February: *Tartuffe* begins a successful run of twenty-eight performances.

25 February: death of Jean Poquelin.

6 October: *Monsieur de Pourceaugnac*, a comedy-ballet with music by Lully, is a triumph.

1670   30 January: *Les Amants magnifiques* (*The Sumptuous Lovers*), a comedy with music and ballet, is staged at Saint-Germain for Louis XIV, who dances in public for the last time.

June: Henrietta of England, on a diplomatic visit to London, sees Molière performed in English.

14 October: exploiting the vogue for 'turqueries' prompted by the visit of Soliman Mustapha in 1669, Molière stages *Le Bourgeois Gentilhomme* (*The Would-Be Gentleman*) with great success.

1671   17 January *Psyché*, a spectacular comedy-ballet, in part written by Corneille.

24 May: *Les Fourberies de Scapin* (*That Scoundrel Scapin*).

2 December: *La Comtesse d'Escarbagnas*.

1672   17 February: death of Madeleine Béjart.

11 March: *Les Femmes savantes* (*Those Learned Ladies*).

Molière quarrels with Lully who persuades the king to grant him the monopoly of entertainments involving music and dance.

15 September: birth of Jean-Baptiste-Armand, who dies aged eleven days.

1673   10 February: *Le Malade imaginaire* (*The Hypochondriac*).

17 February: Molière is taken ill on stage and dies a few hours later.

21 February: he is buried at night in his parish cemetery of Saint-Joseph.

Lully acquires the Palais Royal as the home of French opera and Armande relocates the company in the rue Guénégaud.

1680   Louis XIV merges Molière's former company with the Hôtel de Bourgogne and creates the Comédie Française.

1792   During the Revolution the presumed remains of Molière are removed to the convent of the Petits-Augustins and thence in 1817 to the Père Lachaise.

BIBLIOGRAPHY

Of the currently available standard Works of Molière, the *Oeuvres* (1971) edited by Georges Couton for the Pléiade series is the most readily accessible. Helpfully annotated editions of individual plays have been published in a number of French series (Les Classiques Hachette, Les Petits Classiques Bordas, Les Classiques Larousse, etc.). English editions include *L'Avare*, edited by R. A. Wilson (London, 1949) and by P. J. Yarrow (London, 1959), *L'École des Femmes and la Critique de l'École des Femmes*, edited by W. D. Howarth (Oxford, 1963) and *Don Juan*, also edited by W. D. Howarth (Oxford, 1957).

The fullest survey of the literature of the period is Antoine Adam's *Histoire de la littérature française au XVIIe siècle* (5 vols., Paris, 1956); abridged as *Grandeur and Illusion: French Literature and Society, 1600–1715* (Harmondsworth, 1974). In English, H. Carrington Lancaster's *History of French Dramatic Literature in the Seventeenth Century* (9 vols., Baltimore, 1929–42) may still be consulted but more accessible overviews are provided by Martin Turnell, *The Classical Moment* (London, 1947), W. G. Moore, *The Classical Theatre of France* (Oxford, 1971), John Lough, *Seventeenth-Century French Drama: The Background* (Oxford, 1979) and Robert McBride, *Aspects of Seventeenth-Century French Drama and Thought* (London, 1979). Attitudes to women are analysed by Ian Maclean in *Woman Triumphant* (Oxford, 1977).

Alfred Simon's *Molière, une Vie* (Paris, 1988) is the most recent biography, but highly recommended is Sylvie Chevalley's handsomely illustrated *Molière en son temps* (Paris and Geneva, 1973). Classic studies in French include Jacques Arnavon, *La Morale de Molière* (Neufchâtel, 1945); Antoine Adam's long essay in volume 3 of his general *Histoire*; René Bray, *Molière, homme du théâtre* (Paris, 1954), which views the plays through stage traditions and Molière's role as actor; and Maurice Descotes, *Les Grands rôles du théâtre de Molière* (Paris, 1960). Michel Corvin's *Molière et ses metteurs en scène aujourd'hui* (Lyons, 1985) analyses the way Molière has recently been presented for modern audiences.

There are many studies of Molière in English of which the following are especially recommended: W. G. Moore, *Molière, a New Criticism* (Oxford, 1948); Robert McBride, *The Sceptical Vision of Molière* (London, 1977); W. D. Howarth, *Molière, a Playwright and his Audience* (Cambridge, 1982); P. A. Wadsworth, *Molière and the Italian Theatrical Tradition* (Alabama, 1987); and Peter Nurse, *Molière and the Comic Spirit* (Geneva, 1991). The most recent biography in English is Virginia Scott's *Molière: A Theatrical Life* (Cambridge, 2001).

On individual plays included in this volume, see G. J. Mallinson, *Molière: L'Avare* (London, 1988), J. H. Broome, *L'École des Femmes and Le Misanthrope* (London, 1980), Noel Peacock, *Molière: L'École des Femmes* (Glasgow, 1989), David Whitton, *Molière: Don Juan* (Cambridge, 1985) and David Shaw, 'A secular view of Dom Juan' (*Modern Languages*, 1978, pp. 121–30).

NOTE ON MONEY

1 liard	=	3 deniers
1 sou	=	4 liards
1 livre	=	20 sous
1 écu	=	3 livres
1 louis	=	11 livres

The pistole (a coin minted in Spain and Italy) was worth 10 livres. The franc was the equivalent of the livre, but was used mainly to designate round sums.

TRANSLATOR'S NOTE

John Wood's alert and readable translations first appeared nearly half a century ago and remain very serviceable. However, given the inevitable changes wrought by passing time in register and vocabulary, they stood in need of some revision and modernization. Moreover, John Wood's original selection omitted plays now judged significant and included others which are considered less so. In this volume, *L'École des femmes* (*The School for Wives*) and *La Critique de l'École des femmes* (*The School for Wives Criticized*) are newly translated.

My grateful thanks go to my colleague David Shaw for pointing out my errors so patiently and for providing much invaluable advice.

DAC

The School for Wives, a Comedy

L'École des femmes, Comédie

Performed for the first time on 26 December 1652 at the Palais Royal by the Players of Monsieur, only brother to the King

The School for Wives, Molière's tenth play and the sixth written since his arrival in Paris, created a furore. It pleased the paying public but not the actors of the Hôtel de Bourgogne, for whom its success was a threat, nor the Compagnie du Saint Sacrement which was outraged by what was regarded as an attack on religion. In 1663 Molière replied with the *School for Wives Criticized* and *L'Impromptu de Versailles*, but the affair marked the beginning of a campaign of vilification, some of it very personal, which would resurface in the polemic surrounding *Tartuffe* (1664) and *Don Juan* (1665).

The staging was admired, but Molière's comic performance as Arnolphe, which amused audiences, was judged by the critics to be overwrought. He was further accused of plagiarizing, among others, a tale published by Paul Scarron in 1655, while the play itself was criticized for its implausibility (why does it take Horace so long to realize he is being fooled? is a girl like Agnès likely to drop stones on anyone?) and its lapses of taste: the 'custard pie', children 'born through the ear', a wife as 'a man's stew' and the innuendo of what Horace took from Agnès in Arnolphe's absence. The moral lecture Arnolphe reads to Agnès was construed as an insult to the 'holy mysteries' of religion. Even so, the play was performed over sixty times in 1663 and it remained in Molière's repertoire.

It is not difficult to explain its success. Molière rings the changes on the characters and situations of traditional comedy with a plot which seems mounted on springs. However, the farce is cruder than in his later five-act plays, and the length and style of certain speeches are rather self-conscious attempts at a more 'serious' kind of theatre than the farce and overcomplicated comedy of manners to which audiences were accustomed. Yet not only are borrowed characters and situations developed with great ingenuity, but Molière comments provocatively on a range of cultural issues (middle-class pretension, preciosity, the importance of money, marriage, the education of women and their right to a degree of self-determination) and moral problems (the institutional view of marriage versus young love). It would be wrong to read the play as a libertarian defence of the rights of women, however, for the denouement respects paternal authority, and, moreover, if love is reconciled with marriage it is only by recourse to the artificial conventions of the comedy of intrigue: coincidence, the recognition scene and the inevitable triumph of right over wrong. It is nevertheless clear that Molière challenges as unreasonable the absolute rights of parents, enshrined in law, to do what they willed with their children.

The Arnolphe who mounts a farcical defence of the old values of wifely subordination cuts a comic figure. But his jealousy and fear of cuckoldry give him a psychological depth which, for some, generates sympathies that make it difficult to laugh at him. Molière played Arnolphe as a buffoon. In the eighteenth century he was portrayed as a curmudgeon whose downfall is a just reward for his foolish conduct. The Romantics, however, saw in him something of a tragic figure, as did Lucien Guitry in a notable performance in 1924. But in the wake of Louis Jouvet's production of 1936, Arnolphe has been refigured as a character of farce as Molière seems to have intended. He is the representative of the mean spirit of male, moral and religious conformity against which Molière defends youth and the right to happiness.

Characters

ARNOLPHE, also known as
    Monsieur de la Souche
AGNÈS, a sweet young girl,
    Arnolphe's ward
HORACE, in love with Agnès
ALAIN, a peasant, Arnolphe's
    servant
GEORGETTE, a peasant,
    Arnolphe's maid
CHRYSALDE, friend of Arnolphe
ENRIQUE, Chrysalde's
    brother-in-law
ORONTE, father of Horace and
    old friend of Arnolphe
NOTARY

The scene is set in a square in a town.

Act I

Scene i:

CHRYSALDE, ARNOLPHE

CHRYSALDE: You're here, you say, to marry her?

ARNOLPHE: Yes, and I mean to have it all over and done with tomorrow.

CHRYSALDE: We are alone here and I think, or so it seems to me, that we could talk together without fear of being overheard. Would you like me, as a friend, to tell you exactly what I think? What you are proposing makes me terribly afraid for you. Whichever way you look at it, for you to get married would be a very rash step.

ARNOLPHE: Very true, my friend. Perhaps it's because you have grounds for fear on that score in your own marriage that you are alarmed at my prospects. It seems to me that your forehead has a look about it that suggests that a cuckold's horns are the universal, inevitable accompaniment of marriage.

CHRYSALDE: Such things happen as the result of chance and there's nothing anyone can do about it. In my view, all the fuss people make about these matters is utterly foolish. But when I say I'm afraid for you, I'm thinking of all the jibes so many poor husbands are made to suffer. Because you must be aware that no one, high-born or low, has ever been safe from your strictures. For wherever you go, nothing pleases you more than turning secret affairs into public scandals.

ARNOLPHE: And why not? Is there another city in the whole world where married men are as meek and mild as they are here? Don't you see them, all kinds and in all walks of life, treated with contempt in their own homes? One husband makes a pile of money which his wife then doles out to her hangers-on who promptly turn him into a cuckold. Another, not quite as unfortunate but no less ignoble, sees his wife being given presents daily without his mind ever being troubled by the smallest twinge of jealousy because she tells him that they are the reward of her virtue. Then there's the husband who kicks up a fuss, which does him no good at all, or the one who mildly lets matters take their course and whenever he sees his wife's beau walk through the door, politely takes his gloves and coat. Then there's the wife, cunning like all her kind, who pretends to be quite open about her lover to her faithful spouse who then sleeps soundly, lulled by appearances, feeling sorry for the man who, however, does not let the grass grow under his feet. Another, to account for her extravagance, says that everything she spends she wins at play, and, without thinking to inquire what sort of games she plays, her gullible husband thanks the Lord for the money she wins. In short, there's material for farce and satire everywhere. As a spectator, why shouldn't I laugh at it all? The fools! If only –

CHRYSALDE: Yes, but anyone who laughs at other people must expect to be laughed at in turn. I hear what people say and observe that there are some who delight in gossiping about anything and everything that happens to be going on. But whatever stories are told in the drawing-rooms I frequent, I've never been one to crow over them. I am reticent in that respect and while I might disapprove of the occasional excess, I would never myself put up with what some husbands take without complaining, though I have never gone out of my way to say so. For there is always the fear that the joke might rebound against the joker: in such matters you should never say categorically what you would or wouldn't do. So if the fate which governs all things visited some conjugal disgrace on my forehead, then I'm pretty sure that, given the way I've always behaved, people would make do with laughing behind my back. And maybe I'd even be fortunate enough that a handful of kind persons would say they were sorry. But it's quite different for you, my friend, and I repeat: you are running a devil of a risk. You've always been one to make open fun of long-suffering husbands and acted like a demon let loose in their midst. You'd best watch your step if you don't want to become a laughing-stock. If they were ever to get hold of anything that could be used against you, you'd better look out, for they'll shout it from the roof-tops and –

ARNOLPHE: Good Lord, there's no need to get so worked up, old friend. It'll take a clever man to catch me out on that score. I know all the ploys and underhand tricks women use to deceive their husbands. I know exactly how we are taken in by their cunning ways. I've taken steps to prevent any such thing happening to me. The girl I'm to marry has all the innocence needed to safeguard my husbandly honour against the evil eye.

CHRYSALDE: And what do you imagine a foolish girl can –

ARNOLPHE: I'm marrying a foolish girl so that I'm not made a fool of myself. I'm perfectly prepared to believe that your better half is most respectable. But cleverness in a woman never augurs well. I know what price some men pay for choosing a wife with too many talents. Do you think I intend to saddle myself with some smart woman who never talks about anything except salons and literary clubs, who writes sensitive effusions in prose and verse and opens her doors to wits and men of quality while I, as the husband of Madame, stand around like a saint who has no devotees? Absolutely not! I won't have anything to do with a wife with a mind of her own, who writes more than she needs to. I am determined that mine, sublimely untouched by knowledge, won't even know what a rhyme is. And if the occasion should arise when she's playing party games and gets asked what the cat sat on, I hope she answers 'a custard pie'. In other words, I want her to be utterly ignorant. To be blunt, it will be fine by me if she can say her prayers, if she loves me and knows how to sew and spin.

CHRYSALDE: So you're stubbornly attached to the idea of a stupid wife?

ARNOLPHE: So much so that I'd rather marry a stupid ugly girl than one who was pretty and had brains.

CHRYSALDE: Brains and beauty . . .

ARNOLPHE: It's enough for her to be virtuous.

CHRYSALDE: Come now, how can you expect a silly girl to know what it is to be virtuous? Besides, to my mind it would be very dull to be lumbered with a silly woman for life. Do you think you're going about this sensibly and that your way provides your honour as a husband with adequate safeguards? An intelligent wife may fall short in her duty, but at least she is aware of what she's doing. Whereas a stupid woman may fail in hers as a matter of course, without wanting to or even giving it a second thought.

ARNOLPHE: To that fine argument, to those words of wisdom, I reply as did Pantagruel to Panurge:[1] tell me to marry any wife except a stupid one, preach, quote chapter and verse at me from now until Whitsuntide, and when you're done you'll be amazed to find that you won't have convinced me one bit.

CHRYSALDE: Then I'll not say another word.

ARNOLPHE: Everyone has his own approach and in this matter of a wife, as in all others, I intend to follow mine. I am rich enough, I think, to choose to marry someone for whom I can provide fully, someone who will be so completely dependent on me that she would not be forever reminding me that she came with a large dowry or was better born than me. Her sweet temper and natural poise, more marked in her than in other children of her age, made me fall in love with her when she was just four years old. Since her mother was in very straitened circumstances, it occurred to me to ask if I could adopt her. When she discovered what I wanted, the good woman was only too delighted to be freed of the burden. In a small convent, which has little contact with the world outside, I had the girl raised according to my principles, that is, I gave instructions how she should be treated so that she grew up as unsophisticated as possible. Thank heaven, the result has fully lived up to my expectations. When she was grown up, I found her so perfectly innocent that I gave thanks to God for granting my wish and giving me a wife who is everything I could wish. So I took her away and, since my house is always open to all sorts of people, I arranged for her to live somewhere else, for you can't be too careful, in another house where no one comes to call on me. And to prevent her naturally sweet disposition being ruined, I only keep servants there who are as unspoilt as she is. You must be wondering why I'm telling you all this. It's so you know how careful I've been. And the upshot of it all is that I'm inviting you, as a good friend, to have dinner with her this evening. I'd like you to take a look at her and then tell me if any fault is to be found with my choosing her for a wife.

CHRYSALDE: I accept.

ARNOLPHE: After talking to her, you'll be able to form a judgement about her looks and her innocence.

CHRYSALDE: In that respect, what you've already told me can hardly –

ARNOLPHE: What I've told you falls far short of the whole truth. I'm forever being surprised by her simple ways, and sometimes she comes out with things that make me laugh out loud. The other day – you'll hardly credit this – she came to me very worried and asked in all innocence if it was true that children were born through their mother's ear![2]

CHRYSALDE: I'm very glad to hear it, Seigneur Arnolphe –

ARNOLPHE: Come now! Must you always call me by that name?

CHRYSALDE: I can't help it, it just comes naturally – I never think of you as Monsieur de la Souche. Who on earth ever gave you the idea of changing your name at the age of forty-two, and deriving a title from an old, rotting tree trunk on your farm?

ARNOLPHE: Apart from the fact that the house is known by that name, La Souche sounds better to my ear than Arnolphe.[3]

CHRYSALDE: What on earth is this strange craze for wanting to drop the real family name and adopt one that's based on a passing whim? Lots of people nowadays are going in for it. And, though I don't intend to include you in the comparison, I used to know a peasant farmer called Gros-Pierre who, though he owned nothing except one small piece of land, had a muddy ditch dug all round it and then pretentiously called himself Monsieur de l'Île.

ARNOLPHE: You needn't bother quoting further examples of that sort.[4] Anyhow, La Souche is the name I go by. I think it's a perfectly reasonable name and I like it and I shall be offended if I'm called by the old one.

CHRYSALDE: Nevertheless most people can't get used to it and I still see letters addressed to –

ARNOLPHE: I can put up with it from those who don't know, but you –

CHRYSALDE: As you wish, we won't fall out over it and I'll undertake to train my mouth never to call you anything but Monsieur de la Souche.

ARNOLPHE: Well then, goodbye. I must just stop off here to say hello and let them know I'm back.

CHRYSALDE (*as he leaves*): My word, I do believe he's taken leave of his senses!

ARNOLPHE: He has a bee in his bonnet about some subjects. It's strange to see how passionately attached people are to their own opinions! Ho there!

Scene ii:

ALAIN, GEORGETTE, ARNOLPHE

ALAIN: Who's that knocking?

ARNOLPHE: Open the door. I think everybody's going to be so pleased to see me after an absence of ten days.

ALAIN: Who is it?

ARNOLPHE: Me.

ALAIN: Georgette?

GEORGETTE: What?

ALAIN: Go and open the door.

GEORGETTE: Go yourself.

ALAIN: No, you go.

GEORGETTE: I'm not going.

ALAIN: I'm not going neither.

ARNOLPHE: This is a fine carry on, leaving me standing out here like this. Hey! Excuse me!

GEORGETTE: Who's that knocking?

ARNOLPHE: Your master.

GEORGETTE: Alain?

ALAIN: What?

GEORGETTE: It's the master. Quick, open the door!

ALAIN: Open it yourself!

GEORGETTE: I've got the bellows going on the fire.

ALAIN: I'm seeing my sparrow doesn't get out, in case the cat gets him.

ARNOLPHE: Whichever of the pair of you doesn't open the door won't get anything to eat for four days. Oh, really!

GEORGETTE: Where do you think you're off to? Can't you see I'm going as fast as I can?

ALAIN: Why should you be going rather than me? I can see what you're up to!

GEORGETTE: Get out of the way!

ALAIN: No, you get out of the way!

GEORGETTE: I'm going to open the door.

ALAIN: No, I want to open it.

GEORGETTE: You'll do no such thing!

ALAIN: Nor you neither.

GEORGETTE: Nor you.

ARNOLPHE: This would try the patience of Job!

ALAIN (*opens the door*): There! It's me sir.

GEORGETTE: Good day to you sir. Here I am.

ALAIN: If it wasn't being disrespectful to the master here, I'd give you such a —

ARNOLPHE (*takes a punch from Alain*): Damnation!

ALAIN: Beg pardon!

ARNOLPHE: You clumsy oaf!

ALAIN: Sir, it was her fault –

ARNOLPHE: Both of you, hold your tongues. Stop all this foolishness and give me straight answers. Right then, Alain, how is everybody?

ALAIN (*while Arnolphe removes Alain's hat three times*): Sir, we ... Sir, we are ... Thank heaven, we are all ...

ARNOLPHE: Who taught you, you insolent ruffian, to talk to me with your hat on your head?

ALAIN: You're quite right. I should have known better.

ARNOLPHE (*to Alain*): Ask Agnès to come down. (*To Georgette*) After I went away, was she sad?

GEORGETTE: Sad? No.

ARNOLPHE: No?

GEORGETTE: Oh, yes she was.

ARNOLPHE: Why was that?

GEORGETTE: Strike me dead for a liar if she didn't expect to see you come back any minute. We couldn't hear a horse or a donkey or a mule go past the house without her thinking it was you.

Scene iii:

AGNÈS, ALAIN, GEORGETTE, ARNOLPHE

ARNOLPHE (*aside*): She's got her embroidery with her! That's a good sign! (*To Agnès*) Well, Agnès, I'm back from my travels. Are you glad to see me?

AGNÈS: Yes, sir, heaven be praised.

ARNOLPHE: And I'm very glad to see you too. And have you been keeping as well as I see you now?

AGNÈS: Apart from the fleas, which stopped me sleeping at night.

ARNOLPHE: Don't worry, you'll soon have someone to catch them for you.

AGNÈS: I should like that.

ARNOLPHE: I should think so too. What are you making?

AGNÈS: Mob caps for me. Your night-shirts and night-caps are all ready.

ARNOLPHE: That's all very good. Now go upstairs. Don't get bored, I'll come back soon and talk to you about matters of some importance. (*When they've all gone*) Ah, heroines of today, learned ladies, heavers of tender sighs and spouters of lofty sentiments, I challenge all your poems, novels, epistles, love-letters plus all your theories to equal such honest, modest ignorance!

Scene iv:
HORACE, ARNOLPHE

ARNOLPHE: It's not money that should dazzle us, and as long as honour is . . . But what do I see? Is it . . . yes! No, I'm wrong. No I'm not. Yes I am. No, it's really him, Hor–

HORACE: Seigneur Ar–

ARNOLPHE: Horace!

HORACE: Arnolphe!

ARNOLPHE: I'm so glad to see you! How long have you been here?

HORACE: Nine days.

ARNOLPHE: Really?

HORACE: My first call was at your house, but you weren't there.

ARNOLPHE: I'd gone to the country.

HORACE: Yes, two days before.

ARNOLPHE: Oh, how quickly children grow in just a few years! I'm amazed to see how tall the boy's got. The last time I saw you, you were no higher than that.

HORACE: As you see.

ARNOLPHE: But do tell me about your father Oronte, my old and dear friend whom I admire and respect. What's he doing now? What's he saying these days? Is he still fit and spry? He knows I take a keen interest in everything that concerns him. We've not seen each other for four years, nor, what is worse I think, corresponded.

HORACE: He is in even better heart than you or I, Seigneur Arnolphe. He gave me a letter for you, but he has since written another saying he'll be coming here soon, though I couldn't tell you why. Do you happen to know a fellow townsman of yours who's returning home with a large fortune he made in America where he's been for fourteen years?

ARNOLPHE: No. Have you heard anyone say what his name is?

HORACE: Enrique.

ARNOLPHE: No.

HORACE: My father mentioned him and says he's back, as if I ought to know all about him. He wrote saying they'll be travelling together because of some important piece of business, though what it is his letter doesn't say.

ARNOLPHE: I'll certainly be very pleased to see him and I'll do my best to give him a warm welcome. (*He reads the letter.*) When you write to a friend, there's no need to be so formal as this – all these compliments aren't necessary. Even if he hadn't gone to the trouble of writing to me, you would have been welcome to treat everything I have as your own.

HORACE: I'm just the man to take people at their word. Just now, I need a hundred pistoles.

ARNOLPHE: You oblige me by accepting the offer, indeed you do. Fortunately, I have the money on me. Keep the purse too.

HORACE: I ought to sign –

ARNOLPHE: Let's have none of that talk. Now, what do you think of the town?

HORACE: A large population, superb architecture and, I should think, wonderfully entertaining.

ARNOLPHE: Everyone has his own way of enjoying himself according to his taste. But those they call bucks and beaux have everything they could wish for here, for the women are born flirts. Both the blondes and the brunettes are said to be very willing and the husbands are as easy-going as anywhere in the world. It's entertainment fit for a king. The antics I observe are as good as anything you'd see in a theatre. Maybe you've already turned some girl's head? Have you got anywhere in that line yet? A fine upstanding prospect like yourself was born not just to turn a pretty penny: you're the sort who turns husbands into cuckolds.

HORACE: I won't hide the honest truth from you. I have had something of a sentimental adventure here, and friendship compels me to tell you about it.

ARNOLPHE: Capital! Now for some juicy new story. This will be something to put in my note-book.

HORACE: But please, promise you won't breathe a word.

ARNOLPHE: But of course.

HORACE: As you know in these matters, once the secret gets out, all our careful planning comes to nothing. So I tell you quite frankly that I've fallen in love with a beautiful girl who lives here. From the beginning, my advances met with such success that she sweetly opened her door to me. Without wishing to boast or imply anything against her, it's all coming along very nicely.

ARNOLPHE (*laughing*): And who is she?

HORACE (*pointing to Agnès's house*): A girl who lives in that house, the one with the walls painted red. Actually, she's very naïve, because some man had the extraordinarily silly idea of hiding her away and not letting her have any contact with people outside. Yet despite the ignorance in which she's forcibly kept, she's very attractive, entrancingly so. She has an engaging air about her, with a promise of tenderness in it, which any man would find irresistible. But maybe you've seen her for yourself. She is a star of love, with a constellation of charms. Her name is Agnès.

ARNOLPHE (*aside*): Ah! This will be the death of me!

HORACE: As for the man, I think he's called La Zousse or La Souche, I didn't really catch the name. I was told he's rich but short on common-sense, for they made him out to be a standing joke. Do you know him?

ARNOLPHE (*aside*): This is a bitter pill!

HORACE: Aren't you going to say anything?

ARNOLPHE: Oh! yes, I know him.

HORACE: And is he a fool?

ARNOLPHE: Er . . .

HORACE: What's that? What did you say? Eh? Does that mean yes? Absurdly jealous? A fool? I see that he's everything they said he was. Anyway, the lovely Agnès has made me her slave. I'll not lie to you, she's a pretty little thing, and it would be a sin to leave such a rare jewel in the clutches of a ridiculous booby. As far as I'm concerned, all my efforts and all my fondest hopes shall in future be directed to making her mine, despite her jealous keeper. The money I've just borrowed from you so freely I intend to use to help me bring my plans to a happy conclusion. As you will know far better than I, money, despite our best efforts, is the key that opens all doors, for gold, which goes to most people's heads, paves the way for victory in love as in war. You seem cross. Is it because you disapprove of what I'm planning to do?

ARNOLPHE: No, I was just thinking –

HORACE: You've had enough of this conversation. Goodbye – I'll drop by at your house later to thank you properly. (*He goes.*)

ARNOLPHE: Ah! must I –

HORACE (*returning*): From now on, please be discreet and don't, I beg you, don't breathe a word of my secret to anybody! (*He goes.*)

ARNOLPHE: Oh! I feel as if –

HORACE (*returning*): And especially not to my father who might get angry. (*He goes.*)

ARNOLPHE (*thinking he is about to return*): Eh? . . . Oh! listening to all that was sheer torture! I don't believe anybody has ever been more wretched than I am now! How could he have been so rash, so hasty, as to come here and tell me all about this business? My other name has ensured that he's still in the dark, but surely no young fool ever behaved with so little sense! But, even though I was going through such torment, I should have had enough presence of mind to find out if my fears are real. I should have let his careless chatter run its course and thus got to know exactly how things stand between them. I'll go after him – I don't think he'll have got far. I'll find out by getting him to take me into his confidence. I tremble to think how unhappy this business could make me, for are we not more eager to travel than to arrive?

Act II

Scene i:
ARNOLPHE

ARNOLPHE: Come to think of it, it's just as well I went traipsing all that way without catching him up, because I have such a weight on my heart that I doubt very much if I could have altogether stopped myself from letting him see how I feel. The anguish gnawing away inside me would have come out in to the open and I'd rather he went on not knowing what he doesn't know. But I'm not the sort of man who takes things lying down and leaves the coast clear for some young buck's fancies. I intend to put a spoke in his wheel and, for a start, I'll find out exactly how far things have gone between them. I regard this as a crucial matter of honour, for having brought her to this stage I consider her to be my wife. She can't have been unfaithful without bringing shame on me and everything she's done is my concern. It was fatal to leave her! Why did I go away? (*He knocks at the door.*)

Scene ii:
ALAIN, GEORGETTE, ARNOLPHE

ALAIN: Oh it's you sir. This time –

ARNOLPHE: That'll do. Come here both of you. You go here . . . and you stand there. Come here. Come on, I tell you.

GEORGETTE: Ooh! You're frightening me. My blood's gone all cold.

ARNOLPHE: So is this how you obeyed me when I was away? Did you both get together to betray me?

GEORGETTE: Don't eat me alive, sir, I beg you!

ALAIN (*aside*): I'd swear he must have been bitten by a mad dog!

ARNOLPHE: Oh! I'm so beside myself I can hardly speak. I'm so hot I can't breathe – I wish I could take all my clothes off. So, you pair of wretches, you allowed a man into my house! It's no good trying to run away, you! Here and now you'll . . . Don't you dare budge! . . . I want you to tell me . . . Watch it! . . . Yes! I want both of you . . . by God, I'll wallop whichever of you moves a muscle! How did this man get past my front door? Come on! Out with it! Quickly now, look sharp, at the double, don't stop to think about it. So what have you got to say?

ALAIN and GEORGETTE (*together*): Oo–er!

ARNOLPHE: I feel faint.

ALAIN: This'll be the death of me!

ARNOLPHE: The sweat is pouring off me. I'll stop a moment and catch my breath. I need to get some air, take a walk. How could I have guessed when I knew him as a little boy that he would one day grow up to be capable of this? Heavens! my heart feels as if it's about to burst! I think it would be more sensible to approach Agnès and, by gentle persuasion, find out from her what's going on and how far it concerns me. I'll try to keep control of my temper. I must try to be patient and take it one step at a time. (*To Alain and Georgette*) On your feet and when you go indoors ask Agnès to come down. No, stop. That way I lose the advantage of surprise – they'd warn her I'm in a foul mood. I'll go myself and get her to come down. You two, wait for me here.

Scene iii:
ALAIN, GEORGETTE

GEORGETTE: Mercy! He's in a terrible temper! The way he looked at me made me feel really scared – terrified I was. I never saw a more horrible Christian man.

ALAIN: It's that young gentleman that's made him cross. I told you how it would be.

GEORGETTE: But what the devil is he up to, making us keep the mistress locked up so strict in the house? What reason can he have for wanting to hide her away from everybody? Why won't he let anybody come near her?

ALAIN: Because if they did, he'd be jealous.

GEORGETTE: But wherever did he get such a notion?

ALAIN: He got it . . . he got it from being jealous.

GEORGETTE: Yes, but why's he jealous? And why's he so cross?

ALAIN: Well now, jealousy . . . mark my words Georgette . . . is something . . . er . . . which makes a person worried . . . and stops other folk coming anywhere near the house. I'll give you a for instance so you can have a clearer idea of what I'm on about. Tell me if this isn't true. You get your stew all ready and some hungry tramp shows his face and tries to pinch some. Now, wouldn't you be cross? Wouldn't you want to give him what for?

GEORGETTE: Yes, I understand that.

ALAIN: Well, it's exactly the same thing. A wife is actually a man's stew, and when one man sometimes spots other men who want to dip their fingers in his stew he gets fighting mad in no time.

GEORGETTE: Yes, but why don't everybody feel the same way? How come you see some men who look ever so pleased when their wives are with fine gen'l'men?

ALAIN: That's because not everybody's greedy in love, not the sort that want to hog the whole lot theirselves.

GEORGETTE: If I've not gone cross-eyed, that's him I see coming back.

ALAIN: There's nothing wrong with your eyes, it's him all right.

GEORGETTE: He looks ever so miserable!

ALAIN: That's because he's in an 'orrible temper.

Scene iv:
ARNOLPHE, AGNÈS, ALAIN, GEORGETTE

ARNOLPHE: A certain Greek once said to the Emperor Augustus – and it was as useful a piece of advice as it was sound – that when something happens that makes us lose our temper, we should stop and say the alphabet, to give our anger time to cool and stop us doing things we shouldn't do.[5] I've taken his advice with regard to Agnès. I've brought her out here on purpose, saying we were going for a walk but really so that with all the suspicions going round and round in my sick head I can cleverly lead her up to the subject and, by tackling her about how she feels, set my mind at rest without getting cross. Come along Agnès. You two can go inside.

Scene v:
ARNOLPHE, AGNÈS

ARNOLPHE: It's pleasant strolling like this.

AGNÈS: Very.

ARNOLPHE: It's a lovely day.

AGNÈS: Very.

ARNOLPHE: Tell me what's been happening.

AGNÈS: The kitten died.

ARNOLPHE: What a shame! Still, these things can't be helped. We're all mortal and we must all take our chances. Did it rain at all while I was away in the country?

AGNÈS: No.

ARNOLPHE: Were you bored?

AGNÈS: I never get bored.

ARNOLPHE: What have you been doing these last nine or ten days?

AGNÈS: I finished about six shirts and six mob-caps too.

ARNOLPHE (*thinks for a moment*): The world, dear Agnès, is an odd place. You've seen what scandal-mongering goes on and the way people talk. A couple of neighbours mentioned to me that a young man they'd not seen before came to the house while I was away and said you weren't averse to seeing him and letting him talk to you. But I gave no heed to their nasty tongues and I'd bet that they were wrong when they –

AGNÈS: Merciful heaven! Don't bet: you'd certainly lose.

ARNOLPHE: What! So it's true that a man . . .

AGNÈS: Absolutely true, and he hardly set foot outside the house, I swear.

ARNOLPHE (*aside*): The frankness with which she admits it tells me at least that she's totally without guile. (*To Agnès*) But Agnès, if memory serves, I thought I'd forbidden you to see anybody.

AGNÈS: True. But you don't know why I saw him. If you did, you would have certainly behaved exactly as I did.

ARNOLPHE: Perhaps. But you'd better tell me the story.

AGNÈS: It's quite amazing and hardly creditable. I was working out on the balcony, where it was cool, when I saw this young man, very good-looking, walking by under those trees over there. He caught my eye and immediately gave me a low, very civil bow. Not wishing to appear impolite, I replied with a curtsey. He immediately bowed again, and I gave him another quick curtsey. He answered by bowing a third time and I at once responded for the third time. Then he walked on, came back, walked past again and every time he started all over again and gave me another bow. Meanwhile I, staring at all his comings and goings, curtsied back politely each time. It lasted so long that if it had not grown dark, I'd still be there now going on in the same way, because I did not want to be first to stop and have the mortification of thinking that he would imagine I wasn't as polite as he was.

ARNOLPHE: Quite right.

AGNÈS: The next day, I was standing by the front door when an old woman came up to me and said something along these lines: 'May the Good Lord bless you, my child, and keep you long as beautiful as you are today! He did not make you so pretty so that you should waste the manifold gifts he has bestowed on you. I must tell you that you have wounded a heart which is now left aching.'

ARNOLPHE (*aside*): Ah! instrument of Satan! damned witch!

AGNÈS: 'What, said I amazed, I've wounded somebody?' 'Yes, she said, you've wounded, wounded to the quick, the man you saw yesterday from your balcony.' 'Alas, said I, whatever could have caused it? Did I drop something on him and not notice?' 'No, she said, your eyes did the fatal damage, and their glances are the cause of all his hurt.' 'Good Lord, said I, I've never been so astonished in my life. Is there something in my glance that harms other people?' 'Yes, she said, those eyes of yours will be the death of him for they contain a poison you know nothing of. In short, the poor, unhappy man is wasting away and if, the kind lady went on, if you are cruel enough to refuse to help him, all he'll be fit for a couple of days from now is to be buried six feet deep.' 'Heavens, said I, I'd be very sorry if that happened. What kind of help is he asking me for?' 'My child, she said, all he wants is to see you and talk to you. Only your eyes can save him from wasting away, for they are the antidote to the harm they have done.' 'Oh, with all my heart, said I. And since that's the way of it, he can come and see me here as often as he likes.'

ARNOLPHE (*aside*): Oh! confounded harpy! poisoner of souls! May hell reward you for your charitable interference!

AGNÈS: And that's how he came to see me and got better. Now, in your opinion, wasn't I right? After all, I wouldn't have wanted it on my conscience that I had let him die by refusing him help, because I always feel sorry for anybody who is made to suffer and I can't see a hen die without shedding a tear.

ARNOLPHE (*to himself*): All this is innocence talking. I've only myself to blame for being so foolish as to go away and leave such simple-hearted goodness without guidance and exposed to the wiles of cunning seducers. But I'm afraid the villain might have been bold enough to take his designs beyond a game.

AGNÈS: What's the matter? You seem rather cross. Was I wrong to behave as I told you I did?

ARNOLPHE: No, but tell me what happened next, after he called, and what this young man did when he was with you.

AGNÈS: Ah! If you only knew how delighted he was, and how he got better the moment I set eyes on him and had seen what a pretty casket he gave me as a present, and the money he gave Alain and Georgette, you'd be sure to like him and say, as we do –

ARNOLPHE: Yes, yes, but what did he do when he was alone with you?

AGNÈS: He swore he loved me more than anyone else was ever loved before, and said the prettiest things that were ever said and could never be improved on and sounded so lovely that every time I hear him speak they make me tingle and stir something inside me that leaves me feeling quite flushed.

ARNOLPHE (*aside*): Oh this is intolerable! Here I am trying to get to the bottom of a terrible secret and it's the person asking the questions who feels all the hurt. (*To Agnès*) Apart from all this talk and all the compliments, did he also touch you?

AGNÈS: Oh yes, lots of times! He took my hands and my arms and never got tired of kissing them.

ARNOLPHE: And did he take anything else from you, Agnès? (*Seeing her look disconcerted*) Ah!

AGNÈS: Well yes! He . . .

ARNOLPHE: What?

AGNÈS: Took . . .

ARNOLPHE: What?

AGNÈS: The . . .

ARNOLPHE: Go on!

AGNÈS: I daren't say it. You might be cross with me.

ARNOLPHE: No I won't.

AGNÈS: Yes you will.

ARNOLPHE: Good heavens no!

AGNÈS: Swear you won't.

ARNOLPHE: Very well. I swear.

AGNÈS: He took my . . . You'll be angry.

ARNOLPHE: No.

AGNÈS: Yes.

ARNOLPHE: No, no, no! Devil take it, why all the mystery? What did he take?

AGNÈS: He . . .

ARNOLPHE (*aside*): I suffer the tortures of the damned!

AGNÈS: He took the ribbon you gave me. To tell the truth, I couldn't help myself.

ARNOLPHE (*breathing again*): Never mind the ribbon. What I wanted to know was if he did anything beyond kissing your arms.

AGNÈS: What do you mean? Do people do other things?

ARNOLPHE: Certainly not. But to cure him of the illness he claimed to be suffering from, didn't he ask you for another kind of remedy?

AGNÈS: No. But if he had, you can be sure I'd have done anything to save him.

ARNOLPHE (*aside*): Thanks to the Lord and his mercy, I've come out of this very lightly. If I ever get caught again, I'll deserve everything I get. (*To Agnes*) Not another word Agnès, all this comes of your innocence. I'll say no more about it. What's done is done. I know that by flattering you the young buck only wants to lead you on and then afterwards he'll treat it all as a joke.

AGNÈS: Oh, not at all. He told me it wasn't like that a score of times.

ARNOLPHE: Ah, but you have no idea if he's to be trusted. Never mind, but you must realize that accepting caskets, listening to young bucks and their fancy talk, and being dreamy enough to let your hands be kissed and your heart throb, is a mortal sin, one of the gravest you could commit.

AGNÈS: A sin, you say? And why is that, please?

ARNOLPHE: Why? Because it is written that Heaven is angered by such actions.

AGNÈS: Angered? But why should Heaven be angered? Oh dear! But it's such a nice thing and so pleasant. I'm amazed how happy it can make you feel – I never knew about such things before.

ARNOLPHE: True, all these endearments and sweet nothings and gentle caresses are all very pleasant, but they are to be enjoyed only when everything's above-board. When you get married, the wrong in them is removed.

AGNÈS: So they're not a sin when you're married?

ARNOLPHE: No.

AGNÈS: Then please, let me get married at once.

ARNOLPHE: If that's what you want, then I want it too. It's why I came back: to arrange your marriage.

AGNÈS: Is this possible?

ARNOLPHE: Yes.

AGNÈS: You'll make me so happy!

ARNOLPHE: Yes, I've no doubt that being married will make you very happy.

AGNÈS: You want the both of us . . .

ARNOLPHE: Nothing more certain.

AGNÈS: If it really happens, I'll give you such a hug!

ARNOLPHE: Ah! And I for my part will do the same to you.

AGNÈS: I never know when people are making fun of me. Do you really mean what you say?

ARNOLPHE: Yes, you'll see if I do.

AGNÈS: We'll be married?

ARNOLPHE: Yes.

AGNÈS: But when?

ARNOLPHE: This evening.

AGNÈS (*laughing*): This evening?

ARNOLPHE: This very evening. That makes you laugh?

AGNÈS: Yes.

ARNOLPHE: All I want is to see you happy.

AGNÈS: I'm so grateful to you. I'll be so happy with him!

ARNOLPHE: With who?

AGNÈS: With . . . er . . . him.

ARNOLPHE: Er . . . him? I wasn't thinking of er . . . him. You're rather quick in choosing a husband. But not to mince words, I've got someone else for you and he's ready and waiting. Now as to this er . . . him of yours, please understand that even if this illness he's stringing you along with sends him to an early grave, you must have nothing further to do with him from this day on. If he comes to the house to pay his respects, you will be a good girl and slam the door in his face. Then, if he knocks, you are to throw a large stone at him through the window to let him know he's never to show his face again. Agnès, do you hear? I shall be hiding in a corner and I'll be watching what you do.

AGNÈS: Alas! He's so handsome! He's –

ARNOLPHE: Oh! how you prattle on!

AGNÈS: I wouldn't have the heart!

ARNOLPHE: Not another word! Go upstairs.

AGNÈS: What do you mean? Do you intend –?

ARNOLPHE: That's enough. I am the master here and what I say goes. Go, do what you're told!

Act III

Scene i:
ARNOLPHE, AGNÈS, ALAIN, GEORGETTE

ARNOLPHE: Well now, that all went off very nicely. I'm absolutely delighted. You followed my instructions to the letter and utterly confounded the young buck! That's the advantage of having a wise head to guide you. Your innocence let you be taken unawares, Agnès. You see the predicament you'd got yourself into without intending to? Without my guidance, you were already well on the road to hell and damnation. Everyone knows how these young bucks operate: fancy frills, a lot of ribbons and feathers, long hair, white teeth and smooth talk – but, as I told you, sharp claws just beneath the surface. They're the very devil and have appetites that can only be satisfied by gobbling up a woman's honour. But I repeat: thanks to the help you've been given, you've come out of it still an honest woman. The way I saw you drop that stone on him dashed any hopes he might have had of his schemes, and is further confirmation that we shouldn't put off any longer the wedding I told you to get ready for. But first of all, I think I should have a little talk with you for your own good. Bring a chair out here. (*To Georgette and Alain*) If either of you two –

GEORGETTE: We'll make sure we don't forget any of your orders. That other gentleman pulled the wool over our eyes, but –

ALAIN: If he ever gets in the house again, may I never touch another drop. Besides, he's a rogue. The last time, he gave us two gold crowns that weren't full weight.[6]

ARNOLPHE: Go and get the supper ready just as I like it. And when you've done that, one or other of you can go and fetch the notary who lives at the cross-roads. As I said, I need him for the business of the contract.

Scene ii:

ARNOLPHE, AGNÈS

ARNOLPHE (*sits down*): Agnès, put your work down and listen to me. Raise your head a little and turn your face this way. That's right. Now keep looking at me when I'm talking and mind you take in every word. I'm going to marry you, Agnès. You should give thanks a hundred times a day for the good fortune your fate has brought you. You must reflect on the common condition to which you were born and at the same time admire my generosity which has raised you from your lowly rank of village girl to the position of a respectable lady and now enables you to share the bed and enjoy the affection of a man who has always avoided all such entanglements and refused to grant to a score of very presentable women the honour he proposes to do you. You must never lose sight, I say, of the humble station which you would occupy if it were not for this advantageous offer of marriage, so that the thought of it will teach you more effectively to deserve the position to which I'll have raised you. Always remember what you are and behave in such a way that I shall never have cause but to congratulate myself for taking this step. Marriage, Agnès, is not a game. The rank of wife carries strict duties and I have no intention of elevating you to that estate for you to be flighty and have a good time. Your sex was made to be dependent: power and authority belong with the beards. Men and women might be the two halves of society but these two halves are not equal. One is the upper half and the other the lower. One is subservient to the other which is in charge. The obedience with which the disciplined soldier behaves to the officer who commands him, the valet to his master, children to their father, the lowliest of monks to his superior, comes nowhere near the docility, obedience, humility and profound respect which a wife should show her husband who is her chief, her lord and her master. Whenever he turns a stern eye on her, it is her duty to lower her eyes and never look him in the face until he deigns to pardon her with a kindly glance. That is what women nowadays fail to understand – but you mustn't be led astray by following their example. Be sure you don't imitate them, for they are flirtatious and wicked, and the way they carry on is the talk of the town. Never let yourself be trapped by the snares of the devil, by which I mean you should never listen to what handsome young men tell you. Remember that in making you one half of myself, Agnès, I am entrusting my honour to your care. Now honour is a tender thing and is easily wounded, it's not something to be trifled with. In hell there are boiling cauldrons into which wives who go wrong are thrown for ever. What I'm telling you is no fairy story and you should take all these lessons to heart. If you follow them and shun loose behaviour, your soul will remain as white and as pure as a lily. But if you do anything to the detriment of honour, it will turn as black as coal. Everyone will regard you with horror and one day you will be claimed by the devil and will boil in hell for all eternity, a fate from which may the goodness of heaven preserve you! Bow your head. Just as a novice in a convent must know her duty by heart, so those who enter into marriage should know theirs. I have here in my pocket an important little book (*standing up*) which will instruct you in the whole duty of wives. I don't know who wrote it, but he's clearly a sound man. I want it to be your sole subject of study. Here, take it. Show me how well you read it.

AGNÈS (*reads*):   MAXIMS FOR MARRIAGE
       or The Whole Duty of Wives.
         With daily exercises

First Maxim: She who shares a bed with a husband in lawful matrimony must never forget that, notwithstanding the ways of the modern world, the man who takes her to wife takes her for himself alone.

ARNOLPHE: I'll explain what that means later. For the moment, just read on.

AGNÈS (*reads on*): *Second Maxim*: She must not adorn her person except in a manner which satisfies the husband whose property she is. The care she takes over her appearance is a matter which concerns him alone. It is quite irrelevant if other people find her ugly.

Third Maxim: She must shun all study of artful glances and avoid lotions, powder, potions and the countless ingredients which go into a painted face. Such things are drugs which are fatal to wifely honour each and every day, and the pains taken to appear attractive are rarely undertaken with husbands in mind.

Fourth Maxim: Honour requires that when she goes out, she must stifle under her bonnet any inflaming effects her eyes might produce around her. For if she wishes to please her husband, she had best not please anyone else.

Fifth Maxim: Propriety forbids her to receive any persons other than those who come calling on her husband. Those of a gallant persuasion who have business only with Madame, are not acceptable to Monsieur.

Sixth Maxim: She must not, on any account, take presents from men. In this age we live in, no one gives anything for nothing.

Seventh Maxim: Though she might resent the restriction, her effects must not include a writing desk, ink, paper and pens. According to proper convention, the husband should write everything that is written in his house.

Eighth Maxim: The disorderly routs which are called fashionable assemblies corrupt the minds of women daily. It should be a matter of policy that they should be banned, for it is in such gatherings that plots are hatched against unsuspecting husbands.

Ninth Maxim: The woman who wishes to devote herself to virtue must avoid gambling as she would the plague. For gambling is very hazardous and often tempts a woman to risk her all.

Tenth Maxim: She must not share the present taste for promenading and picnics in the country. Wise minds hold that in such outings, it is invariably the husband who foots the bill.

Eleventh Maxim: . . .

ARNOLPHE: You can read the rest for yourself. I'll explain it all properly later, step by step. I've remembered a little business I must attend to. I just need to have a word with someone. I shan't be long. Go in now, and mind you take good care of that book. If the notary comes, ask him to wait for a moment.

Scene iii:
ARNOLPHE

ARNOLPHE: I couldn't do better than have her for my wife. I can mould her into exactly what I want. She's like a piece of wax in my hands: I can turn her into whatever shape I like. When I was away, she was very nearly snatched away from me through her excessive innocence. But to tell the truth, it's far better for a man's wife to err in that direction. Mistakes like hers are easily remedied: anyone who's simple-minded is easy to teach, and if she's been led astray from the right path, a couple of words will soon bring her back to it. But a clever woman is a different kettle of fish. Our fate hangs on her will. Once she's made up her mind nothing can alter it, nothing we say will have the slightest effect. Her quick brain means that she laughs at our principles. She turns her crimes into virtues and, to achieve her nefarious goals, she dreams up tactics which foil the ingenuity of the cleverest man. We wear ourselves out pointlessly trying to avoid the inevitable: a clever woman who plots and schemes is a fiend. Once the fancy takes her to pass silent sentence on our honour, we might as well give up – as many respectable husbands can testify. Still, that young buck won't get the last laugh. He's got his comeuppance because he blabbed too much. It's the usual trouble with Frenchmen: when things are going their way, they can't bear to keep it secret. Their silly vanity has such a hold on them, that they would rather be hung than keep their mouths shut. Oh, women must surely be tempted by the devil when they set their caps at such empty-headed fools and ... But here he is ... I won't show my hand and I'll try and find out how badly he's taking it.

Scene iv:
HORACE, ARNOLPHE

HORACE: I've just come from your house. Fate has clearly decreed that I shall never find you at home. But I'll keep trying and in the end, one day –

ARNOLPHE: Oh come now, let's dispense with these pointless formalities. Nothing irritates me more than all this ceremonial nonsense. If I had my way, it would be done away with. It's a vexatious habit – and a stupid waste of two thirds of most people's time. So let's put our hats back on our heads without more ado. Now then, these love affairs of yours – may I know how you are getting on with them, Seigneur Horace? When we spoke last, my mind was on other things but since then I've been thinking. I am impressed by the speed of your early progress and I'm interested in seeing how you go on.

HORACE: Ah! Since I opened my heart to you, my love has suffered a setback.

ARNOLPHE: Oh? What sort of setback?

HORACE: Cruel fate has brought the girl's guardian back from the country!

ARNOLPHE: That's unfortunate.

HORACE: Moreover, to my great regret, he has discovered that we've been seeing each other in secret.

ARNOLPHE: And how the devil did he find out about it so soon?

HORACE: I don't know, but there's no doubt about it. I thought I'd go and call on the captivating creature at the usual time, but both the maid and the valet, adopting a very different attitude to me in the way they looked and spoke, barred my way, said 'Go away, you're pestering us', and then very rudely slammed the door in my face.

ARNOLPHE: Slammed the door!

HORACE: In my face.

ARNOLPHE: That's a bit strong!

HORACE: I tried talking to them through the door. But every time I tried to say anything, they replied: 'You can't come in. The master's forbidden it.'

ARNOLPHE: So they didn't open the door?

HORACE: No. And from a window Agnès confirmed that her guardian was back by sending me packing with some very high and mighty remarks and a stone thrown by her own fair hand.

ARNOLPHE: How do you mean, a stone?

HORACE: A stone, and not a small one either, with which she personally acknowledged my visit.

ARNOLPHE: The devil she did! This is no trifling matter. I'd say you're in a pretty pickle.

HORACE: That's true. Things are going badly for me, all because her guardian chose the wrong moment to return.

ARNOLPHE: I feel really sorry for you, I do assure you.

HORACE: That man has ruined everything for me.

ARNOLPHE: Quite. But it's nothing – you'll find a way of picking up the pieces.

HORACE: I must try and think of some scheme which will allow me to evade the strict vigilance of this jealous old man.

ARNOLPHE: That should be easy enough. After all, the girl's in love with you.

HORACE: Of course she is.

ARNOLPHE: You'll get there in the end.

HORACE: I hope so.

ARNOLPHE: The stone made you turn tail but you shouldn't let that worry you.

HORACE: Of course not. I realized immediately that the man was there, orchestrating it all without being seen. But what did surprise me, and it will surprise you too, was another development that I'll tell you about – something bold which that beautiful young creature did that you would not have expected from such innocence. You must admit, love is a great mentor: it teaches us to be what we never were and as a result of its lessons a complete transformation in our behaviour is but the work of a moment. It breaks down nature's barriers in us and the effect can be so sudden that it seems like a miracle. Love instantly turns misers into the souls of liberality, makes cowards brave, changes boors into gentlemen, gives a nimble turn to the most sluggish brain, and wit to the most innocent mind – and yes, this last miracle took place in Agnès. For when she gave me my marching orders with these express words: 'Go away: I don't want you to visit me. I know everything you're going to say and here is my answer', the stone or rock that startled you dropped at my feet with a note attached to it. I was amazed to see that the letter chimed both with the sense of what she'd said and with the stone she'd thrown. Aren't you surprised she should do such a thing? Doesn't this show how good love is at sharpening wits? Can you deny that its prodigious power produces astonishing changes in the human heart? What do you say to this ploy and her brief note? Eh? Don't you admire the ingenuity of her mind? Don't you reckon that Mr Jealousy has come out of this little game looking pretty ridiculous? Tell me.

ARNOLPHE: Yes, quite ridiculous.

HORACE: So why aren't you laughing? (*Arnolphe gives a forced laugh.*) That man, waging war on my love from the start, retreats inside his house and puts up a show of resistance with rocks, as though I intended to take the place by storm! Quaking foolishly in his boots, he turns all his servants against me in an attempt to drive me away and is then foiled under his nose and with his own tactics by the girl he wishes to keep in a state of complete ignorance! For myself, even though his return has thrown my plans into disarray, I don't mind saying I think it's the funniest thing I ever heard. I can't think about it without laughing. But you don't seem to be laughing very much.

ARNOLPHE (*with a forced laugh*): Forgive me, I'm laughing as much as I can.

HORACE: But I must, as one friend to another, show you the letter. Her hand put into it everything her heart feels and did so in very touching terms and with such kind regard, such tender innocence and simplicity – I mean in a way that conveyed everything an unspoilt nature feels when it is wounded by love for the first time.

ARNOLPHE (*aside*): So this, you wicked girl, is the use you make of your pen! It was not part of my plans that you were to be taught to write in the first place.

HORACE (*reads*): 'I want to write to you, but am at a loss to know where to start. I have thoughts which I would like you to know, but have no idea how I should set about expressing them and I mistrust my own words. Since I am beginning to realize that I have always been kept in a state of ignorance, I am afraid I might put down on paper something which is not right or say more than I ought. In all honesty, I do not know what you have done to me, but I am aware of feeling extremely upset by what I have been told to do to you. It is going to be very hard for me to live without you and I would dearly like to be yours. Perhaps it's wicked to say that, but I can't stop myself saying it. How I wish I could say it without doing anything wrong. I am forever being told that all young men are deceivers, that they should not be listened to and that everything you tell me is intended to lead me on. But I assure you that I have never been able to believe that of you, and I have been so moved by your words that I could never think they were false. Please tell me frankly whether they are. For you know, I have no wicked intentions and you would be committing the greatest wrong in the world if you really were to deceive me. And I think I should die of grief.'

ARNOLPHE (*aside*): Oh! the snake in the grass!

HORACE: What's the matter?

ARNOLPHE: Matter? Nothing's the matter. I just coughed.

HORACE: Did you ever hear a more tender declaration of love? And despite the abominable interference of an unjust tyrant, could you ever hope to find a sweeter nature? Is it not criminal to set out with a wicked intention to pervert so noble a soul and throttle its intelligence under a heap of ignorance and stupidity? Love has begun to tear down the veil. If with the help of some kindly star, I can, as I hope, thwart that utter beast, the scoundrel, the cad, the villain, the swine . . .

ARNOLPHE: Goodbye.

HORACE: What, going so soon?

ARNOLPHE: I have just this minute remembered a pressing engagement.

HORACE: But you wouldn't happen to know, since she is so closely guarded, of someone who might have access to the house? I make no bones about asking you, for it's not out of the way for friends to lend each other a helping hand at moments like this. I've got no one on the inside except people who are to keep an eye out for me. As I've discovered, no matter how I approach them, both the maid and the valet are not prepared to modify their rudeness and listen to me. I used to have an old woman up my sleeve for situations like these – she was a real genius, more than human. She was very useful to me at first, but the poor woman died four days ago. Can't you think of some way of helping me?

ARNOLPHE: No, really. You'll manage very well without me.

HORACE: Goodbye, then. You see how much I trust you.

Scene v:
ARNOLPHE

ARNOLPHE: Having to stand there and let myself be humiliated! It was torture keeping my pain and anguish to myself! Fancy a simple-minded chit like that having such a ready turn of mind! Either she pretended to be innocent when she was with me, the hussy, or else it was the devil who put all that deviousness into her head. But either way, that fatal letter has done for me. I see the villain has taken control of her mind and by ousting me he has found his place in her affections. Oh, I am in despair, the pain of it will kill me! I am hit twice by having her heart stolen from me, since both my love and my honour suffer as a result. I am furious to discover that my territory has been invaded, and incensed to see my precautions circumvented. I know that to punish her wantonness, all I need do is to let her evil destiny take its course: she herself will provide me with my revenge! And yet it is infuriating to lose the woman we love. But heavens! did I choose her after all that philosophizing only to find myself now totally besotted by the girl? She has no family, no friends, no money. She abuses my prudence, my generosity and my affection. And yet I love her even after this underhand trickery, and cannot live without loving her. You fool! Have you no shame? Oh! I am furious, outraged, I could slap my face a thousand times! I think I'll go inside now, but only to see how she behaves after doing such a terrible thing. Heaven grant that my forehead show no mark of dishonour. Or if it is written that I must come to such a pass, then at least give me the fortitude which some men show in such circumstances!

Act IV

Scene i:

ARNOLPHE

ARNOLPHE: I don't mind admitting it: I just can't seem to settle anywhere. My head's spinning with all sorts of plans for stamping my authority on my house, both inside and out, which would wreck all the efforts of that young buck! How sweetly the hussy looked me in the eye! She wasn't the least bothered by all the things she's done. And though she's brought me within two steps of an early grave, anyone would think to look at her that she didn't care. I saw her – the calmer she seemed the angrier I got. The boiling fury that rose up in me seemed to stoke the flames of my love even higher. I felt bitter, angry, desperate towards her and yet I never saw her look more beautiful. Never did her eyes seem so bright, never did they arouse such keen desire in me. I know in my heart that I shall die if my sorry fate rules that everything is to end in dishonour for me. So that's how it is! I supervised her education with so much affection and prudence, brought her to live in my house when she was a child, entertained the fondest hopes of her, my heart built on the foundation of her growing beauty and for thirteen years I've cosseted her for myself – and all that so that some young clod she falls for can just turn up and steal her from under my very nose, when she is already half married to me! No, by God! No! Ah, my fine friend, you silly young fool, you'll be wasting your time going round in circles. Either my efforts will come to nothing or I shall smash all your hopes to smithereens, that I swear. You won't get the better of me.

Scene ii:

NOTARY, ARNOLPHE

NOTARY: Ah! there he is. Good afternoon! I've come all ready to draw up the contract you wanted.

ARNOLPHE (*not seeing him*): How shall I set about it?

NOTARY: It must be done according to the usual form.

ARNOLPHE (*not seeing him*): I must think carefully what precautions I'll have to take.

NOTARY: I won't draw up any deed that goes against your interest.

ARNOLPHE (*not seeing him*): I shall need to guard against the unexpected.

NOTARY: Your affairs will be quite safe in my hands. To avoid being misled, you shouldn't sign the contract before you've got your hands on the dowry.

ARNOLPHE (*not seeing him*): I'm afraid, if I do anything that attracts attention, the whole business will be the talk of the town.

NOTARY: Oh, we can easily avoid attracting attention by drawing up your contract in secret.

ARNOLPHE (*not seeing him*): But how am I going to settle matters with her?

NOTARY: Any settlement you make on her is determined by the amount of dowry you receive.

ARNOLPHE (*not seeing him*): I love her, and that's my biggest problem.

NOTARY: If that's the case, a wife may be treated more generously.

ARNOLPHE (*not seeing him*): How should I treat her in the circumstances?

NOTARY: The rule is that the groom should settle on the bride a third of the dowry that comes with her. But that rule is not hard and fast. If you want to give her more, you can.

ARNOLPHE (*not seeing him*): If . . . (*He sees the notary.*)

NOTARY: As for what may be settled on a husband who survives his wife, that is a matter for both to decide. But I should say that the groom may settle on the bride whatever he likes.

ARNOLPHE: What?

NOTARY: He can be more generous if he loves her deeply and wishes to make her happy. This may take the form of a provision, by what is called a preamble to the marriage contract, which reverts to the husband with the decease of the wife, or may not revert but become the legal entitlement of the said wife's heirs, or it may take the form of a common-law settlement according to their several wishes, or by deed of gift in the marriage contract itself, which may be single or joint. Why are you shrugging your shoulders? Am I talking like a fool? Am I not familiar with the forms of contracts? Who will teach me them? No one can, I tell you. Don't I know that when people marry, they have joint title by customary law and practice to all personal effects, real estate and acquired property, unless they renounce such rights by special deed? Don't I know that one third of the property of the bride becomes part of the joint estate so that . . .

ARNOLPHE: Yes, no doubt of it, you know it all. But who asked you?

NOTARY: You did. You try and make me look a fool by shrugging your shoulders and scowling.

ARNOLPHE: Devil take the man and his silly face. Goodbye – it's the only way to make you stop.

NOTARY: Didn't you send for me to draw up a contract?

ARNOLPHE: Yes, I sent for you. But the matter has been postponed. I'll send for you again when another time has been fixed. Did you ever see such a devil of a man for prattling on! (*He goes out.*)

NOTARY: If I said he was mad, I don't think I'd be far wide of the mark.

Scene iii:

NOTARY, ALAIN, GEORGETTE

NOTARY: Didn't you come to fetch me for your master?

ALAIN: Yes.

NOTARY: I have no idea what you make of him, but you can go this minute and tell him from me that he is a blithering idiot.

GEORGETTE: We won't forget.

Scene iv:

ALAIN, GEORGETTE, ARNOLPHE

ALAIN: Sir . . .

ARNOLPHE: Come here. You are my good, faithful, true friends, as I have cause to know.

ALAIN: The notary . . .

ARNOLPHE: Let's leave him for some other time. Someone has designs on my honour. Think what a disgrace it would be for you my children if that person took away your master's honour! You wouldn't dare show your faces in public after that and, if you did, everyone would point at you and jeer. So since this business concerns you as much as me, you on your side must keep up a strict watch so that this young spark can't in any way –

GEORGETTE: You told us what to do a little while ago.

ARNOLPHE: But you must be careful not to yield to his fine words.

ALAIN: Oh! really –

GEORGETTE: We know how to take care of ourselves against him.

ARNOLPHE (*to Alain*): What if he approached you on the quiet and said: 'Alain, there's a good fellow, won't you ease my aching heart by lending me a hand?'

ALAIN: 'You're an ass.'

ARNOLPHE: Good. (*To Georgette*) 'Georgette, my pet, you seem to me to be such a sweet, kind person.'

GEORGETTE: 'You're a fool.'

ARNOLPHE: Good. (*To Alain*) 'But what harm can you see in an honest and perfectly respectable plan?'

ALAIN: 'You're a rogue.'

ARNOLPHE: Very good. (*To Georgette*) 'I shall die for sure if you don't take pity on the anguish I suffer.'

GEORGETTE: 'You're a ninny, and cheeky with it.'

ARNOLPHE: Very good. 'I'm not the sort of man who expects something for nothing. I've a very good memory for anyone who does me a good turn. So take this, Alain, as an advance, and have a drink on me. And here's something for you, Georgette, to buy yourself a new petticoat with. (*Both put out their hands and take the money.*) That's just a sample of my generosity. The only favour I ask of you is to let me see your beautiful mistress.'

GEORGETTE (*pushing him away*): 'Not likely!'

ARNOLPHE: That's good.

ALAIN (*pushing him away*): 'Get out!'

ARNOLPHE: Excellent.

GEORGETTE (*pushing him away*): 'And be sharp about it!'

ARNOLPHE: Good! Stop, that's enough!

GEORGETTE: Did I do it properly?

ALAIN: Is that the sort of thing you meant?

ARNOLPHE: Yes, very good, apart from the money which you shouldn't have taken.

GEORGETTE: We didn't remember that bit.

ALAIN: Would you like us to do it again now?

ARNOLPHE: No, that'll do. Go into the house, both of you.

ALAIN: You've just got to say the word.

ARNOLPHE: No, I said. Go inside when I tell you. You can keep the money. Go on, I'll catch you up. Keep your eyes open and back me up in what I do.

Scene v:
ARNOLPHE

ARNOLPHE: I need a spy with sharp eyes: I'll ask the cobbler who lives at the corner of our street. I intend to keep her in the house all the time, maintain a watch and, above all, bar the door to ribbon-sellers, wig-makers, hair-dressers, women who make handkerchiefs and gloves, second-hand dealers and all those shady characters who busy themselves every day advancing the cause of love's mysteries. Oh, I've been about a bit and know all the tricks. My man will need to be pretty damn clever if a message or note from him is to get through!

Scene vi:

HORACE, ARNOLPHE

HORACE: This must be my lucky spot: I always seem to find you here. I've just had a narrow squeak and no mistake! When I left you, not expecting anything of the sort would happen, I saw Agnès by herself step out on to her balcony for a moment to enjoy the cool air under those overhanging trees there. She waved and then somehow managed to get down into the garden and open the gate for me. But we had no sooner got to her room when she heard that jealous keeper of hers coming up the stairs. All she could do in the circumstances was to shut me inside a large wardrobe. He came straight in. I couldn't see him, but I heard him striding around the room, not saying anything, heaving pitiful sighs from time to time, thumping tables now and then, kicking a little dog which felt sorry for him and angrily throwing all the clothes he could find on the floor. He even lashed out furiously with his hand and smashed several vases with which the lovely girl had decorated her mantelpiece. It's clear the old goat must somehow have got wind of the trick she played on him. Anyhow, when he'd marched round and round for some time, venting his anger in this way on things that could not fight back, the jealous fiend, very agitated but not saying what was worrying him, left the room and I my wardrobe. We decided we wouldn't risk staying together any longer, for we were afraid of the man. It was too dangerous. But tonight, very late, keeping as quiet as I can, I'm to go to her room. I shall cough three times to let her know it's me. When I give this signal, I shall see her window open and through it, by means of a ladder and with Agnès's help, love will assist me to get inside. I wanted to tell you all this, for you're the only friend I have. A happy heart grows happier when its joy is shared, for even if we could attain perfect bliss over and over again, we'd still not be content if no one else knew about it. I'm sure you'll be delighted by this happy turn my affairs have taken. Goodbye. I must go and think about what needs to be done next. (*He goes out.*)

Scene vii:

ARNOLPHE

ARNOLPHE: So! The hostile fate which seems determined to drive me to despair will not give me a moment to breathe! Am I to see all my prudent, careful plans upset one by one through their collusion? Am I, in my prime, to be made a fool of by a simple-minded girl and a young hothead? For twenty years I've been contemplating the sorry fate of husbands and taken careful note of all the pitfalls which can lead the wisest of them to stumble and end in misery. My mind has benefited from the misfortunes of others, and, when I decided to take a wife myself, I looked for the best way of ensuring that my forehead remained free of dishonour and thus ensure I was different from the rest of the cuckolds. To this noble end, I believed I had set in train everything human prudence could devise. But as though fate had decreed that no man here below shall be exempt, and after all the experience and insight I could gather in these matters, after twenty years and more of reflecting how I should proceed with all due caution, have I avoided following in the footsteps of so many husbands only to end up in the same mess after all? Oh! cursed fate, I shall prove you wrong yet! I am still in charge of the girl he's after. That malignant young puppy may have robbed me of her heart, but I will at least see to it that he doesn't get the rest. Tonight, which they've chosen for their amorous encounter, will not pass off as agreeably as they think. It gives me some satisfaction to know, amid so much misery, that I've been warned about the trap that's been set for me and that this young fool, who wants to get the better of me, has chosen his own rival to confide in!

Scene viii:

CHRYSALDE, ARNOLPHE

CHRYSALDE: Well, shall we have dinner before we take our stroll?
ARNOLPHE: No. Tonight I'm not eating.
CHRYSALDE: Is that a joke?
ARNOLPHE: Please excuse me. I've got something else on my mind.

CHRYSALDE: Won't this marriage you were planning be taking place?

ARNOLPHE: You poke your nose into other people's business far too much!

CHRYSALDE: Oh, so touchy! What's worrying you? Has something untoward happened, old friend, to complicate the course of true love? I'd swear it had by the look on your face.

ARNOLPHE: Whatever happens to me, I shall at least have the advantage of not being like some husbands who meekly tolerate seducers in their houses.

CHRYSALDE: It's a strange fact that, for all your knowledge of these matters, you always get worked up about them, equating them with the ultimate happiness and believing there is no other kind of honour in the whole world. To be a miser, a brute, a rogue, a villain or a coward is nothing, in your view, compared with this stigma, so that however a man may have lived his life, he must be by definition honourable provided he has not been deceived by his wife. If you think it through, why do you insist on believing that a husband's reputation depends on such chance events? Why assume a noble mind should feel guilty for something it could not have prevented? Why, I ask you, do you think that when a man takes a wife, it should be she who determines whether he deserves praise or blame? Why should he turn the affront of her infidelity into some monstrous, dreadful spectre? You should get it into your head that a wise man can take a less gloomy view of cuckoldry, that such occurrences are neutral in themselves since no one is immune to the vagaries of chance, that, to put it in a nutshell, whatever people might say, the only harm done comes from the way we take these things? To behave well in such difficult circumstances, as in all others, we must avoid extremes and not imitate those excessively accommodating husbands who pride themselves on affairs of this sort, are forever talking about their wives' lovers, singing their praises wherever they go, boasting of their talents, making a show of being close friends with them, attending all their soirées and parties and behave in such a way that people are amazed that they should have the nerve to show their faces in such gatherings. Such conduct is clearly quite wrong, but the other extreme is no less to be condemned. If I disapprove of husbands who make friends with their wives' lovers, I have no time either for the obstreperous sort who are unwise enough in their unhappiness to storm and rage and thereby attract the attention of everyone to the noise they make and, by stirring up a fuss, seem determined that no one shall remain ignorant of what has happened to them. Between these two extremes, there is a middle path which a sensible husband will take in such cases. And if he can follow it, he has no need to feel ashamed of the worst a wife can do to a man. So in spite of what people say, it is easy to regard cuckoldry in a much less dire light. I repeat: the secret is merely knowing how to make the best of it.

ARNOLPHE: After such an excellent speech, the whole brotherhood of cuckolds owes Your Lordship a vote of thanks. Any husband who listened to you spout would be only too happy to enrol as a member.

CHRYSALDE: That's not what I meant – it's what I was criticizing. Look, since it's Fate that gives us our wives, I maintain that we should act in this as though we were playing dice: if you don't get what you want, you've got to play a canny game and resign yourself to improving the odds by behaving sensibly.

ARNOLPHE: By which you mean sleeping soundly, eating your share and pretending to yourself that none of it matters.

CHRYSALDE: You think it's a joke. But to tell the plain truth, I see plenty of things around me that are much more frightening and which I myself would consider far greater calamities than this kind of mishap which terrifies you so much. Do you think that if I had to choose between these two alternatives I would not prefer to be what you say than see myself married to one of those fine, upstanding women whose wicked temper turns the smallest thing into an inquisition, a dragon of purity, a she-devil of respectability, the kind who always hide behind their womanly virtue and, because of one minor wrong they refrain from doing us, assume they have the right to browbeat all and sundry and insist, on the grounds that they have been faithful to us, that we should put up with everything they care to do? Once again, old friend, you should realize that cuckoldry is only what we make it, that there are circumstances which may even be desirable, and that it has its compensations like everything else.

ARNOLPHE: If you have the temperament to settle for so little, I don't. It's not in my character to give it a try and rather than submit to such humiliation, I'd –

CHRYSALDE: Heavens! don't swear! You'll only perjure yourself. If fate

has made up its mind, then nothing you do will be any use. Nobody's
going to ask for your opinion.

ARNOLPHE: So I shall be a cuckold?

CHRYSALDE: My, you are in a state! Many people have been reduced
to it and, without wishing to do you down, they don't compare with
you in looks, courage, wealth and birth.

ARNOLPHE: And I have no wish to be compared with them. To tell you
the truth, I'm getting rather sick of your needling. So let's have no
more of it, if you don't mind.

CHRYSALDE: You're angry. No doubt we shall find out why. Goodbye.
But remember, whatever your sense of honour prompts you to do,
that anyone who swears that what we've been talking about will
never happen to him is already half way there.

ARNOLPHE: And I swear again that it won't. And now I'm going to
find a way of preventing any such eventuality.

Scene ix:
ALAIN, GEORGETTE, ARNOLPHE

ARNOLPHE: My friends, I beg you to help me now. I know how devoted
you are but at this juncture you must be unstinting in your loyalty.
If you serve me as I trust you will, you can be assured that I shall
reward you. I've discovered that the man you know (not a word to
anyone) intends to catch me out tonight by getting into Agnès's
room by means of a ladder. The three of us are going to have to set
a trap for him. I want each of you to find a stout stick and when he
gets to the top rung – I'll open the window at the right moment –
both of you, in your own time, will set about the scoundrel in a
manner his back won't forget. That should teach him never to come
here again. Now, without mentioning my name in any way or giving
any hint that I shall be standing behind you, do you think you have
wit enough to serve my anger?

ALAIN: If it's just a matter of walloping him, you can leave it to us.
You'll see, when I get started, if I go at it heavy-handed or not.

GEORGETTE: And my hand might not look as heavy, but it'll certainly
do its share of the walloping.

ARNOLPHE: Go back inside now and, mind, no wagging tongues. (*They go.*) This business will be a useful lesson to others. If all the husbands living in the city gave their wives' lovers a welcome like this, there would be a lot fewer cuckolds about.

Act V

Scene i:
ALAIN, GEORGETTE, ARNOLPHE

ARNOLPHE: You wretches! What have you done? Why were you so violent?

ALAIN: We were only following orders, sir.

ARNOLPHE: It's no good trying to trying to hide behind that as an excuse. My orders were to thrash him, not kill him. And it was on his back not his head that I told you to let the storm burst. Merciful heavens, what a predicament fate has landed me in! How can I bear to go and look at the corpse? Go indoors – and mind you don't breathe a word about the perfectly harmless instructions I gave you. (*They go.*) It will soon be day and now I must think how I can face up to this disaster. Help! What's to become of me? And what will the boy's father say on learning about this business when he least expects it?

Scene ii:
HORACE, ARNOLPHE

HORACE: I must get closer and find out who that is.

ARNOLPHE: Who could have foreseen . . . ? Who's that, may I ask?

HORACE: Is that you Seigneur Arnolphe?

ARNOLPHE: Yes. But who are you?

HORACE: It's Horace. I was on my way to your house to ask a favour. You're up and about early!

ARNOLPHE (*aside*): What's the meaning of this? Is it a dream? is it an illusion?

HORACE: To tell you the truth, I'd got myself into terrible trouble and

I thank the Lord and his infinite goodness for letting me meet you just when I need you. I was coming to tell you that everything went off perfectly, even better than I could have dared hope, as the result of a development which was intended to ruin everything. I've no idea how word got out about the assignation I'd been granted, but just as I'd almost got up to the window I saw, against all expectations, several servants appear from nowhere, who suddenly started waving their arms about threateningly. This made me lose my footing and fall all the way back down again. My tumble cost me a few bruises but saved me from a solid whacking. These servants, and I think my jealous friend was among them, attributed my fall to the effect of the battering they'd given me. And since the pain forced me to lie where I was for some time without moving a muscle, they were quite convinced that they'd done for me and each of them fell into an instant panic. It was very quiet and I could hear them bickering. They all accused each other of murder and, cursing fate and not pausing to fetch a lamp, crept down quietly to feel if I was dead. You can be sure that in the darkness of the night I managed to give a fair impression of a corpse. They went away absolutely petrified. Just as I was thinking of making off myself, young Agnès, dreadfully upset by my supposed death, came hurrying up to me. For she had heard straightaway what the servants had been saying to each other and, since she had been less closely guarded while all the hullabaloo was going on, she had managed to slip out of the house without difficulty. But when she found I was not hurt, she burst into an explosion of joy which I can't really put into words. What can I say? That lovely creature has finally heeded the dictates of her heart, decided never to return home again and has entrusted her fate entirely to my word of honour. Think for a moment and judge by the innocence of her reaction how vulnerable she has been left by the folly of a madman! What grave dangers would she run if I now turned out to be the sort of man who'd care less for her! But my heart burns with a love too pure for that: I'd rather die than wrong her. In my eyes, her beauty deserves a better fate and nothing except death shall ever part me from her. I anticipate this business will make my father furious, but we shall choose our time to placate his anger. I shall surrender to sweeter delights, for after all we must make do with what life sends us. What I'm asking you to do is, without betraying our secret, to let me give this beautiful creature into your keeping, to look kindly on my feelings for her and allow her to stay safely in your house for at least a day or two. Apart from the need to conceal from prying eyes that she's run away and to prevent a full search for her being started, you must see that it would be suspicious if a girl as gorgeous as she is were to be seen with a young man. And since in matters of the heart I have taken you completely into my confidence, knowing that I can rely on your prudence, it is only to you, as my faithful friend, that I can entrust this precious burden.

ARNOLPHE: Rest assured: I am entirely at your disposition.

HORACE: So you really agree to do me this good turn?

ARNOLPHE: Most willingly, I say. I'm glad to have an opportunity of being of use to you and I thank heaven for putting it my way. Nothing I ever did will give me greater pleasure.

HORACE: I am greatly in your debt for all your kindness. I had feared you might make difficulties. But you're a man of the world and wise enough to make allowances for the hot blood of youth. One of my servants is looking after her just round that street corner.

ARNOLPHE: But how shall we manage it, for it's almost daylight? If I take charge of her here, I may be seen. And if you're spotted coming to my house, the servants will talk. To be on the safe side, you must bring her to some place where it is darker. My garden's handy. I'll go and wait for her there.

HORACE: We'd be very wise to take precautions. I'll simply hand her to you and then go home immediately, being careful not to attract attention. (*He goes.*)

ARNOLPHE: O Fortune! This stroke of good luck will make up for all the bad turns your whims have done me! (*He muffles his face in his cloak.*)

Scene iii:
AGNES, HORACE, ARNOLPHE

HORACE: Don't worry about where I'm taking you. I've found you a safe place to stay. If you remained in my house, it would ruin everything. Pass through that gate and go wherever you're taken. (*Arnolphe takes her hand. She does not recognize him.*)

AGNÈS: Why are you leaving me?

HORACE: I must, dearest Agnès.

AGNÈS: Please try and come back soon, then.

HORACE: The love in my heart will urge me to do so.

AGNÈS: I'm not happy when you're out of my sight.

HORACE: I'm sad too when you're not there.

AGNÈS: If that were true, you'd stay here.

HORACE: Ah! Do you doubt that I love you madly?

AGNÈS: No, you don't love me as much as I love you. (*Arnolphe pulls her.*) Ouch! that hurts!

HORACE: It's only because it would be dangerous if the two of us were seen here together dearest Agnès. The trusty friend who leads you by his hand is only being careful. He's zealously committed to our cause.

AGNÈS: But following a man I don't know who . . .

HORACE: Don't be afraid. You'll be perfectly all right in his capable hands.

AGNÈS: I'd rather be in the hands of Horace, and I'd have . . . (*To Arnolphe who pulls her again*) Just a moment!

HORACE: Goodbye. It grows light and I must go.

AGNÈS: When shall I see you, then?

HORACE: Soon, I swear.

AGNÈS: Until that moment I shall worry all the time!

HORACE: Thank heavens, my happiness is no longer in jeopardy and I can now rest easy.

Scene iv:

ARNOLPHE, AGNÈS

ARNOLPHE (*hiding his face in his cloak*): Come, I'm not going to lodge you here. I've got a room all ready for you somewhere else. I intend to keep you in a safe place. (*He lowers his cloak.*) Do you recognize me?

AGNÈS (*recognizing him*): Oh!

ARNOLPHE: So, you hussy, seeing my face like this frightens you. You don't seem very pleased to find me here. I'm spoiling the plans concocted by this infatuation of yours. (*Agnès looks round to see if she can catch sight of Horace*.) Don't look to your lover for assistance: he's too far away to help you. Oh, so young, and yet you go behind my back! You ask with a rare innocence if children are born through the ear, and then make assignations at night and creep out of the house to go off with your lover without attracting attention. My God, how your tongue wags when you're with him! Where on earth did you learn to do that? Who the devil taught you so much so quickly? So you've stopped being afraid of meeting ghosts, then? Is it a paramour who comes by night that's made you bold? Ah! you minx, how could you be so two-faced? How could you plan such a thing after all I've done for you? You're like a viper I cherished in my bosom: the moment it feels it's strong enough, it shows its gratitude by trying to bite the hand that feeds it!

AGNÈS: Why are you shouting at me?

ARNOLPHE: Oh of course, I'm the one who's in the wrong!

AGNÈS: I never meant any harm by what I did.

ARNOLPHE: Isn't running away with a lover an unworthy action?

AGNÈS: He's a man who told me he wanted me to be his wife. I was only doing what you said – you told me that by marrying we remove the sin.

ARNOLPHE: Yes. But I intended that you should marry me! I seem to think I made my meaning sufficiently clear.

AGNÈS: Yes. But if I may speak frankly between ourselves, he is more to my taste in that respect than you are. You make marriage out to be tedious and trying, and the way you talk presents it in the most terrible light. Whereas he on the other hand makes it sound so full of joys that I long to be married.

ARNOLPHE: Ah! that's because you love him, you ungrateful girl!

AGNÈS: Yes, I do love him.

ARNOLPHE: And you have the effrontery to tell me to my face?

AGNÈS: Why shouldn't I say it if it's true?

ARNOLPHE: But should you be in love with him, you baggage?

AGNÈS: But I couldn't help it. He's the one who did it. I'd never given it a thought – then it happened all by itself.

ARNOLPHE: But you ought to have fought against those feelings.

AGNÈS: How can anyone fight against something that's so nice?

ARNOLPHE: But didn't you know I wouldn't like it?

AGNÈS: I didn't know any such thing. What harm can it do you?

ARNOLPHE: None at all — I suppose it should make me deliriously happy. So by all accounts, you don't love me?

AGNÈS: Love you?

ARNOLPHE: Yes.

AGNÈS: Alas, no.

ARNOLPHE: What do you mean, no?

AGNÈS: Do you want me to lie?

ARNOLPHE: Why don't you love me, Miss Impudence?

AGNÈS: Good heavens, it's not me you should be blaming. Why didn't you make me love you as he did? I don't think I did anything to stop you.

ARNOLPHE: I did everything I could to make you. But all my efforts have come to nothing.

AGNÈS: In that case, he obviously knows far more about it than you do, because he had no difficulty whatsoever in making me love him.

ARNOLPHE: Listen to the way the hussy argues back and answers me! Dammit, would one of your clever modern women have any more to say for herself? Ah! How little I know you! Or maybe, by Jove, any silly woman knows more about these things than the cleverest man. But if your brain is so good at answering back, Little Miss Argument, do you think I've brought you up all these years at my expense simply to hand you over to him?

AGNÈS: No. He'll pay everything back, down to the last penny.

ARNOLPHE: She has a way of saying certain things that makes me twice as cross as I was before. But is it in his power, you baggage, to repay all the debts you have incurred?

AGNÈS: I don't owe you as much as you think.

ARNOLPHE: Do you call nothing all the trouble I've taken to raise you since you were a little girl?

AGNÈS: And a fine job you made of it, I must say! You saw to it that I got a pretty kind of general education! Do you think I have any illusions on that score? that in my head I don't know that I am very stupid? It makes me feel ashamed, and at my age I don't want to be taken for a fool any longer if I can help it.

ARNOLPHE: So you reject ignorance! And you'd rather be given lessons by that young buck, whatever the cost might be?

AGNÈS: Certainly I would. He's shown me that I could know so much, and I consider I owe more to him than to you.

ARNOLPHE: I don't know what's stopping me giving you a cuff with the back of my hand to repay such defiant talk. Seeing you so provokingly cool is infuriating and giving you a good thrashing would relieve my feelings!

AGNÈS: Oh, you can, if that would make you feel better.

ARNOLPHE (*aside*): Her words, and the way she looks disarm my anger and revive all the old tenderness and love which blots out the abominable thing she's done. Being in love is a strange business! How vulnerable men are to women who betray them, how prone to such weakness! Everyone knows they are not perfect – they're all excess and indiscretion. Their minds are mean and their souls are brittle. There's nothing so frail or so moronic, nothing so faithless. And yet despite it all, we will do anything for these serpents. Ah well, let's make peace. (*To Agnès*) Come, you little minx, I forgive you for everything and give you back all my affection. Judge by this how much I love you and when you observe how kind I am, love me in return.

AGNÈS: I would like to comply with all my heart. If I could, what price would I have to pay?

ARNOLPHE: But my sweet, you could if you really wanted to. (*Sighing*) Just hear me sigh for love, see the languishing look in my eye, consider the man I am, and forget that snivelling wretch and the love he offers you. He must have cast a spell on you: you'll be so much happier with me. You love being smartly dressed and elegantly turned out – and of course you always will be, I swear. I'll not stop billing and cooing day and night. I'll pet you, I'll cuddle you and I'll gobble you up. You shall do exactly as you please. I won't say another word because, well, I've said it all. (*Aside*) To what extremities does passion lead us! (*To Agnès*) Truly, there never was a love like mine! What proof of it do you want from me, ungrateful girl? Do you want to see me weep? Do you want me to beat my breast? Would you like me to tear out half my hair? Do you want me to kill myself? Yes, just say if you do. I'm ready, you cruel girl, to do anything to prove how much I love you.

AGNÈS: Stop it. Everything you're saying leaves me cold. Horace could do more for me in two words than you.

ARNOLPHE: Ah! you provoke me too much! You try my anger too far! I shall persist with my plan, you obstinate fool! You shall leave town at once. You reject my proposal and drive me beyond endurance. But the depths of a convent shall give me my revenge!

Scene v:
ALAIN, ARNOLPHE

ALAIN: I dunno if it's true, sir, but it looks as if Agnès and the corpse went off together.

ARNOLPHE: She's here. Go upstairs and lock her up in my room for me. He won't come looking for her there and anyway it'll only be for half an hour. I'm going to fetch a cab to take her to a place where she'll be safe. Now you be sure you don't let her out of your sight. Perhaps a change of scene will snap her out of her infatuation.

Scene vi:
HORACE, ARNOLPHE

HORACE: Ah! I've come looking for you! I'm in despair! Heaven, Seigneur Arnolphe, has decreed that I am to be unhappy: through a fatal twist of the ultimate injustice, the woman I love is to be torn from my arms. I discovered that my father had travelled here in the cool of the night and was about to land somewhere hereabouts. Briefly, the reason for his coming, which as I say I knew nothing about, is that he has found me a wife without writing to let me know, and he's here to celebrate the marriage. You've shared all my worries, so you can judge whether a worse disaster could have befallen me. This Enrique I told you about yesterday is the cause of all the misfortune which has struck me. He has come with my father to complete my undoing, since it is his only daughter that I'm to marry. I thought I'd faint the moment they starting speaking of it. My father talked of coming to see you, so, not being able to stand hearing any more, I immediately raced on ahead of him, fearing the worst. I beg you, don't breathe a word about my engagement: it might make him angry and, since he has the greatest respect for you, try to talk him out of this other marriage.

ARNOLPHE: Oh absolutely.

HORACE: Advise him to delay matters for a while and, like a true friend, do my cause a good turn.

ARNOLPHE: I won't fail you.

HORACE: I shall entrust my hopes to you.

ARNOLPHE: Excellent.

HORACE: I think of you as my true father. Tell him that at my age . . . Oh! I see him coming! Come, listen. I'll give you some arguments you can use. (*They withdraw to a corner of the stage.*)

Scene vii:

ENRIQUE, ORONTE, CHRYSALDE, HORACE,
ARNOLPHE

ENRIQUE (*to Chrysalde*): I would have recognized you the moment I set eyes on you, even if nobody had told me who you were. I see in you the image of your sweet sister who was once, long ago, mine by marriage. And I would have been happy if the cruel Fates had allowed me to bring back my faithful wife to share with me the joy of seeing all her family after our many tribulations. But since the implacable force of destiny has deprived me forever of her loving presence, I must try to be resolute and be content with the only fruit of our love which remains to me. She is very dear to you and I would be wrong to give her in marriage without your approval. In the son of Oronte I have made a choice which is illustrious in itself, but the final decision must be as acceptable to you as it is to me.

CHRYSALDE: You must have a poor opinion of my judgement if you doubt whether I approve such a suitable choice.

ARNOLPHE (*to Horace*): Yes, I shall do my very best for you.

HORACE: Don't forget, be careful not to –

ARNOLPHE: Don't worry.

ORONTE (*to Arnolphe*): Ah! there is such warmth in the way you greet me!

ARNOLPHE: Seeing you fills me with great joy.

ORONTE: I came here –

ARNOLPHE: No need to say any more. I know what's brought you here.

ORONTE: Someone has told you already?

ARNOLPHE: Yes.

ORONTE: Good.

ARNOLPHE: Your son is opposed to this marriage. His heart is promised elsewhere and sees only misery in the prospect. He has even begged me to try to change your mind. As for myself, the only advice I can give you is not to allow the wedding to be postponed and to exert your authority as a father. Young people must be made to obey with a firm hand and we do them no service by indulging them.

HORACE: Ah! the traitor!

CHRYSALDE: If he feels the least reluctance, then I don't believe we should try to force him. I suspect that my brother shares my opinion.

ARNOLPHE: What? Is he prepared to let himself be governed by his son? Do you think a father should be so weak that he cannot make the younger generation do what they're told? It would be a fine thing, I must say, to see him ruled by someone who should be ruled by him! No, no! He is my dear friend and his honour is my honour. He has given his word. He must keep it. Let him now be seen to stand firm and put an end to all his son's attachments.

ORONTE: That is well said. In the matter of this marriage, I will answer for his obedience.

CHRYSALDE (*to Arnolphe*): I must say I am surprised by the enthusiasm you show for this marriage. I have no idea what motive you can have to . . .

ARNOLPHE: I know what I'm doing and I've said what needed to be said.

ORONTE: Yes, yes Seigneur Arnolphe, it's –

CHRYSALDE: He doesn't like being called by that name. He is Monsieur de la Souche, as we explained to you.

ARNOLPHE: It's of no consequence.

HORACE: What's that I hear?

ARNOLPHE (*returning to Horace*): Oh yes, you have there the key to the mystery. Do you really think I should have behaved differently?

HORACE: What further trouble . . .

Scene viii:

GEORGETTE, ENRIQUE, ORONTE, CHRYSALDE,
HORACE, ARNOLPHE

GEORGETTE: Oh sir, if you don't come now, we'll have a terrible time keeping hold of Agnès. She's trying all sorts to get away and she might even jump out of the window!

ARNOLPHE: Bring her here to me. I intend to take her away at once. (*To Horace*) It's no use getting upset. Being happy all the time would make any man arrogant. Every dog has its day, as the proverb has it.

HORACE: Merciful heaven, was there ever misfortune greater than mine? Was anyone ever plunged into the depths of such misery?

ARNOLPHE (*to Oronte*): Press on quickly with fixing a time for the wedding. I have an interest in it and shall certainly attend.

ORONTE: That's exactly what I mean to do.

Scene ix:

AGNÈS, ALAIN, GEORGETTE, ORONTE, ENRIQUE,
ARNOLPHE, HORACE, CHRYSALDE

ARNOLPHE (*to Agnès*): Come here my dear, come along. So you can't be kept in, you rebel, do you? Here is your lover. You may drop him a meek and humble curtsey as a reward for his trouble. (*To Horace*) Goodbye. This development may have got a little in the way of your wishes, but not all lovers end up happy.

AGNÈS: Are you going to let him take me away like this, Horace?

HORACE: I'm in such despair that I don't know where I am.

ARNOLPHE: Come along, prattlebox, let's go.

AGNÈS: I want to stay here.

ORONTE: Won't you tell us what all this mystery is about? We're standing here, looking at each other, with no idea of what's going on.

ARNOLPHE: When I've got more time, I might tell you. Until then, goodbye.

ORONTE: Where do you intend to go? The way you're talking to us is not very civil.

ARNOLPHE: I advised you, despite his protestations, to get this marriage over and done with.

ORONTE: Yes, but before we can do that, if you've been told everything, were you not also informed that the young person in question, without whom it cannot happen, is living under your own roof, I mean the daughter born all those years ago to the lovely Angélique whom Seigneur Enrique had secretly married? So when you talked the way you did, what exactly were you referring to?

CHRYSALDE: I too was surprised by his manner of proceeding.

ARNOLPHE: What . . .

CHRYSALDE: My sister married in secret and had a daughter whose fate was hidden from the whole family . . .

ORONTE: . . . and so that nothing got out, she was put out to nurse in the country by her father under a false name . . .

CHRYSALDE: . . . and at that time, Fate declared war on him and forced him to leave his native land . . .

ORONTE: . . . and face a thousand different dangers in lands beyond so many seas . . .

CHRYSALDE: . . . where his bravery earned him honour which treachery and envy would have robbed him of in his own country . . .

ORONTE: . . . and on returning to France, his first thought was to find the woman to whom he had entrusted his daughter . . .

CHRYSALDE: . . . and this woman told him candidly that she had given her into your keeping when she was four years old . . .

ORONTE: . . . and that she had done this and accepted your charity because she did not know which way to turn in her extreme poverty . . .

CHRYSALDE: . . . and Enrique, absolutely delighted and with joy in his heart, has brought her to this place . . .

ORONTE: . . . and you shall soon see her, for she's coming here to clear up the mystery in front of everyone.

CHRYSALDE (*to Arnolphe*): I think I have a good idea of what you are going through. But Fate has not smiled on you in this business. If you believe not being a cuckold is such a fine thing, the best policy is not to get married at all.

ARNOLPHE (*he goes out fuming, incapable of speaking*): Aaargh!

ORONTE: Why is he rushing off without saying a word?

HORACE: Ah, father, you shall be fully acquainted with this strange tale. Chance has enacted here what you in your wisdom had planned. By gentle bonds of mutual affection, I pledged my word to marry this lovely girl. In fact, it is she whom you have come looking for and for whose sake I almost made you angry by my disobedience.

ENRIQUE: I had no doubt about who she was the moment I first saw her, and ever since my heart has not stopped being full. Come, daughter, I surrender to joy and happiness!

CHRYSALDE: I would do the same as you, brother, with all my heart. But this place and your joy are ill-suited to each other. Let us go into the house to unravel these mysteries, thank our friend for all the trouble he's gone to and give thanks to Heaven which invariably arranges everything for the best.

The School for Wives Criticized, a Comedy

La Critique de l'École des femmes, Comédie

*First performed in Paris at the Palais Royal on Friday
1 June 1663 by the Players of Monsieur, only brother
to the King*

The School for Wives unleashed a 'comic war' which lasted for more than a year. Molière's critics – the defenders of literary orthodoxy, fashionable wits, prudes and zealots, rival authors and actors – joined forces to decry the play, deplore its bad taste and denounce its disrespect for religion. In the preface to his published text, Molière indicated that he intended to reply to his detractors with 'a dissertation . . . written in the form of dialogue'. The result was *The School for Wives Criticized* which was first performed with *The School for Wives* on 1 June 1663. In the weeks that followed it was staged thirty-five times at the Palais Royal and at Court, after which Molière abandoned it, returning to the fray with *L'Impromptu de Versailles* (18 or 19 October 1663) which gave a no less tart response to actors that he had already made to writers.

The School for Wives Criticized was revived after his death but it was not performed again between 1691 and 1835. It was published on 7 August 1663 with a preface addressed to the Queen, Anne of Austria, in which he observed that her favour 'proves beyond question that true devotion is not incompatible with innocent amusements', an argument which he would repeat during the controversy surrounding *Tartuffe* in 1664.

It is a very literary comedy and is set in new social territory for Molière, who moves from stagy kings, impertinent valets and the well-to-do middle class to the aristocratic milieu which was connected both to the Court at the Louvre and the salons of the capital. There is no plot but Molière deals sharply with individuals (various models have been proposed for the characters of Lysidas and Damon) and with clearly differentiated types who articulate the argument. The Marquis is a fop, Climène is precious to a degree and Lysidas a pedant. Against them are ranged the measured judgements of Uranie and Dorante who represent the common-sense point of view which, at least in theatrical terms, was Molière's own. For the satire here is far from negative and this 'dissertation' is a pondered statement of Molière's concept of comedy. He argues for 'natural' dialogue, simplicity in taste and plain judgements uncontaminated by prejudice and preconceived ideas. He mocks the politically correct *précieuses* and pedants who can only be amused 'according to the rules', and prefers to be judged by spectators who have no axe to grind: the neutral parts of the Court, the non-aligned intelligentsia, and the pit with its uncomplicated good sense. Above all, Molière asserts the moral function of comedy which allowed observation from nature but avoided personal vilification. The purpose of comedy must always be to mock, with a view to their correction, our collective and personal vices.

Characters

URANIE, cousin to Élise
ÉLISE, cousin to Uranie
CLIMÈNE, a lady of fashion
GALOPIN, a page
The MARQUIS, a gentleman of
    fashion
DORANTE, or the Chevalier
LYSIDAS, a poet

The play is set in Paris, in the drawing-room of Uranie.

Scene i:

URANIE: What's this, cousin? Hasn't anyone been to call on you?

ÉLISE: Not a soul.

URANIE: Really! I'm amazed both of us have been left to ourselves all day.

ÉLISE: I'm surprised too, it's hardly what we're used to. Your house, thank God, is usually a refuge for all the idlers of the Court.

URANIE: To tell the truth, I found the afternoon very long.

ÉLISE: I thought it very short.

URANIE: The fact of the matter, cousin, is that clever people like being alone.

ÉLISE: Oh, I bend my knee in deference to cleverness, but as you know clever is not what I aim to be.

URANIE: Myself, I like company and don't mind admitting it.

ÉLISE: I like company too, but only the best. All those tiresome callers we have to put up with are often the reason why I like being alone.

URANIE: It means you're too fussy if you can only put up with the best people.

ÉLISE: It means a lack of discrimination if you put up with all sorts of people regardless.

URANIE: I enjoy the company of the sensible ones and amuse myself with the fools.

ÉLISE: But it doesn't take the fools long to become very boring and most of them stop being amusing after the first visit. But, talking of fools, wouldn't you like to disentangle me from your bothersome Marquis? Or do you intend to saddle me with him all the time, or suppose I can put up with his puns for ever? It's too, too gross.

URANIE: Now you're falling into the fashionable way of talking. It's considered very amusing at Court.

ÉLISE: Too bad for those who go in for it. They wear themselves ragged trying to keep up their incomprehensible gibberish all day long. It's a fine thing, I must say, the way people slip into a conversation they're having at the Louvre hoary old double meanings fresh from the gutters of the market place and the Place Maubert![1] A pretty poor kind of badinage for courtiers! A man thinks he's being witty if he comes up to you and says: 'Madame, here you are in the Place Royale,[2] and yet everybody can see you from a distance of three leagues outside Paris, because everyone sees you *de bon oeil*,'[3] because Bonneuil is a village three leagues away. Now isn't that terribly smart and clever? And shouldn't the people who come up with such sparkling witticisms have every reason to feel pleased with themselves?

URANIE: But they don't say them as though they believed they're witty. Most of the people who talk in that affected way are perfectly well aware that it's ridiculous.

ÉLISE: I repeat: too bad for them if they go to all that trouble to talk rubbish and make bad jokes on purpose. That's why I think there's even less excuse for them and, if it was up to me, I'd know what to do with them and their waggish in-talk.

URANIE: Let's drop the subject. It's getting you a little too worked up. Let us instead observe that, in my view, Dorante is very late for the supper we're all supposed to be having.

ÉLISE: Perhaps he's forgotten and . . .

Scene ii:

GALOPIN, URANIE, ÉLISE

GALOPIN: Madame! Madame Climène is on her way to call on you.

URANIE: Oh God! Not her!

ÉLISE: But you were only just complaining about being left alone: it's Heaven's punishment on you.

URANIE: Quick, go and say I'm not at home.

GALOPIN: She's already been told you are.

URANIE: And what idiot told her that?

GALOPIN: Me, Madame.

URANIE: Devil take you, you villain! I'll teach you not to take it on yourself to give answers.

GALOPIN: I'll go and tell her that you've decided to be out, Madame.

URANIE: Stop, you stupid oaf! Let her come up since the damage is done.

GALOPIN: She's still talking to a gentleman in the street. (*He goes out.*)

URANIE: Oh, cousin, having her coming to call just now is very awkward for me.

ÉLISE: It's true, the lady is awkward by nature. Never been able to stand the ghastly creature myself and, with all due respect to her rank, she's the stupidest woman who ever took it into her head to have opinions.

URANIE: That's rather strong language.

ÉLISE: No, no, she deserves it and something stronger too, to do her full justice. Is there a woman alive who is a more perfect instance of what is called 'precious', taking the word in its worst sense?

URANIE: But she objects to having the word applied to her.

ÉLISE: True. She objects to the word but not to the thing. She's precious from head to foot. She's the most affected creature in the whole wide world. It's as if her whole body is double-jointed and the movement of her hips and shoulders and head seems to be controlled by springs. She always affects a languid, silly drawl, pouts to show off her little mouth and rolls her eyes to make them look big.

URANIE: Not so loud. If she heard you . . .

ÉLISE: It's all right, she's not on her way up yet. I still remember the evening she wanted to see Damon[4] on account of his reputation and the plays he's had staged. You know what he's like and how lazy he is at keeping up his end of a conversation. She'd invited him to supper, because he's a wit, but he never seemed less witty than when he was with the half-dozen people she'd asked along to hear him perform. They stared at him with eyes like saucers, as though he was some kind of freak. The whole company thought he was there to entertain them with witticisms, that every word which dropped from his lips must be extraordinary, that he was bound to improvise in verse on everything they said and thought he wouldn't ask for more wine without uttering an epigram. But he completely fooled them by not saying anything and remaining silent, and the lady was as displeased with him as I was with her.

URANIE: That's enough. I'm going to stand by the door to greet her there.

ÉLISE: Just one more thing. I wouldn't mind seeing her married to the marquis we were talking about. Now that would be a pretty match – a precious flower and a court jester!

URANIE: Oh do be quiet. Here she is.

Scene iii:

CLIMÈNE, URANIE, ÉLISE, GALOPIN

URANIE: Really, it's terribly late to be —

CLIMÈNE: Oh! For heaven's sake, my dear, have a chair brought for me, quickly.

URANIE: Quick, a chair. (*Galopin brings a chair and goes out.*)

CLIMÈNE: Oh, dear God!

URANIE: What is it?

CLIMÈNE: I cannot bear it any longer.

URANIE: What's the matter?

CLIMÈNE: I think I'm going to faint.

URANIE: Is it the vapours?

CLIMÈNE: No.

URANIE: Would you like to be unlaced?

CLIMÈNE: Good God no! Ah!

URANIE: What's wrong with you? When did it start?

CLIMÈNE: Just over three hours ago. I caught it in the Palais Royal.[5]

URANIE: Caught what?

CLIMÈNE: For my sins, I've just seen that dreadful hodge-podge, *The School for Wives*. I still feel queasy from the effect it had on me. I think it'll take me a couple of weeks to get over it.

ÉLISE: It's amazing how illness strikes when it's least expected.

URANIE: I can't think what stuff my cousin and I must be made of. We went to the same play the day before yesterday and both of us came away feeling well and cheerful.

CLIMÈNE: You mean you've seen it?

URANIE: Yes, sat through it from beginning to end.

CLIMÈNE: And it didn't give you convulsions, my dear?

URANIE: I'm not that sensitive, thank goodness. And as far as I could see, I thought the play more suited to making people better than to making them ill.

CLIMÈNE: Good heavens, what are you saying? How could such an idea be put forward by anyone with a modicum of common-sense? How could anybody fly in the face of reason as you do and hope not to be corrected? And in the last analysis, is there a mind anywhere with such a craving for jokes that it would relish the insipid fare with which the play is peppered? For myself, I confess I did not find the smallest trace of Attic salt[6] in it. The passage about 'children being born through the ear' seemed to me in the most appalling taste, the 'custard pie' made me feel quite queasy and at 'a man's stew' I thought I was actually going to retch.

ÉLISE: Heavens, how elegantly that was put! I'd have said it was a good play. But you have such an eloquent turn of phrase, Madame, and you express things so delightfully that I'm forced to agree with you, despite what I may have thought.

URANIE: Well, I'm not so easily swayed. To give you my honest opinion, I think this comedy is one of the funniest the author has written.

CLIMÈNE: Oh, you make me grieve when you talk like that. I cannot let you get away with such clouded judgement. Can a respectable woman take any pleasure in a play which keeps maidenly modesty in a constant state of alarm and pollutes the imagination at every turn?

ÉLISE: What a pretty way of putting things you have! Madame, you are a formidable critic and I pity poor Molière for having you as an enemy!

CLIMÈNE: Believe me, my dear, you should make a positive effort to correct your view. For the sake of your reputation, don't go telling people you liked the play.

URANIE: Well, I can't think what you found in it that could offend anybody's modesty.

CLIMÈNE: Alas, everything! And I maintain that no decent-minded woman could see it without feeling very uncomfortable, so numerous were the dirty, foul things I found in it.

URANIE: You must have a special gift for detecting filth that other people don't have, for I didn't notice any myself.

CLIMÈNE: That's obviously because you didn't want to see it. For the filth is there and, thank heaven, it's quite bare-faced. There's not the flimsiest veil to conceal it and the boldest eyes are shocked by its utter nakedness.

ÉLISE: I say!

CLIMÈNE: Oh yes, yes indeed!

URANIE: That's as maybe, but please give me an example of the filth you mentioned.

CLIMÈNE: Dear me, do I need to spell it out for you?

URANIE: Yes. I'm just asking for one passage which shocked you to the core.

CLIMÈNE: Does it take anything more than the scene with Agnès, where she talks about what the young man has taken?[7]

URANIE: Well? What's filthy about that?

CLIMÈNE: Ah!

URANIE: Please say.

CLIMÈNE: Shame on you!

URANIE: Out with it.

CLIMÈNE: I've nothing to say to you.

URANIE: Myself, I can't see the harm in it.

CLIMÈNE: That's all the worse for you!

URANIE: All the better for me, I should say. I look at the side of things that's shown me. I don't turn them over and peer underneath to see what's not intended to be seen.

CLIMÈNE: A woman's virtue –

URANIE: A woman's virtue has nothing to do with putting on airs. It ill becomes us to try to be purer than the genuinely pure. Affectation in this matter is worse than in any other. I don't think there's anything more ridiculous than that prickly sense of female honour that interprets everything the wrong way, attributes a guilty meaning to the most innocent words and takes offence at imagined slights. Believe me, women who kick up a fuss about such things aren't thought to be any more high-principled for it. On the contrary, their ambiguous primness and affectation make others all the more critical of the way they lead their lives. People are only too happy when they discover things to criticize in their behaviour. To give you an example, the other day in the theatre there were some women over the way from our box who acted in the most affected manner throughout the entire performance, turning their heads away and hiding their faces, thus giving rise all round them to silly comments about their behaviour which otherwise would not have been made. One of the footmen even shouted out that their ears were more chaste than all the rest of their bodies.

CLIMÈNE: So, when you see that play, you've got to be blind and pretend not to notice what's in it?

URANIE: But you shouldn't try to see things that aren't there.

CLIMÈNE: Oh! I maintain once more that the filth is there all right and it stares you in the face.

URANIE: Well I just don't agree with that.

CLIMÈNE: What! Isn't decency visibly outraged by what Agnès says in the passage we were talking about?

URANIE: Not at all. She doesn't say a single word that isn't perfectly decent, and if you want to read something else into it then it's you who're supplying the filth, not her, for she's only talking about a ribbon that's been taken from her.

CLIMÈNE: Oh, you can ribbon away as long as you like. But that 'the' where she pauses isn't put there for nothing. That 'the' starts some very peculiar thoughts. That 'the' is shockingly scandalous. Say what you like, you can't defend the outrageousness of that 'the'.

ÉLISE: That's true, coz, I side with Madame against that 'the'. That 'the' is offensive to the highest degree and you're wrong to defend that 'the'.

CLIMÈNE: There is a lubriciousness in it that is not to be tolerated.

ÉLISE: What was that word you used, Madame?

CLIMÈNE: Lubriciousness, Madame.

ÉLISE: Oh good Lord! Lubriciousness! I've no idea what it means, but I think it's a perfectly lovely word.

CLIMÈNE (*to Uranie*): You see? Even your own flesh and blood is on my side.

URANIE: Good heavens, she just prattles on. She never says what she thinks. If you want my advice, don't place too much faith in what she says.

ÉLISE (*to Uranie*): Oh, how unkind of you to try and make Madame suspicious of me. Just think where it would leave me if she were to believe what you say. Shall I be so unfortunate, Madame, that you would entertain such thoughts of me?

CLIMÈNE: Of course not. I pay no attention to anything she says. I believe that you are more sincere than she makes out.

ÉLISE: Oh, how right you are, Madame, and you'd do me justice by believing that I regard you as a most persuasive person, that I share all your opinions and am captivated by every word you speak.

CLIMÈNE: But I only say what I think, without affectation.

ÉLISE: That's perfectly obvious, Madame. Everything you say or do is natural. There is in your words, your tone of voice, the way you look and walk, your manner and dress sense the indefinable stamp of distinction which so delights people. I've been studying you, watching and listening, and I'm so taken with what I find that I try to copy you and imitate you in every respect.

CLIMÈNE: You're laughing at me, Madame.

ÉLISE: Excuse me, Madame, but who would want to laugh at you?

CLIMÈNE: I am not a good model, Madame.

ÉLISE: Oh, but you are, Madame!

CLIMÈNE: You flatter me, Madame.

ÉLISE: Not at all, Madame.

CLIMÈNE: Please spare me this, Madame.

ÉLISE: But I'm sparing you as it is. I haven't said the half of what I think, Madame.

CLIMÈNE: For heaven's sake, let's leave it there, if you don't mind. Otherwise, you'll make me feel most frightfully embarrassed. (*To Uranie*) Anyway, we're both against you and it ill becomes intelligent persons to stick stubbornly to . . .

Scene iv:

The MARQUIS, CLIMÈNE, GALOPIN, URANIE, ÉLISE

GALOPIN: Stop, sir, please!

MARQUIS: You obviously don't know who I am.

GALOPIN: Oh yes I do, but you can't go in.

MARQUIS: Ah! You're making a great fuss for a page!

GALOPIN: It's not right, trying to barge in when you've been told otherwise.

MARQUIS: I wish to see your mistress.

GALOPIN: She's not at home. I told you.

MARQUIS: She's there, in her room.

GALOPIN: She may be there, but she's not at home.

URANIE: What's the meaning of all this?

MARQUIS: It's your page Madame, playing the fool.

GALOPIN: I told him you weren't at home Madame, but he still keeps on trying to come in.

URANIE: But why did you tell this gentleman that I wasn't there?

GALOPIN: You told me off the other day for telling him you were.

URANIE: The impudence of the boy! I beg you sir, don't believe a word of what he says. He's not very bright and mistook you for somebody else.

MARQUIS: I realized that Madame, and, had it not been discourteous to you, I would have taught him not to mistake people of rank for somebody else.

ÉLISE: My cousin is extremely obliged to you for your civility.

URANIE: A chair you insolent boy!

GALOPIN: Isn't that one there?

URANIE: Bring it closer. (*Galopin drags the chair roughly and goes out.*)

MARQUIS: Your young page doesn't think much of me Madame.

ÉLISE: That would be quite wrong of him.

MARQUIS: Could his disapproval be a *tax* I pay on my *acts*? Ha ha ha ha!

ÉLISE: As he grows older, he'll learn to recognize the right people.

MARQUIS: What were you ladies talking about when I interrupted you?

URANIE: That play, *The School for Wives*.

MARQUIS: I've only just come from seeing it.

CLIMÈNE: Well sir, and what did you make of it, if I may ask?

MARQUIS: An absolute shocker.

CLIMÈNE: Oh! I'm delighted to hear it.

MARQUIS: It's the most disgraceful thing you could imagine. But devil take it, I could hardly get in to see it. I thought I was going to be crushed at the door and never had my feet trod on so often. Just look at the state of my knee tassels and ribbons. Really!

ÉLISE: They are clearly the most damning indictment of *The School for Wives*. You are quite right to disapprove of it.

MARQUIS: I don't think there's ever been such a bad play.

URANIE: Ah! Here's Dorante. We've been expecting him.

Scene v:
DORANTE, *the* MARQUIS, CLIMÈNE, ÉLISE, URANIE

DORANTE: Please don't move. Don't stop what you were saying. You're discussing a topic which has been the talk of every house in Paris for the last four days. There has rarely been anything funnier than the great variety of opinions that have been expressed about it. For I have heard some people denounce the play for exactly the same things for which I have seen others praised the most.

URANIE: The Marquis is being very critical of it.

MARQUIS: That's true. I think it's lamentable, dammit, lamentable, it's as lamentable as you can get. It's what you might call lamentable.

DORANTE: And I, Marquis, find your opinion lamentable.

MARQUIS: Why Chevalier, you're not proposing to defend the play?

DORANTE: Yes, I do propose to defend it.

MARQUIS: By God, you have my guarantee that it's lamentable!

DORANTE: Your guarantee wouldn't stand up in a court of law. But tell me, Marquis, if you will, why the play is what you say it is.

MARQUIS: Why it's lamentable?

DORANTE: Yes.

MARQUIS: It's lamentable, because it's lamentable.

DORANTE: Well, after that there's no more to be said. The case has been heard and sentence passed. Even so, enlighten us, tell us what's wrong with it.

MARQUIS: How should I know? I didn't even bother to listen. But dammit, I know I never saw anything so bad. Dorilas, who was sitting next to me, thought the same.

DORANTE: Now there's an authority! You've got sound support!

MARQUIS: You only had to hear the constant roars of laughter from the pit. It's all the proof I need to know the play is worthless.

DORANTE: So I take it, Marquis, that you are one of those superior persons about town who refuse to admit that the pit has any common-sense at all and would be mortified to find themselves joining in and laughing with it, even if it was the funniest play ever written? The other day I saw a friend of ours in the theatre, sitting on the stage, making himself quite ridiculous for exactly that reason. He listened to the play from beginning to end with the most solemn and sombre expression on his face. Everything that made other people laugh made him frown. Every time they laughed, he shrugged his shoulders and looked down sadly at the pit. And occasionally, glancing scornfully at the people there, he'd say aloud: 'Go on, laugh, you there in the pit, laugh away!' His irritation was as good as another play. He was civil enough to perform it to the entire audience and everybody agreed that no one could have carried it off better. Listen Marquis if you will, and others like you too. There's no special place reserved for common-sense in a comedy. The difference between a gold half-louis and fifteen sous has nothing to do with taste, and people can be poor judges whether they're sitting down or standing up.[8] And in general terms, I'd rather trust the judgement of the pit because among the people who make up that part of the audience there are some who are quite capable of judging a play according to the rules, and because the rest form an opinion by the right method of judging, which is to let yourself be carried along by the play, without blind prejudice, or affected enthusiasm, or silly squeamishness.

MARQUIS: So now Chevalier, you're the champion of the pit! By God, I'm glad to hear it. I shall not fail to inform it that you're one of its friends! Ha ha ha ha!

DORANTE: You can laugh all you like. I stand up for good sense and can't abide people with cranky ideas, like the Marquis de Mascarille.[9] It makes me very angry when I see them making fools of themselves despite their rank. They always lay down the law and talk fearlessly about all manner of subjects, though they don't know the first thing about them. They cheer the worst parts of a play but never stir during the good passages. When they see a painting or hear a concert, they scatter praise and blame on all the wrong things, pick up here and there the technical terms of the art they're criticizing and invariably mangle and misuse them. Ah! by heaven! Gentlemen, if the Almighty has not given you a proper understanding of such things, hold your tongues! Don't give those who hear you expatiate grounds for laughing at you, and remember: if you say nothing at all, other people might think you're really very clever.

MARQUIS: I say Chevalier, you're taking this —

DORANTE: Good Lord, Marquis, I don't mean you — I'm referring to a dozen other gentry who bring Court society into disrepute by their bizarre behaviour and make the common people think we're all alike. I myself intend to distance myself from them as much as I can and shall go on poking fun at them whenever I come across them until they finally see sense.

MARQUIS: Just tell me this Chevalier: do you reckon Lysandre is clever?

DORANTE: Yes I do. Very.

URANIE: There's no denying it.

MARQUIS: Ask him what he thinks of *The School for Wives*. You'll find he'll tell you he doesn't like it.

DORANTE: Well, there are lots of people who are too clever for their own good, too dazzled by their own brilliance to see clearly. They'd be extremely put out if they found themselves agreeing with anyone, since they feel obliged to give the lead in these matters.

URANIE: That's true. Friend Lysandre is clearly one of them. He must be the first with his opinion and likes other people to hold back respectfully until he comes out with it. Any expression of approval given before his is an insult to his intelligence, and he takes his revenge publicly by adopting the opposite view. He thinks he should be consulted in all intellectual matters and I'm convinced that if the author had shown him his play before having it staged, he'd have thought it the finest that was ever written.

MARQUIS: And what do you make of Milady Araminte who goes round telling everybody it's disgraceful and claiming she couldn't stomach it because it's crammed full of filth?

DORANTE: I'd say her remarks were consistent with the character she plays nowadays and that there are people who make themselves ridiculous through trying to be too high-minded. She's clever enough I grant you, but she has followed the bad example of those women who on reaching a certain age cast around for something to put in the place of what is slipping away from them and imagine that a show of strict prudery can be a substitute for youth and beauty. Araminte goes further in that direction than the rest of the breed and her scruples are so sensitive that she detects filth in places where no one else has ever seen any. They say that these scruples of hers even extend to trying to cripple our language. The lady is so strict that she'd willingly chop the head and tail off just about every word there is because she finds those syllables indecent.[10]

URANIE: You can't be serious Chevalier.

MARQUIS: So Chevalier, you think you can defend this play of yours by being sarcastic about those who condemn it.

DORANTE: Not at all. But I do think the lady is wrong to be so shocked —

ÉLISE: Just one moment Chevalier, there might be others besides her who hold the same views.

DORANTE: Well at least I know you are not one of them, and when you went to see it —

ÉLISE: That's true, but I've changed my opinion. Madame Climène has supported hers with such convincing reasons that she has brought me round to her way of thinking.

DORANTE (*to Climène*): Ah Madame, I do beg your pardon. If you wish, I shall, out of regard for you, take back everything I said.

CLIMÈNE: I wouldn't wish you to do so out of regard for me but out of a regard for what is right. For when properly considered, this play is totally indefensible and I cannot conceive how –

URANIE: Ah, here's Monsieur Lysidas, the author.[11] He's come just at the right moment to discuss this question. Monsieur Lysidas, draw up a chair and sit down here.

Scene vi:
LYSIDAS, DORANTE, *the* MARQUIS, ÉLISE, URANIE, CLIMÈNE

LYSIDAS: I'm rather late Madame, but I had to read out my play at the house of Madame la Marquise – you know, I told you about her – and the warm reception I was given detained me an hour longer than I had anticipated.

ÉLISE: Applause does have a magical power to detain an author.

URANIE: Do be seated Monsieur Lysidas. We shall read your play after supper.

LYSIDAS: Everybody who was there intends to come to the first performance and have promised to do their duty by it.

URANIE: I'm sure they will. But please, do sit down. We're in the middle of a subject that I'd like to see taken further.

LYSIDAS: I trust Madame that you will also take a box for the opening night?

URANIE: We'll see. But please let's go on with the discussion.

LYSIDAS: I must inform you, Madame, that they're nearly all taken.

URANIE: But that's splendid. Now, you came just when I needed you. Everyone here was against me.

ÉLISE: The Chevalier was on your side to begin with but now he knows that Madame is leading the opposition, I think you're going to have to look for support elsewhere.

CLIMÈNE: No, no, I wouldn't want him to be ungallant to your cousin. I shall permit his head to line up on the same side as his heart.

DORANTE: With this permission, Madame, I shall be bold and defend myself.

URANIE: But first, let us be told Monsieur Lysidas's sentiments.

LYSIDAS: On what, Madame?

URANIE: On *The School for Wives*.

LYSIDAS: Ah!

DORANTE: What do you make of it?

LYSIDAS: I have nothing to say about it. You know, we authors should be very circumspect when talking about each other's work.

DORANTE: But, just between ourselves, what do you think of the play?

LYSIDAS: I, sir?

URANIE: Give us your honest opinion.

LYSIDAS: I think it's excellent.

DORANTE: Really?

LYSIDAS: Yes, really. Why not? Isn't it quite clearly the best play ever staged?

DORANTE: Aha! You're a sly devil, Monsieur Lysidas. You're not saying what you think.

LYSIDAS: I beg your pardon?

DORANTE: Good Lord, I know you. Don't pretend with us.

LYSIDAS: I, sir?

DORANTE: It's clear to me that you're only saying the nice things you say about this play out of politeness. In your heart of hearts you agree with most people who consider it bad.

LYSIDAS: Ha ha ha!

DORANTE: Come now, be frank now and admit it's a terrible play.

LYSIDAS: It's true that the best judges do not approve of it.

MARQUIS: My word, Chevalier, that's you sorted out! See where all your scoffing gets you! Ha, ha, ha, ha!

DORANTE: That's right, my dear Marquis, laugh as much as you like!

MARQUIS: You see we've got the experts on our side.

DORANTE: True, a verdict from Monsieur Lysidas does carry considerable weight. But Monsieur Lysidas will permit me not to yield for all that. Since I have the temerity to defend myself against Madame's way of thinking, he will not take it amiss if I combat his.

ÉLISE: What? So now you have it: Madame Climène, the Marquis and

Monsieur Lysidas are all against you and yet you still won't give in! Really, it's most ill-bred.

CLIMÈNE: Honestly, it's beyond me that reasonable people can take it into their heads to try to defend the wicked nonsense in that play.

MARQUIS: Dammit, Madame, it's deplorable from one end of it to the other.

DORANTE: That's pretty sweeping, Marquis. Nothing's easier than dismissing matters out of hand like that. I don't think anything is safe against that kind of categorical judgement.

MARQUIS: By God, all the actors from the other theatres who went to see it hadn't a good word to say for it.

DORANTE: Oh, then I won't say any more. You're right, Marquis. Since the other actors tore it to shreds, then obviously we should take their word for it. They're all very knowledgeable and quite unprejudiced.[12] So there's nothing more to be said. I give in.

CLIMÈNE: Whether you give in or not, one thing I am sure of: you'll not get me to tolerate the indecencies in the play, nor the offensive way it satirizes women.

URANIE: I myself shall take good care not to be offended by it or to take everything that's said in it personally. That kind of satire is aimed at manners in an overall way and is only indirectly relevant to individuals. So let's not apply the barbs of a general criticism to our particular selves, but, if we can, let's try to learn from the lesson without letting on that we think it was aimed at us. We shouldn't take all these ridiculous pictures of manners performed in the theatre too seriously. They are public mirrors in which we should never admit we can see our own reflections. And to be offended by what's in it is to make a public confession of our shortcomings.

CLIMÈNE: For my own part, I do not mention these things because they might in any way concern me personally, for I think my way of life is such that I need not fear to be identified in any of the representations of women who behave badly.

ÉLISE: Of course not, Madame. No one would try to look for you in that quarter. Your character is well known: it is one of those things that no one would argue about.

URANIE: Which is why, Madame, nothing I said was meant for you. My words, like the satire in this play, were intended in a general sense.

CLIMÈNE: I'm sure they were, Madame. But let's not linger further on this topic. I don't know how you take the insults made against our sex at one point in the play, but personally I don't mind admitting that it makes me frightfully angry to observe that this impertinent author calls us *serpents*.[13]

URANIE: But don't you see, he puts the word in the mouth of a ridiculous character?

DORANTE: Besides, Madame, are you not aware that the insults of lovers never give offence? that love may be tempestuous as well as sweet? and that in such circumstances the strangest words – and even worse – are often taken as marks of affection by the very women at whom they are directed?

ÉLISE: Say what you like, I can't stomach the word any better than the 'man's stew' and 'custard pie' that Madame was talking about earlier.

MARQUIS: Ah, by Jove! Yes, 'custard pie'! That's something I noticed myself. Custard pie indeed! I am grateful to you, Madame for reminding me of the custard pie. Are there enough apples in Normandy to throw at the actors when they say 'custard pie'? Custard pie indeed, custard pie!

DORANTE: How do you mean: custard pie?

MARQUIS: By God, Chevalier! Custard pie!

DORANTE: What about it?

MARQUIS: Custard pie!

DORANTE: Tell us what you have in mind.

MARQUIS: Custard pie!

URANIE: But it seems to me you really ought to explain what you mean.

MARQUIS: Custard pie, Madame!

URANIE: What do you find to object to in that?

MARQUIS: Me? Nothing. Custard pie!

URANIE: Oh, I give up.

ÉLISE: The Marquis has gone about it the right way and beaten the pair of you into submission. But I'd like Monsieur Lysidas to finish you off with a few thwacks of his own.

LYSIDAS: It's not my habit to pick faults in anything: I usually go very easy on other people's work. But still, without wanting to trample on the Chevalier's evident partiality for the author, you must admit that this kind of comedy isn't proper comedy at all, and that there's a great deal of difference between all these trifling amusements and the beauties of serious drama. Yet these days people can't get enough of them. It's all they go to see. You see appallingly thin audiences for great plays while the whole of Paris flocks to the flummery. I confess there are times when it makes my heart bleed. It's a disgrace to the nation.

CLIMÈNE: It's true. People's taste is strangely debased in these matters. Our times are becoming abysmally vulgarified.

ÉLISE: That's another good word – 'vulgarified'. Did you coin it, Madame?

CLIMÈNE: Well . . .

ÉLISE: I thought so.

DORANTE: So you take the view, Monsieur Lysidas, that all the intelligence and beauty go into serious drama and that comic plays are footling affairs that have nothing whatsoever to commend them?

URANIE: That's not the way I see it. Of course tragedy is a beautiful thing when it's done properly. But comedy has its charms and I think that the one is no less difficult to do than the other.

DORANTE: Certainly, Madame. You say difficult, but if you were to add 'more' on the side of comedy, you wouldn't be far wrong. For indeed I think it's a good deal easier to wax eloquent over noble sentiments, to defy Fate in verse, to rail at Destiny and take the gods to task than to get to proper grips with human folly and put the failings we all have on a stage in a congenial way. When you portray heroes, you can do as you please. They are pure invention and no one expects them to resemble real people. All you need to do is follow the promptings of a free-wheeling imagination which often departs from the truth and sets off in pursuit of the extraordinary. But when you portray people, you must paint from nature. Audiences want your characters to be true to life and you won't get anywhere unless you make the men and women of your own times recognizable on stage. What I mean is that in serious theatre, all you need do to avoid criticism is to say sensible things and express them well. But that's not enough with comedy: you must be amusing. And making decent people laugh is a very peculiar business.

CLIMÈNE: I believe I am one of those decent people. But I didn't find anything to laugh at in any of what I saw.

MARQUIS: By God, neither did I.

DORANTE: Coming from you, Marquis, that doesn't surprise me – it's because you couldn't find any puns in it.

LYSIDAS: Lord, sir, what you could find in it was hardly any better. All the witticisms fell pretty flat, to my mind.

DORANTE: That was not the view at Court.

LYSIDAS: Oh sir, the Court . . .

DORANTE: Go on Monsieur Lysidas, finish what you were saying. I can see you mean that the Court is no judge of these things. To accuse the injustice of the times and the ignorance of courtiers is the usual refuge of you authors, sir, when your plays do not succeed. I would have you please remember, Monsieur Lysidas, that the eyesight of courtiers is as good as anyone else's, that a man with a lace collar and feathers in his hat can be as shrewd as another in a short wig and a short, plain cravat, that the great test for any play is the view taken of it at Court, that you must study its taste if you want to get anywhere, that nowhere else do you get such fair judgements, and, without wishing to drag in all the learned persons who congregate there, remember that the natural good sense and conversation of elegant society breeds a special cast of mind which judges with incomparably greater subtlety than all the pedants with their rusty learning.

URANIE: It's true that however short a time you spend there, you see so many things going on every day that you do acquire discerning habits of mind, especially in telling good wit from bad.

DORANTE: There are some absurd people at Court, I agree, and I am the first, as you observe, to deride them. But, for heaven's sake, there are also plenty of the same sort among the professional wits. If a play makes fun of marquises, I think there's a much better case for making fun of authors. It would be hilarious to put their pedantic affectation and ludicrous fussing on a stage, their nasty habit of killing off the characters in their works, their appetite for applause, their reluctance to say what they think, the things they do to further their reputation and their defensive and offensive cliques, not forgetting their wars of wit and battles in prose and verse.

LYSIDAS: Molière is very fortunate, sir, to have such an enthusiastic supporter as you. But to come to the point, the question before us is whether his play is good or bad, and I am prepared to identify many glaring faults everywhere in it.

URANIE: It's an odd thing but you dramatic poets always dismiss the plays everyone goes to see and never say anything good except about plays nobody goes to. You show unquenchable hatred for the former and a quite incomprehensible affection for the latter.

DORANTE: That's because it is charitable to side with the afflicted.

URANIE: But please, Monsieur Lysidas, do point out these faults. I missed them.

LYSIDAS: Those who know their Aristotle and their Horace can see, Madame, that the play sins against the rules of art.

URANIE: I confess I am not acquainted with those gentlemen. I don't know the rules of art.

DORANTE: Men like you make me laugh with your rules which you are forever trumpeting in our ears, to confuse the ignorant. To hear you talk, anyone would think that the rules of art are the greatest mysteries in the world. Yet they are no more than a set of simple observations which common-sense has formulated about what can spoil the pleasure we find in works of this sort. And the same common-sense that made these observations long ago still goes on making them every day, without any help from Horace and Aristotle. I should very much like to know if the greatest of all the rules is not simply to please and if a performance of a play which has achieved that goal did not set about it in the right way. Do you think the entire public is wrong about these matters, and that no one can be the best judge of his own pleasure?

URANIE: I've noticed one thing about those gentlemen, which is that those who talk the most about the rules and know more about them than anybody else, write plays that nobody thinks are any good.

DORANTE: And that shows, Madame, just how little attention we need pay to their complicated quarrels. For after all, if the plays which observe the rules do not please, and those which do please do not observe the rules, then it must of necessity follow that there must be something wrong with the rules. So let's not worry about the pettifogging dogma which they would like to see dominate public taste. Let's judge a play only by the effect it has on us. Let us have the confidence to surrender to whatever grips our emotions and not look for reasons to prevent us from enjoying it.

URANIE: Personally, when I see a play, my only concern is whether it moves me. And if I've been thoroughly entertained, I don't ask if I'm wrong or if Aristotle's rules forbade me to laugh.

DORANTE: It's exactly like the man who finds a sauce delicious and insists on looking to see if it's any good by checking it against the recipes in the *Cuisinier français*.[14]

URANIE: True, and I wonder about the sophistication of some people who split hairs about things we should make our minds up about ourselves.

DORANTE: You're right, Madame, to find all their mysterious nuances peculiar. For if the distinctions they make are real, then we are left no longer trusting ourselves – our very senses will be their slaves in everything, even eating and drinking, and we won't dare to call anything good any more without the approval of the experts.

LYSIDAS: In short, sir, your only argument is that *The School for Wives* is a success. You're not in the least interested in whether it follows the rules, provided that . . .

DORANTE: Just a moment, Monsieur Lysidas, I can't allow that. I do say that the great art in all this is to please, and that since this comedy pleased those people for whom it was intended, I think that is quite enough as far as this play is concerned and there's no need to look any further. But at the same time I maintain that it does not offend against any of the rules you're talking about. I've read them, thank heaven, as closely as the next man and I could easily prove that perhaps we have no play in the repertoire more regular than this one.

ÉLISE: Courage, Monsieur Lysidas! We're lost if you back down now!

LYSIDAS: What sir? The protasis, the epitasis, the peripeteia . . .

DORANTE: Ah, Monsieur Lysidas, you beat us into submission with your long words! Please, couldn't you wear your learning a little more lightly? Bring what you say down to the level of ordinary mortals and speak in a way that people understand. Do you think that a Greek name lends more weight to your argument? And don't you think it would be just as effective to say 'the exposition' rather than the protasis, the 'development of the plot' for the epitasis, and the 'climax' instead of the peripeteia?

LYSIDAS: They are technical terms which it is legitimate to use. But since the words grate on your ears, I shall explain what I mean another way. I shall ask you to respond positively to three or four observations I am about to make. Should we tolerate a play which runs counter to the definition of what a play is? For the term 'drama' comes from a Greek word meaning 'to act', which indicates that the nature of this kind of composition consists of action. And in this particular play, there is no action and the whole thing is made up of monologues either by Agnès or Horace.

MARQUIS: Aha, Chevalier!

CLIMÈNE: That's very cleverly observed, and it gets to the nub of the thing.

LYSIDAS: Is there anything less witty or, to put it more accurately, more vulgar than some of the jokes which make everyone laugh and in particular the one about 'children through the ear'?[15]

CLIMÈNE: Excellent!

ÉLISE: Ah!

LYSIDAS: And isn't the scene with the valet and the serving woman inside the house[16] tedious, too long and quite out of keeping with the rest?

MARQUIS: That's true.

CLIMÈNE: Absolutely.

LYSIDAS: And doesn't Arnolphe give his money to Horace far too readily?[17] And since he's the ridiculous character in the play, should he be allowed to perform the action of a good and worthy man?

MARQUIS: Good. Another excellent point.

CLIMÈNE: Splendid!

ÉLISE: Marvellous!

LYSIDAS: And are not the sermon and the maxims[18] ludicrous and even lacking in respect for the mysteries of our religion?

MARQUIS: Well said!

CLIMÈNE: That's the way to talk!

ÉLISE: Nothing could be better.

LYSIDAS: And finally, this Monsieur de la Souche who we are told is an intelligent man and seems so serious-minded in a number of passages, doesn't he descend into something far too comic and exaggerated in the fifth act[19] when he explains the violence of his feelings to Agnès, with all that wild rolling of the eyes, and the ridiculous sighs and silly tears which make everybody laugh?

MARQUIS: By God! Wonderful!

CLIMÈNE: Miraculous!

ÉLISE: Bravo, Monsieur Lysidas!

LYSIDAS: I'll pass over a large number of other points, for I do not wish to bore you.

MARQUIS: By Jove, Chevalier, that's you put in your place!

DORANTE: We shall see.

MARQUIS: Upon my soul, you've met your match!

DORANTE: Perhaps.

MARQUIS: Answer, answer, answer, answer!

DORANTE: Gladly. He . . .

MARQUIS: Come on, please answer.

DORANTE: Let me do so, then. If . . .

MARQUIS: By heaven, I defy you to answer!

DORANTE: I shan't be able to if you talk all the time.

CLIMÈNE: Please, let's hear his arguments.

DORANTE: First, it is not correct to say that the play consists entirely of narration. We see plenty of action on stage and the monologues themselves recount actions, as is required by the nature of the plot. Moreover, all these long speeches are made naturally to the person concerned. As a result, he is plunged at every turn into a state of deepening confusion, which amuses the audience, and with each new revelation he takes whatever steps he can to ward off the disaster he fears.

URANIE: My own view is that the beauty of the plot of *The School for Wives* lies in all the confiding that goes on constantly. What seems very amusing to me is that an intelligent man who is kept informed of everything, both by the simple girl he loves and his blundering rival, still for all that can't avoid what happens to him.

MARQUIS: Nonsense! Nonsense!

CLIMÈNE: A feeble answer.

ÉLISE: A poor argument.

DORANTE: As for 'children through the ear', that's only funny in relation to Arnolphe. The author didn't put it in as a joke in itself but only as a way of showing the character of the man, of depicting his folly, since he repeats a silly, banal remark Agnès has made as though it were the most wonderful thing in the world, which fills him with utter delight.

MARQUIS: That's no answer.

CLIMÈNE: It's not satisfactory.

ÉLISE: Might as well not say anything.

DORANTE: As to the money he gives so freely, not to mention the fact that the letter from his best friend is an adequate guarantee, it's not inconsistent that someone might be ridiculous in certain matters and sensible in others. And to take the scene with Alain and Georgette inside the house, which some people have found long and dull, there is certainly a good reason for it. In the same way that Arnolphe has been duped while he was away by the sheer innocence of the girl he loves, so, when he gets back, he is kept for some considerable time outside his front door by the innocence of his servants, so that he is seen at every turn to be punished by the very thing he had assumed would make his precautions unassailable.

MARQUIS: These are arguments that carry no weight.

CLIMÈNE: It won't wash.

ÉLISE: It's pitiful.

DORANTE: As for the moral observations you call a sermon, it's a fact that sincerely religious people who heard them didn't find they profaned any of the mysteries you mentioned. And it's obvious that the words 'hell' and 'boiling cauldrons' are sufficiently justified by both Arnolphe's extravagant behaviour and the innocence of the girl he's talking to. As to the amorous outburst in act five which you accused of being too exaggerated or too farcical, I'd like to know if it isn't a satire of the way lovers carry on, and if even the most upright and proper people in similar circumstances do not do things –

MARQUIS: Upon my soul, Chevalier, you'd be well advised to say no more.

DORANTE: Very well, but if we could only take a look at ourselves when we're head over heels in love –

MARQUIS: I simply won't listen to you.

DORANTE: Please, do listen. Isn't it in moments of raging passion –

MARQUIS (*singing*): Tra la la la, Tra, la, la, la, la, la, la.

DORANTE: What –

MARQUIS: Tra la la la, Tra, la, la, la, la, la, la.

DORANTE: I don't know if –

MARQUIS: Tra la la la, Tra, la, la, la, la, la, la.

DORANTE: It seems to me –

MARQUIS: Tra la la la, Tra, la, la, la, la, la, la.

URANIE: Amusing things keep happening during our little quarrel. I think someone could turn them into a short play that would work quite well as an afterpiece to *The School for Wives*.

DORANTE: You're right.

MARQUIS: By heaven, Chevalier, you'd have a role in it that wouldn't reflect much credit on you.

DORANTE: True, Marquis.

CLIMÈNE: I should really like it to be done – but only if it were treated exactly as it happened.

ÉLISE: And I'd be glad to supply my character for it.

LYSIDAS: I wouldn't refuse to let mine be in it, on the contrary.

URANIE: Since everyone would be pleased, Chevalier, do write notes on everything and give them to your friend Molière so that he can turn them into a play.

CLIMÈNE: He'd certainly do no such thing – it's hardly something that would enhance his reputation.

URANIE: Not at all. I know what he's like. He doesn't care if people criticize his plays provided they go to see them.

DORANTE: Yes. But what ending could he come up with for this? For he couldn't have a marriage or the discovery of a long-lost relative. I don't see how our discussion could be concluded.

URANIE: He'd have to think up some event or other.

Scene vii:
GALOPIN, LYSIDAS, DORANTE, *the* MARQUIS, CLIMÈNE, ÉLISE, URANIE

GALOPIN: Madame, supper is served.

DORANTE: That's it! It's just what we need for the ending we're looking for! We couldn't find anything more natural. They'll argue long and hard, just as we've been doing, and no one will give in. Then a page will enter and say Madame, supper is served, and they'll all troop off to eat.

URANIE: There couldn't be a better ending for the play and we'd be well advised to stop there.

Don Juan

or,

The Statue at the Feast

Don Juan,
ou
Le Festin de pierre

First performed on 15 February 1665 at the Palais Royal by the Players of Monsieur, only brother to the King

Don Juan, with Molière in the role of Sganarelle, began its extraordinary career with fifteen highly successful performances. The acting and production values, particularly the spectacular effects devised for despatching Don Juan to hell, were greatly admired. Yet from the start the play was controversial and after the first performance Molière cut the scene (III.ii) in which Don Juan tries to force the Poor Man to blaspheme. Following the annual Easter closure of the Paris theatres the play was withdrawn in the face of mounting opposition. It was said to defend free thought and 'atheism'. Here, said one critic, was a play in which 'an unbeliever, who is seemingly struck down, in fact strikes at and overturns the very foundations of religion'. It was argued too that Sganarelle was such a feeble defender of the faith that he was no better than Don Juan himself.

Though *Don Juan* was not banned, Molière never performed it again, nor, though authorized to print the text, did he publish it. An edited version was staged in Paris in 1676 and the following year, at the request of Molière's widow, it was modified and turned into verse by Thomas Corneille and performed with great success. Though the original text was included in an edition of the complete plays in 1682, it was censored before publication and only a handful of uncut copies survived. The cuts, together with other passages probably discarded by Molière himself, were restored in the edition of Molière's works published the following year in Amsterdam. But it was Thomas Corneille's version which continued to be performed for nearly two hundred years. It was not until 1847 that the Comédie-Française gave *Don Juan* its sixteenth performance. It was staged again only 136 times before 1953 when, having been revived by Louis Jouvet, it was performed with great success by Jean Vilar at the Théâtre National Populaire. Since then it has been fully rehabilitated and is now recognized as one of Molière's greatest masterpieces.

The figure of Don Juan de Tenorio, the aristocrat who rebels against God and is punished for his audacity, made his first appearance in the

1620s in Spain, in a play by a monk, Tirso de Molina, whose purpose was to show that eleventh-hour conversions cannot compensate for an immoral life. Tirso's play was adapted several times in Italy, notably by Cicognini before 1650 and Giliberto in 1652. In 1658 the Italian actors based in Paris performed a version of the story in the farcical style of the *commedia dell'arte*, and, in Lyons, an actor named Dorimond staged a tragi-comedy on the theme, which he called not 'the guest of stone' as his predecessors had done, but *Le Festin de pierre, ou le Fils criminel* (*The Feast of Stone, or the Criminal Son*). It was published in 1659 and performed in Paris in 1661. Another version with the same title, a tragi-comedy by the actor Villiers, was staged in 1659 while the Italian actors performed their comic version throughout the 1660s: one revival was given only a month before the curtain went up on Molière's *Don Juan*. And despite the controversy, the subject remained popular. Rosimond's *Nouveau Festin de pierre* was staged in 1669.

Molière, far from setting out to make an intellectual stand, plainly sought to exploit a subject which had proved successful with audiences, and his *Don Juan* has clear debts to the French versions of Villiers, Dorimond and the Italians. But while Dorimond made Don Juan a believer who revolts against God, Molière more provocatively made him a rationalist who believes in nothing. His contempt for religion is made clear in his attitude to marriage, by which he refuses to be bound. As a seducer he exhibits a heartless libertinism which, in its rejection of spiritual and moral values, resembles the free thought which the Church equated with atheism. Yet though Molière seems to play with fire, his interest in Don Juan is not doctrinal but human.

He developed the role of Don Juan's father and invented Elvira. Both are reminders of the emotional side of life and the harm which Don Juanism and atheism can do. Moreover, Don Juan is hardly made happy by his constant pursuit of women, for his life is a mechanical series of physical conquests, each forgotten as new victims cross his path. But he is more than an emotional cripple, for he is a hypocrite. He is not without courage, yet he simply deserts Elvira, cannot speak honestly to his father whom he despises and hides behind the cloak of religion when it suits him. The progress of Don Juan – from libertinism, to philosophical atheism and finally to mealy-mouthed hypocrisy – suggests that Molière's point of view was less concerned with denouncing disbelief than with pointing to the need for settled human values.

Even so, it does not seem at first sight a suitable subject for comedy. Elvira has a sombre dignity and it is not easy to be amused by the honourable valour of her brothers. Yet the mood is constantly relieved by injections of farce (the comic peasants of Act II, or Monsieur Dimanche in Act IV), amusing stage business (the plates in Act V) and, above all, through the anchor-character of Sganarelle, a very French comic valet who brings the audience down to earth along with the final curtain by wondering who will pay his wages.

For despite Don Juan and the ghostly Statue he defies, this is a play which covers the range of theatrical colours, from slapstick to high drama. It is, moreover, the least regular of the Molière canon. The chronology is uncertain and the setting switches silently from town to beach, from tavern to mausoleum, with a freedom which prepares us for the mysterious drama of Don Juan's fate.

Characters

DON JUAN, son of Don Louis
SGANARELLE, valet to Don Juan
ELVIRA, wife of Don Juan
GUSMAN, squire to Elvira
DON CARLOS ⎱ Elvira's brothers
DON ALONSO ⎰
DON LOUIS, Don Juan's father
FRANCISCO, a poor man
CHARLOTTE ⎱ peasant girls
MATHURINE ⎰

PIERROT, a peasant
STATUE of the Commander
LA VIOLETTE ⎱ servants of
RAGOTIN ⎰ Don Juan
MONSIEUR DIMANCHE, a
   tradesman
LA RAMÉE, a soldier of fortune
RETINUE of the brothers Don
   Carlos and Don Alonso
A SPECTRE

The action is set in Sicily.

Act I

Scene i:
SGANARELLE, GUSMAN

SGANARELLE (*holding a snuff-box*): Aristotle and all the philosophers can say what they like, there's nothing like tobacco.[1] It's an honest man's habit. Anyone who can live without tobacco doesn't deserve to live at all. It not only stimulates and purges the human brain, it also teaches people to be virtuous, and from it you learn how to act like a gentleman. Surely you've noticed that the moment a man starts taking it, how polite he is to everybody and is only too pleased to offer it around right and left wherever he happens to be? He doesn't even wait to be asked but goes right in and anticipates people's wishes. Which just goes to show that snuff breeds sentiments of honour and virtue in everyone who takes it. But enough of that now. Let's get back to what we were talking about. You were saying, my dear Gusman, that your mistress Dona Elvira, surprised by our departure, set out in pursuit. You said my master had managed to make her fall so deeply in love with him that she couldn't live another moment without coming to look for him here. Shall I tell you, between our two selves, what I think? I'm afraid she won't get much joy from being in love with him. Travelling to this town won't do much good. You'd have done just as well staying where you were.

GUSMAN: Yes, but what's the reason for it? Do tell me Sganarelle, exactly what it is about this ominous situation that makes you afraid? Has your master taken you into his confidence? Did he say he felt he had to leave us on account of something we'd done to cool his feelings for us?

SGANARELLE: Not at all. But knowing how the land lies, I have a fair idea of how these things usually go. He hasn't said anything to me yet, but I'm almost tempted to bet that's exactly the way they're going now. I could be wrong, but after all I've had a lot of experience and I know a bit about this sort of thing.

GUSMAN: What? Are you saying the reason for Don Juan's sudden departure was that he has been unfaithful? You think he could be so callous as to betray Dona Elvira's innocent love like that?

SGANARELLE: No, it's just that he's still young and hasn't the heart . . .

GUSMAN: But how could a gentleman do such a cowardly thing?

SGANARELLE: Oh yes, he's a gentleman all right, and a lot of difference
it makes! That won't stop him doing anything he wants to!

GUSMAN: But surely he's bound by the obligations of holy matrimony.

SGANARELLE: Ah Gusman, my poor friend, believe me, you still don't
know what sort of man Don Juan is.

GUSMAN: No, I certainly don't know what sort of man he could possibly
be if he has really practised such a deception. I simply do not
understand how, after being so affectionate, after showing such
impatience, after all his tender declarations, vows, sighs and tears,
after all those impassioned letters, ardent protestations and repeated
promises, in a word, after behaving with so much fire and displaying
such passion that he went as far as invading the holy calm of a
convent to carry off Dona Elvira – I repeat, I simply cannot understand
how, after all that, he could be so heartless as to go back on his
word.

SGANARELLE: I don't find it at all hard to understand, and if you knew
our slippery friend as well as I do, you'd find that this sort of thing
comes easily to him. I'm not saying his feelings for Dona Elvira have
changed. I can't be sure yet. I left before he did you know, on his
orders, and he's not spoken to me since he got here. But I will say
this much, as a warning – *inter nos* – that in Don Juan my master
you see that greatest villain the world has ever known, a maniac, a
cur, a devil, a Turk, a heretic, who doesn't believe in Heaven or
Hell or things that go bump in the night. He spends his life like a
brutish beast, a swinish Epicurean,[2] a second Sardanapalus,[3] shutting
his ears to anyone who remonstrates with him and ridiculing everything we believe in. You tell me he's married your mistress. Take it
from me: to satisfy his lust, he'd have done a lot more than that –
as well as her, he'd have married you, and her dog and her cat too.
A wedding doesn't mean a thing to him. It's the only sort of trap he
sets for ensnaring women: he weds them left, right and centre, ladies,
their daughters, shopkeepers' wives, peasant girls, there's none too
bold or too shy for him. If I told you the names of all the women
he's married in one place or another, it would take from now till
tonight. What I'm telling you comes as a surprise – you've gone
quite pale. But this is only a faint outline of the man. To complete

the picture would take a great deal more work. So let's just settle for saying that the wrath of Heaven is bound to catch up with him some day and that, as far as I'm concerned, I'd rather serve the devil himself than Don Juan. He's made me witness so many horrible things that I wish he was already – I don't know where! Oh, a nobleman who is wicked, now there's a terrible thing! I've got to do what he tells me whether I like it or not. Fear makes me serve him so well, it silences my real feelings and more often than not reduces me to pretending I approve of things which in my heart of hearts I hate. But there he is, taking a turn in the palace. Let's separate now, but just let me say this: I've talked to you frankly and in confidence, and I let it all out a bit too quickly. But if any word of it ever came to his notice, I'd say you were lying.

Scene ii:

DON JUAN, SGANARELLE

DON JUAN: Who was that man who was talking to you? I seem to think he looked very much like our friend Gusman, Dona Elvira's man.

SGANARELLE: That's more or less the size of it.

DON JUAN: What do you mean? Was it him?

SGANARELLE: The very same.

DON JUAN: And how long has he been in town?

SGANARELLE: Since yesterday evening.

DON JUAN: What brings him here?

SGANARELLE: I'd have thought you'd have a pretty good idea of what might be bothering him.

DON JUAN: Our departure, no doubt?

SGANARELLE: The poor man's very upset by it. He was asking me what was the reason for it.

DON JUAN: And what answer did you give him?

SGANARELLE: I told him you hadn't said a word to me on the subject.

DON JUAN: Well then, and what do you think was the reason? What do you make of this business?

SGANARELLE: I think, not wishing to do you an injustice, that you've got some new love-affair on the go.

DON JUAN: You think that?

SGANARELLE: Yes.

DON JUAN: Well now, you're not wrong. I confess: another woman has driven all thought of Elvira out of my head.

SGANARELLE: Lord, yes! I know my Don Juan like the back of my hand. I know you've got the most roving eye that ever was, always flitting from one entanglement to another and never content to settle anywhere for long.

DON JUAN: Tell me, don't you think I'm right to behave the way I do?

SGANARELLE: Well sir . . .

DON JUAN: Go on, out with it!

SGANARELLE: Of course you're right, if you like. There's no denying it. But if you didn't like, then maybe it would be a different matter.

DON JUAN: Really? I give you my permission to speak freely and tell me exactly what you think.

SGANARELLE: In that case sir, I'll be frank and say that I don't at all approve of the way you carry on. I think it's very wicked to go round falling in love right, left and centre the way you do.

DON JUAN: What! Would you restrict a man to staying chained to the first woman who takes his fancy, have him give up everything for her and never look at any others again? The idea is ludicrous – making a bogus virtue out of being faithful, being trapped for ever in the same relationship and as good as dead from youth onwards to the other pretty faces that might catch our eye! No no: fidelity is for imbeciles. All beautiful women are entitled to our love, and the accident of being the first on the scene shouldn't deprive the rest of the rightful claims they have on our affections. Speaking for myself, beauty enchants me wherever I find it and I surrender unresistingly to the sweet savagery it stirs in us. No matter how far I'm committed, the fact that I'm in love with one beautiful woman shall never make me unfair to the rest. I always keep an eye open so that I can see the merits of all of them and give each and every one due homage and tribute as nature demands. Come what may, I cannot refuse love to what I find lovable. The moment I see a pretty girl asking to be loved, then if I had ten thousand hearts I'd give them all to her. After all, there's something inexpressibly charming about falling in love, and the whole pleasure of it lies in variety. There's a rare satisfaction to be got from laying siege to a young woman's affections with endless compliments, seeing day by day the small advances we make, pitting our fervour, tears and sighs against the naïve innocence of a heart unwilling to lay down its weapons, overturning one by one the little obstacles she puts in our way, overcoming the scruples she is so proud of, and leading her gently to the point to which we want to bring her. But once we've mastered her, what more is there? What else could we possibly want? The bloom of passion is dulled and we will nod off, gently sedated by love, unless some new affair comes along to wake our desire and offer the delightful prospect of another conquest. In a nutshell, there is no pleasure to compare with overcoming the resistance of a beautiful woman and in this my ambition is the same as that of all great conquerors who march continually from one victory to the next and are incapable of even thinking of setting a limit to what they want. There is nothing that can put a stop to my impulsive desires. I feel I could love the whole world and, like Alexander the Great, I wish there were other worlds so that I could extend my amorous conquests to them.

SGANARELLE: God! how you do go on! Anyone would think you'd learned that off by heart. You talk like a book.

DON JUAN: And what have you got to say about it?

SGANARELLE: Well now, what I say is ... I don't know what to say. You twist things round in such a way that you seem to be right, even though it's clear you're not. I did have some pretty fine thoughts, but you've muddled me up with all your talk. Never mind, next time I'll write my notions down on paper and then I'll be able to argue properly with you.

DON JUAN: Good idea.

SGANARELLE: But is it all right, seeing you gave me permission, if I say I'm the teeniest bit shocked by the kind of life you lead?

DON JUAN: What do you mean? What sort of life do I lead?

SGANARELLE: Oh, it's a very good life. But, for instance, seeing you getting married again once a month as you are doing ...

DON JUAN: Well, what could be more agreeable?

SGANARELLE: True. I can see that it's very agreeable – and very amusing. I wouldn't mind doing the same myself if there was no harm in it. But you know sir, trifling like that with a holy sacrament and –

DON JUAN: Don't fuss, that's a matter for Heaven and me, and we can work it out between us without you worrying your head about it.

SGANARELLE: Upon my word sir, I've always heard it was a bad thing to make mock of God, and that unbelievers come to no good.

DON JUAN: Stop there, you stupid oaf. You know what I told you: I hate people who preach at me.

SGANARELLE: But I'm not talking about you, heaven forbid – you know what you're doing, and if you don't believe in anything, you've got your reasons. But there are some pretentious people about who are unbelievers without knowing why. They claim they're free-thinkers because they imagine it makes them look clever. Now if I had a master like that, I'd look him in the eye and tell him straight: 'How dare you set yourself up against Heaven? Aren't you afraid of mocking the holiest things the way you do? What right have you, you worm, you pygmy (I'm talking to the master I mentioned), what right have you to want to scoff at everything that men hold most sacred? Do you think that, just because you're a gentleman and wear the latest style of wig, because you have feathers in your hat and gold lace on your coat and ribbons as red as fire (it's the other master I'm talking to, not you), do you think, I ask, you're any the cleverer for it, that you can do as you like and that nobody's going to dare tell you a few home truths? Take it from me, though I'm just your servant, that sooner or later Heaven punishes the wicked, those who lead godless lives come to a bad end and –'

DON JUAN: Be quiet!

SGANARELLE: Why, what's up?

DON JUAN: This is what's up. I must tell you that I have fallen in love with a lady and that, impelled by her beauty, I followed her here to this town.

SGANARELLE: But sir, weren't you afraid of coming here where you killed the Commander six months ago?

DON JUAN: Why should I be afraid? Didn't I kill him stone dead?

SGANARELLE: Very dead, none deader. He's got no cause to complain.

DON JUAN: I was pardoned for that business.

SGANARELLE: True, but the pardon may not have ended the resentment felt by his friends and family, and –

DON JUAN: Oh, let's not dwell on all the disagreeable things that can happen. Let's just think of the pleasant ones. The young lady I mentioned, a prettier creature you couldn't imagine, has just got engaged and she's been escorted here by the man she's going to marry. It was by chance that I noticed these lovebirds three or four days before they were due to leave. I never saw two people so devoted, so completely in love. The visible tenderness of their affection for each other awakened certain feelings in me. I was smitten – but my love started as jealousy. Yes, from the start, I could not bear to see them so happy together. Resentment stirred my desires and I thought what a very great pleasure it would give me to come between them and break up a relationship which so offended my sensibilities. But so far, all my efforts have failed and I've had to resort to desperate measures. Today, this husband-to-be has organized a little outing for his future wife: he's taking her out for a sail on the sea. Without telling you anything of what was afoot, I've got everything ready to gratify my passion. I've hired men and a little boat, and with this laid on I expect to carry the beautiful creature off without any trouble.

SGANARELLE: Oh sir!

DON JUAN: What is it?

SGANARELLE: You've done splendidly and you've got the right attitude. There's nothing in this world like getting what you want.

DON JUAN: Then get ready to come with me. Make sure you hold yourself personally responsible for bringing all my weapons along, so that . . . Oh! what a moment for our paths to cross! You villain, you didn't tell me she was here too!

SGANARELLE: Sir, you never asked me.

DON JUAN: Is she out of her mind, not changing her clothes and coming to town dressed for the country?

Scene iii:

DONA ELVIRA, DON JUAN, SGANARELLE

DONA ELVIRA: Don Juan, won't you do me the kindness of acknowledging my presence? Is it too much to hope that you will at least turn and look at me?

DON JUAN: Madame, I confess I am surprised. I did not expect you here.

DONA ELVIRA: Yes, I can see that you were not expecting me, and though you are surprised, it is not in the way I had hoped. Your

manner of showing it entirely convinces me of what I could not bring
myself to believe. I wonder at my own naïvety, at my foolish heart
which refused to believe in your duplicity, though you gave me so
many proofs of it. I was good-natured enough, I admit – no, foolish
enough – to want to deceive myself and do all I could, against my
better judgement, to deny the evidence of my own eyes. I tried to
find justifications to calm my tenderest feelings and sought excuses
for the growing coldness I noticed in you. I deliberately invented a
thousand good reasons to explain your abrupt departure and absolve
you of the crime which common-sense told me you were guilty of.
My well-founded suspicions gave me warnings every day, but in
vain: I refused to heed the voice inside me which made you guilty
in my eyes and I listened eagerly to all manner of absurd fancies
which convinced me that you were innocent. But your manner just
now leaves me no room for doubt and the way you looked when
you saw me again tells me far more than I wish to know. Even so,
I should like to hear from your own lips what reasons you had for
going away. Speak Don Juan, I beg you. Let me hear how you will
manage to justify yourself.

DON JUAN: Madame, Sganarelle here knows why I left.

SGANARELLE: Me sir? Excuse me – I don't know a thing about it.

DONA ELVIRA: Very well. Come Sganarelle, speak up. It doesn't matter
from whose lips I hear his excuses.

DON JUAN (*indicating to Sganarelle to step forward*): Come along! Speak
to the lady!

SGANARELLE: What do you want me to say?

DONA ELVIRA: Come here, since that's what he wants, and tell me his
reasons for leaving in such a hurry.

DON JUAN: Aren't you going to answer?

SGANARELLE: I can't answer. You're just making a fool of your servant.

DON JUAN: Give her an answer, I tell you!

SGANARELLE: Madame . . .

DONA ELVIRA: Well?

SGANARELLE (*turning to Don Juan*): Sir –

DON JUAN (*threateningly*): If you . . .

SGANARELLE: Madame, the reasons we left were the great conquerors,
Alexander and those other worlds. (*To Don Juan*) There sir, that's
the best I can do.

DONA ELVIRA: Would you be good enough, Don Juan, to throw some light on these mysteries?

DON JUAN: To tell the truth Madame . . .

DONA ELVIRA: Ah! For a man who has lived at Court and must surely be used to this sort of thing, you put up a poor defence. I'm sorry to see you so embarrassed. Why not put on a brave face and bluster your way out of it like a gentleman? Why not swear that your feelings for me have not changed, that you still love me more than man ever loved woman, and that nothing but death can part you from me? Why don't you say that extremely urgent business forced you to leave without giving you a chance to let me know, that you have to stay here for some time against your wishes, and that if only I go back where I came from I can be sure you will follow at the first possible opportunity? Can't you say that you truly yearn to be by my side once more and that when I am far away you suffer the agonies of a body that is separated from its soul? That's how you should be defending yourself instead of saying nothing and looking disconcerted.

DON JUAN: I assure you Madame that I have no gift for dissembling and that I am entirely sincere. I won't say that my feelings for you have not changed and that I yearn to be by your side, since it is patently obvious that I only left to get away from you, not for the reasons you might imagine, but on grounds of conscience alone: I left because I had come to believe it would be a sin to go on living with you any longer. I was attacked by scruples Madame, and I saw clearly the error of my ways. I reflected that to marry you I carried you off from the seclusion of a convent, that you broke vows which committed you to a higher love, and that these are things which God does not forgive. I was overtaken by repentance and dreaded the wrath of Heaven. I realized that our marriage was no more than another name for adultery, that it must bring down a punishment from on high and, in short, that I should try to forget you and give you a way of returning to your former duty. Do you wish Madame to stand in the way of such a holy purpose? Would you have me take you back and in so doing bring Heaven's fury down around my ears and by –

DONA ELVIRA: Ah, villain! Now I know you for what you are! And, to my misfortune, the knowledge comes too late, when it serves only to drive me to despair! But be assured: your crime will not go unpunished and that same Heaven you mock will find a way of avenging your villainy!

DON JUAN: Note that Sganarelle: Heaven!

SGANARELLE: Oh absolutely. But we don't reckon much to Heaven, oh no, not us.

DON JUAN: Madame —

DONA ELVIRA: Enough! I will not listen to another word! Indeed, I reproach myself for having heard too much already. Only cowardly spirits stand by while their shame is flaunted like this. In such moments noble minds decide upon a course of action at the first sign. Do not expect an outburst of reproaches and insults from me! No, my anger is not the kind that vents itself in pointless words but saves its fury for vengeance. I say again: Heaven will punish you for the perfidious wrong you have done me. And if Heaven holds no terrors for you, then beware at least the fury of a woman scorned! (*She goes out.*)

SGANARELLE (*aside*): If only he could feel some remorse!

DON JUAN (*after a moment's thought*): Come along, we must give some thought to how we're going to manage that other piece of business.

SGANARELLE: Oh, what an abominable master am I forced to serve!

Act II

Scene i:
CHARLOTTE, PIERROT

CHARLOTTE: Lawks-a-mercy Pierrot, you got there jes' in time.

PIERROT: Lor' lumme, yes! Within a whisker o' being drownded they was, the pair of 'em.

CHARLOTTE: So it'd be that there squall this mornin' as wot tipped 'em up in the sea?

PIERROT: Listen good, Charlotte, an' I'll tell you straight 'ow it come about, 'cos in a manner o' speakin' it was me wot spotted 'em first: first to spot 'em I was. Any road, we was down on the beach, me and fat ol' Lucas, and we was muckin' about, havin' a bit o' fun, chuckin' clodges at each other for a lark, you know how Lucas likes a bit of a lark, and I don't mind a bit of a lark meself neither now and then. Any road, there we was larkin' about, you know, for a lark, when far away I sees summat bobbin' up and down in the water a long way out wot looks like it's comin' towards us in fits an' starts. I'm keepin' an eye fixed on her and then all at once I sees as how I can't see nothin' no more. 'Ay up, Lucas,' says I, 'I reckon that there is fellers swimmin'.' 'Get on,' says he, 'you been boozin', you be seein' double.' 'Get away,' says I, 'I ain't seein' double, them's fellers out there.' 'No it ain't,' says he, 'you got the sun in your eyes.' 'Fancy bettin',' says I, 'as how I ain't got no sun in my eyes,' says I, 'an' as how that's two fellers,' says I, 'an' as how they're swimmin' our way,' says I. 'God's teeth,' says he, 'I bet it ain't.' 'Right then, fancy a bob on it?' 'Don't mind if I do,' says he, 'an' to show I'm willin', there's me shillin',' says he. Now I'm not stupid, never been a fool with me money, but I plonks down me bet quick as you like, six pennies and two thruppeny bits by God, all bold I was, like I'd just downed a pint in one, 'cos I'm one to chance me arm, me, I jes' put me head down an' chaaarge! But I knew wot I was doin' though. There's no flies on me. Any road, the stakes is no sooner down when I sees these two fellers plain as day. They starts wavin' their arms for us to go out and fetch 'em in. So I pockets the stakes first an' 'Look sharp, Lucas,' says I, 'you can see 'em clear as anythin' now, callin' us. Come on, let's go an' fish 'em out.' 'Not me,' says he, 'they made me lose,' an' on an' on he goes till in the finish, cuttin' a long story short, I gives 'im a good talking to an' in the end we jumps into a boat, then after a lot of pushin' and shovin' we fish 'em out of the water, then we takes 'em home to be by the fire, then they strips off stark naked to get dry, then in comes two more wot had been with 'em an' fished theirselves out, then Mathurine comes in and one of 'em starts makin' eyes at 'er. An' that's how it all come about Charlotte, exackly.

CHARLOTTE: Did I 'ear you say Pierrot as 'ow there's one wot's better-lookin' than the rest?

PIERROT: Ay, that'd be the master. He'll be some great big toff for sure, 'cos he got all gold on 'is coat from top to bottom. And even them wot's his servants is gents. Howsomever, toff or no toff, by God he'd have drownded if I 'adn't bin there.

CHARLOTTE: Oh, get on with you!

PIERROT: By stars, if it 'adn't been for us, his goose would have been cooked and no mistake!

CHARLOTTE: He's not still there in your 'ouse is he, in the altogether?

PIERROT: That he's not. They dressed him all up again with us there. I never seen a man bein' dressed up before. Wot a lot of fussin'! Them toffs at Court go in for all sorts of bits an' pieces, I'd get lost in 'em, I would – fair gobsmacked I was at the sight of it. Fancy Charlotte, they got hair that's not fast to their head! Plonk it on last thing they do, like a cloth 'at. They got shirts with sleeves you an' me could hide in, no trouble. 'Stead of breeches, they got skirts as wide as from 'ere to Christmas. 'Stead of doublets, they got skimpy little weskits wot don't reach half way down their chest. 'Stead of neck-bands, they got a great big neckerchief, like webbing, with four great big frilly dollops of linen wot hangs all the way down to their belly. They got more little frills at the end of their sleeves, an' yardsanyards o' lace wrapped round an' round their legs, an' altogether such a clutter and tangle of ribbons as 'ow you feel sorry for them that 'as to wear 'em. There ain't a single bit of 'em, from one end of 'em to the other, even the shoes on their feet, that ain't all ribbons. If it was me that 'ad to wear 'em, I'd trip over 'em and break me neck.

CHARLOTTE: Lawks Pierrot, I got to go an' have a look at that.

PIERROT: Jest a minute Charlotte. I got somethin' I want to say to you first.

CHARLOTTE: Oh, go on then. Tell me what it is, but be quick.

PIERROT: Look 'ere Charlotte, I gotter get somethin' off of me chest, as the sayin' goes. I loves you, you know I do, and I want us to be wed. But Lord love us, I ain't satisfied with you.

CHARLOTTE: Whatever d'you mean by that?

PIERROT: What do I mean? I mean you aggravate me, an' I don't mind saying so.

CHARLOTTE: And 'ow do you make that out?

PIERROT: Lord 'elp me, I do believe you don't love me one little bit.

CHARLOTTE: Ha ha! Is that all?

PIERROT: Ay, that's all and it's plenty.

CHARLOTTE: Oh Lord, Pierrot, you're for ever harpin' on to me about the same ol' thing.

PIERROT: I'm forever harpin' on to you about the same ol' thing because it's always the same ol' thing. If it wasn't always the same ol' thing, I wouldn't be forever harpin' on to you about the same ol' thing.

CHARLOTTE: But wot are you after? Wot d'you want?

PIERROT: God 'elp me, I wants you to love me.

CHARLOTTE: And don't I love you?

PIERROT: No, that you don't! And there's me that does me very best to make you. Don't I buy you – no offence intended – ribbons from all the pedlars as comes round? Don't I just about break me neck fetchin' you blackbirds' nests? Don't I get the fiddlers to play tunes for you when it's your birthday? An' it's all the same as if I was bangin' me 'ead against a brick wall. Look 'ere, it ain't right or decent goin' round not lovin' the folks wot's in love with us.

CHARLOTTE: Lordy, but I do love you too!

PIERROT: Aye, an' you've got a funny way o' showin' it!

CHARLOTTE: 'Ow do you want us to love you?

PIERROT: I wants you to love me the same as folks love each other when they're in love with each other, proper like.

CHARLOTTE: Don't I love you proper?

PIERROT: That you don't. When it's proper love, you can tell – there's no end o' ways o' showin' it to folk when you love 'em with all your heart. Look at that great lump Thomasina, she's right daft about young Robin, always hangin' round 'im, pesterin' 'im, never lets 'im be. Forever playin' some trick on 'im she is, or givin' 'im thumps for nothing. Jest the other day 'e was sat sittin' on a stool, when she whips it out from under 'im and down 'e goes flat on 'is back on the floor. By God, that's 'ow folks carry on when they're in love. But you don't never say nothin' to me, you jest stand there like a block o' wood. I could walk up and down in front o' you till I was blue in the face and you wouldn't shift yourself long enough to give us a clip on the 'ead or spare me a word. By George! it ain't good enough! You behave too cold-hearted to folks.

CHARLOTTE: What d'you expect me to do? It's me nature and I can't do nothin' to alter it.

PIERROT: I don't give tuppence about your nature. When folks is in love with other folks, they always show it somehow.

CHARLOTTE: Right then, I love you all I can, and if that ain't good enough for you, you can go an' fall in love with somebody else.

PIERROT: Ah, that's me put to rights, I don't think! Damn it all, if you was really in love with me, you wouldn't talk like that.

CHARLOTTE: Why d'you have to go gettin' me all flustered?

PIERROT: Blow me, 'ow 'ave I gone an' upset you? I'm not askin' for anything but a bit more lovin'.

CHARLOTTE: Well why don't you let me alone instead of pesterin' me so much? P'raps it'll come over me sudden one of these days, all by itself.

PIERROT: Give us your 'and on it then Charlotte.

CHARLOTTE: Right ho, there it is.

PIERROT: Only promise you'll try to be a bit more lovin'.

CHARLOTTE: I'll do everythin' I can, but it's got to come by itself. Pierrot, is that the gen'l'man?

PIERROT: That it is.

CHARLOTTE: Lawks! He ain't 'alf 'andsome! It would 'ave been a downright shame if he'd been drownded.

PIERROT: I'll be back again soon. I'm just off for a noggin to set me up again after all I been through.

Scene ii:

DON JUAN, SGANARELLE, CHARLOTTE

DON JUAN: So Sganarelle, our scheme misfired. That unexpected squall upset the boat and the plan we devised with it. But to tell the truth, that little peasant girl I've just left has made up for everything. She was so charming that I can almost forget the disappointment of failing in our other business. She mustn't slip through my fingers. I've already paved the way so that I shan't be kept sighing too long.

SGANARELLE: I must say you astonish me sir. No sooner do we escape death by the skin of our teeth than, instead of thanking the Lord for taking pity on us, you're already starting up all over again, going out of your way to attract his wrath by your usual goings-on and crim— Shut up, you knave! You don't know what you're talking about! The Master knows what he's doing. Get along with you.

DON JUAN (*notices Charlotte*): Aha! Where did this one come from Sganarelle? Did you ever see a prettier little thing? Tell me, don't you think she's even lovelier than the other one?

SGANARELLE: Absolutely. (*Aside*) Here we go again!

DON JUAN: To what do I owe the pleasure of this charming encounter, my dear? I'm amazed! Can there really be creatures as lovely as you to be found among these woods and cliffs?

CHARLOTTE: You can see for yourself sir.

DON JUAN: Are you from the village?

CHARLOTTE: Yes sir.

DON JUAN: And you live there?

CHARLOTTE: Yes sir.

DON JUAN: And your name is?

CHARLOTTE: Charlotte sir, at your service.

DON JUAN: What a pretty girl! What fire in her eyes!

CHARLOTTE: Sir, you're makin' me blush!

DON JUAN: You mustn't blush when you hear the truth. What do you say Sganarelle? Did you ever see a prettier picture? Turn round a little would you? Ah! such a lovely figure! Just lift your chin an inch, if you'd be so good. Oh! such a sweet face! Open your eyes wide. Aren't they beautiful! Now a glimpse of your teeth, please. Quite delicious – and what inviting lips! Speaking personally, I am captivated. I never met a more entrancing creature.

CHARLOTTE: If it pleases you to say so sir, but, I dunno whether you be making fun of me or no.

DON JUAN: Me, make fun of you? Heaven forfend! I'm far too much in love with you for that, and I mean that most sincerely.

CHARLOTTE: If that be so, I'm much obliged.

DON JUAN: Not at all. You must not feel in any way obliged to me for anything I say. It's no more than what is due to your beauty.

CHARLOTTE: All this fine talk is over my head sir. I don't know wot to say. I ain't clever enough.

DON JUAN: Sganarelle, just look at her hands.

CHARLOTTE: Don't sir. They're as dirty as anything!

DON JUAN: What are you talking about? They're the loveliest hands in the world! Please, do say I can kiss them?

CHARLOTTE: Oh sir! you're too kind. If I'd known about this beforehand, I'd 'ave given 'em a good scrub in bran-water.

DON JUAN: Tell me one thing pretty Charlotte, you're not married by any chance?

CHARLOTTE: No sir. But I soon will be, to my intended, Pierrot. He's the son of Simonette from next door.

DON JUAN: Is it possible? A girl like you marry a rough peasant? Never! It would be a desecration of beauty – you weren't born to live in a village. You deserve a far better fate. Heaven knows it and has sent me here for the very purpose of stopping this marriage and doing justice to your loveliness. Because, Charlotte, I love you with all my soul. You only need say the word and I shall take you away from this ghastly place and raise you to the position that is rightly yours. No doubt such a declaration sounds rather sudden, but what of that? It all comes of your being so utterly ravishing. I have fallen more in love with you in a quarter of an hour than I might with anyone else in six months.

CHARLOTTE: True as I'm standin' 'ere sir, when you goes on like that I dunno wot to do. I love it the way you talk and I'd give anything so as I could believe you. But I was always told never to believe what gen'l'men say and as 'ow all them that come from the Court be sweet talkers and only want to lead a girl astray.

DON JUAN: I'm not one of them.

SGANARELLE: Oh, far from it!

CHARLOTTE: You see sir, it ain't funny when you let yourself be led astray. I'm just a poor country girl, but I got me virtue for a recommendation. I'd die sooner'n have my honour spoiled.

DON JUAN: Now, would I be so wicked to take advantage of a girl like you? Would I be so base as to despoil your honour? Never! My conscience wouldn't allow it. I love you Charlotte, truly and honourably, and to show you that I'm speaking the truth, let me tell you that all I have on my mind is marriage. Could you want any clearer proof? I'm ready whenever you wish and I call upon my man here to bear witness that I have given you my word.

SGANARELLE: Oh no, no need to be afraid. He'll marry you as often as you want.

DON JUAN: I see you don't know me yet Charlotte. You do me a great wrong if you judge me by other men. There may be rogues about, men who think only of taking advantage of young girls, but don't include me in their number, don't ever doubt the sincerity of my love. Besides, your beauty should give you all the reassurance you want. When a girl is as pretty as you are, she should feel safe from all such fears. Take it from me, you don't look the sort of girl who lets herself be taken advantage of, and as far as I am concerned, I declare I'd rather die a thousand deaths than harbour the slightest thought of deceiving you.

CHARLOTTE: Oh Lor'! I dunno if you're tellin' the truth or no, but the way you go on makes a person believe you.

DON JUAN: Just trust me, and you'll do me justice. I hereby repeat the promise I made you. Won't you accept my word? Won't you say you'll be my wife?

CHARLOTTE: Yes, if my auntie says yes.

DON JUAN: Then Charlotte, since you yourself are willing, give me your hand.

CHARLOTTE: But please sir, you won't play fast an' loose with me will you? 'T'would be a wicked thing to do, for you see how much I trust you.

DON JUAN: What! It appears you still doubt my sincerity. Do you want me to swear the most awesome oaths? May Heaven –

CHARLOTTE: Oh Lor', please don't swear, I believe you!

DON JUAN: Then give me a little kiss to show you mean to keep your promise.

CHARLOTTE: Oh no sir! Wait till we be wed, please, and then I'll kiss you all you want.

DON JUAN: Very well sweet Charlotte, what you want I want too. Only give me your hand and allow me to smother it with kisses to show how entranced I am by your . . .

Scene iii:

DON JUAN, SGANARELLE, PIERROT, CHARLOTTE

PIERROT (*coming between them and pushing Don Juan*): Half a mo' sir, steady on, if you don't mind. You're gettin' a bit 'ot under the collar – catch your death o' cold, you will.

DON JUAN (*pushing Pierrot away roughly*): Where did this insolent clod come from?

PIERROT: I'm tellin' you to keep off – you can't go round kissin' my intended!

DON JUAN (*goes on pushing him*): What are you making all this fuss about?

PIERROT: By stars! You mustn't go pushin' folk around like that.

CHARLOTTE (*holding Pierrot back by his arm*): Leave 'im alone Pierrot.

PIERROT: Leave 'im alone? I ain't goin' to leave 'im alone, not me!

DON JUAN: Ah!

PIERROT: Dammit! Just because you're a gen'l'man, d'you think you can come 'ere an' kiss our women under our noses? Why don't you go somewhere else an' kiss your own?

DON JUAN: Eh?

PIERROT: Eh yourself. (*Don Juan boxes his ear.*) Dammit, don't you 'it me! (*Another slap*) Hey, what the . . . (*Another*) God's teeth! (*Another*) By the saints! Damn it all, it ain't right 'ittin' folks like that. It ain't no way to pay a feller back wot saved you from bein' drownded!

CHARLOTTE: Now don't get mad Pierrot.

PIERROT: I'll get good an' mad if I want. You should be ashamed of yourself girl, lettin' 'im talk so sweet to you.

CHARLOTTE: Oh Pierrot, it ain't what you're thinkin'. This gen'l'man wants to wed me an' you got no call to get mad.

PIERROT: But dammit! you're promised to me.

CHARLOTTE: That don't matter Pierrot. If you love me, you should be glad for me to become a lady.

PIERROT: Oh should I? Hell's teeth! I'd sooner see you dead than wed to somebody else.

CHARLOTTE: Get away Pierrot, don't you go frettin' none. When I'm a lady I'll see you right, you can bring butter an' cheese to our 'ouse.

PIERROT: By George! I wouldn't bring you anythin', no, not if you was to pay me double. Is that why you been givin' 'eed to wot he been sayin'? Blow me down, if I'd a-known that afore, I wouldn't 'ave fished 'im out of the drink – I'd have fetched 'im one over the 'ead with a oar I would.

DON JUAN (*closing on him and getting ready to strike*): What's that you say?

PIERROT (*retreating behind Charlotte*): Look 'ere, I ain't afraid of anyone.

DON JUAN (*going round after him*): Wait a minute you.

PIERROT (*dodging round Charlotte*): I don't care nothin' for nobody.

DON JUAN (*running after Pierrot*): We'll see about that.

PIERROT (*taking refuge again behind Charlotte*): I've seen many a better man than –

DON JUAN: Let me get my hands –

SGANARELLE: Oh come on sir, let the poor devil alone. It would be wicked to give him a good hiding. Listen lad, just go away and don't say another word to him.

PIERROT (*rushes in front of Sganarelle and says defiantly to Don Juan*): I got plenty to say to 'im, I'll —

DON JUAN (*raises his hand to slap Pierrot who ducks and Sganarelle gets hit*): I'll teach you!

SGANARELLE (*looking at Pierrot who ducked to avoid the slap*): Devil take the oaf!

DON JUAN: That's what you get for trying to be helpful.

PIERROT: Phew! I'm off to tell 'er auntie about all this carry-on. (*He goes out.*)

DON JUAN: At last I am about to become the happiest of men! I wouldn't exchange my happiness for anything in the world. Oh what pleasure we'll have when you're my wife and . . .

Scene iv:
DON JUAN, SGANARELLE, CHARLOTTE, MATHURINE

SGANARELLE (*seeing Mathurine*): Aha!

MATHURINE: Sir, wot are you doin' there with Charlotte? You ain't courtin' 'er too?

DON JUAN (*aside to Mathurine*): No, on the contrary: it was she who was suggesting she'd like to be my wife and I was telling her I was engaged to you.

CHARLOTTE: And wot do Mathurine want with you?

DON JUAN (*aside, to Charlotte*): She's jealous seeing me talking to you. She wants me to marry her, but I was telling her you're the one I want.

MATHURINE: Why, Charlotte —

DON JUAN (*aside, to Mathurine*): You won't get anywhere talking to her. She's got the idea firmly fixed in her head.

CHARLOTTE: Why, Mathurine —

DON JUAN (*aside, to Charlotte*): It's no good trying to talk to her — you'll never get her to see sense.

MATHURINE: Can she —

DON JUAN (*aside, to Mathurine*): There's no way you'll ever make her listen to reason.

CHARLOTTE: I'd like to —

DON JUAN (*aside, to Charlotte*): She's as stubborn as the very Devil.

MATHURINE: Really —

DON JUAN (*aside, to Mathurine*): Don't say anything to her, she's mad.

CHARLOTTE: I think —

DON JUAN (*aside, to Charlotte*): Let her be, she's out of her mind.

MATHURINE: No, no, I got to talk to 'er.

CHARLOTTE: I want to know why she —

MATHURINE: Why wot?

DON JUAN (*aside, to Mathurine*): I bet she tells you that I've promised to marry her.

CHARLOTTE: I —

DON JUAN (*aside, to Charlotte*): What do you bet she'll make out I've given her my word to make her my wife.

MATHURINE: Look 'ere Charlotte, it ain't fair goin' round queerin' other people's pitches.

CHARLOTTE: It ain't right Mathurine to be jealous because the gen'l'man is talkin' to me.

MATHURINE: It was me the gen'l'man seen first.

CHARLOTTE: If 'e seen you first, 'e seen me second, an' it's me wot 'e promised to wed.

DON JUAN (*aside, to Mathurine*): You see? What did I tell you?

MATHURINE: Get away with you. I'm the one 'e promised to wed, not you.

DON JUAN (*aside, to Charlotte*): Didn't I guess as much?

CHARLOTTE: Not likely! I'm telling you: it's me.

MATHURINE: You're havin' me on. I'll say one more time: it's me.

CHARLOTTE: Well, there 'e is. 'E can tell us if I'm right.

MATHURINE: Aye, let 'im say as 'ow I'm wrong if I ain't speakin' the 'onest truth

CHARLOTTE: Did you promise to marry 'er sir?

DON JUAN (*aside, to Charlotte*): Now you're teasing me.

MATHURINE: Is it true sir as 'ow you gave 'er your word to wed 'er?

DON JUAN (*aside, to Mathurine*): How could you think such a thing?

CHARLOTTE: See? She's stickin' to it.

DON JUAN (*aside, to Charlotte*): Let her ramble on.

MATHURINE: You're a witness to 'ow she will have it so.

DON JUAN (*aside, to Mathurine*): Let her prattle away.

CHARLOTTE: No no. We gotter know the truth.

MATHURINE: Yes, it's gotter be settled.

CHARLOTTE: That's right Mathurine, I want the gen'l'man to show you wot a silly little fool you are.

MATHURINE: Yes Charlotte, and I want the gen'l'man to take you down a peg.

CHARLOTTE: Settle the argument sir, please.

MATHURINE: Decide for us sir.

CHARLOTTE (*to Mathurine*): Now you'll see.

MATHURINE (*to Charlotte*): You'll be one the one to see.

CHARLOTTE (*to Don Juan*): Tell us.

MATHURINE (*to Don Juan*): Speak to us.

DON JUAN (*embarrassed, speaking to both of them*): What do you want me to say? You both claim that I've promised to marry you. But doesn't each one of you know the truth without my needing to spell it out? Why make me go over the same ground again? Surely the one I have really given my promise to can afford to laugh at anything the other one says. Why should she worry, as long as I keep my promise to her? All the explanations in the world aren't going to get us any further forward. Actions speak louder than words, and what we do cuts more ice than what we say. There's only one way I'm prepared to try to settle this between you: when I do marry, you'll see which one I love. (*Aside, to Mathurine*) Let her think whatever she wants. (*Aside, to Charlotte*) Leave her to her fond imaginings. (*Aside, to Mathurine*) I worship you! (*Aside, to Charlotte*) I'm yours to command. (*Aside, to Mathurine*) All other faces are ugly compared with yours. (*Aside, to Charlotte*) From the moment I first saw you, I haven't had eyes for anyone else. (*To both*) I have some business to attend to. I'll be back in a quarter of an hour. (*He goes out.*)

CHARLOTTE (*to Mathurine*): There now, I'm the one 'e's in love with.

MATHURINE: But I'm the one 'e's goin' to wed.

SGANARELLE: Oh poor deluded girls! I pity your innocence. I won't stand by and watch you rushing to your ruin. Believe me, the pair of you: don't be taken in by all the tales he's told you. Stay at home in your village.

DON JUAN (*returning*): I'd like to know why Sganarelle didn't follow me.

SGANARELLE: My master's a rogue. His only intention is to deceive you as he has deceived many others. He's the biggest one for marrying in the whole human race and ... (*Seeing Don Juan*) That's not true and you can tell anybody who says so that he's a liar. My master isn't the biggest one for marrying in the whole human race, not at all. He isn't a rogue, it's not his intention to deceive you and he never deceived a woman in his life. Oh look! there he is. You can ask him for yourselves.

DON JUAN (*to himself*): Yes.

SGANARELLE: Sir, since there's so many wagging tongues about nowadays, I thought I'd do a bit of anticipating. I was just saying that if anybody started telling them nasty tales about you, they were not to believe it and shouldn't hesitate to tell him he was a liar.

DON JUAN: Sganarelle.

SGANARELLE: Yes! My master's a man of honour, you can take my word for it.

DON JUAN: Hm.

SGANARELLE: People like that are a load of good-for-nothings.

Scene v:

DON JUAN, LA RAMÉE, CHARLOTTE, MATHURINE, SGANARELLE

LA RAMÉE: Sir, I've come to warn you that it's not safe for you to stay here.

DON JUAN: What do you mean?

LA RAMÉE: A dozen men on horseback are looking for you. They'll be here any moment. I don't know how they managed to follow you to this spot. But I got the information from a peasant they'd been questioning. They'd given him your description. You must be quick. The sooner you get away from here the better.

DON JUAN (*to Charlotte and Mathurine*): I've been called away on urgent business, but I want you to remember the promise I gave you and be sure that you'll hear from me before tomorrow evening. (*Charlotte and Mathurine go out.*) Since the odds are stacked against us I must think of some clever plan to escape the danger that threatens me. I want Sganarelle to put on my clothes, and I –

SGANARELLE: Sir, you can't mean it. Do you want to expose me to the risk of getting myself killed dressed in your clothes and –

DON JUAN: Come on, quickly now! You should take it as an honour. A servant should think himself lucky to have the privilege of dying for his master.

SGANARELLE: Thanks a lot for the honour. Oh Lord! If I must die, grant that I don't die because I was mistaken for somebody else!

Act III

Scene i:

DON JUAN *dressed for the country*, SGANARELLE *in doctor's robes*

SGANARELLE: My word sir, you must admit I was right: both of us are provided with foolproof disguises. Your first idea wouldn't have done the trick at all. This little get-up will hide our identity much better than what you had in mind.

DON JUAN: You certainly look the part. I can't imagine where you managed to dig up that ridiculous outfit.

SGANARELLE: Yes, absurd isn't it? They're robes that belonged to an old doctor who left them in a pawnshop where I picked them up. Cost me a pretty penny too. But would you believe it sir, I'm already treated with respect on account of these clothes? People I meet take their hats off to me, and some are coming to consult me because I look like a man of learning.

DON JUAN: How do you mean?

SGANARELLE: Five or six country people, men as well as women, spotted me on the road and came up to me asking for my advice about their various ailments.

DON JUAN: And you told them you knew nothing about such things?

SGANARELLE: Me? Not at all! I felt obliged to uphold the honour of my robes. I held forth to them about their complaints and gave each one a prescription.

DON JUAN: And what remedies did you prescribe?

SGANARELLE: Upon my word sir, I just went along with whatever came into my head and handed out prescriptions at random. It would be funny if my patients got better and came back to thank me!

DON JUAN: And why not? Why shouldn't you enjoy the same prerogatives as other doctors? They're no more responsible for curing their patients than you are. Their skill is a lot of flim-flam. All they do is take the credit when things turn out well. You might as well make the most of the patient's good luck and ensure that your remedies are held responsible for wreaking whatever good is done by chance and the workings of nature.

SGANARELLE: Why sir, are you a heretic in medical matters too?

DON JUAN: It's one of the greatest mistakes made by the human race.

SGANARELLE: What — you don't believe in senna pods nor in rhubarb nor in antimony?

DON JUAN: Why should I believe in them?

SGANARELLE: You're a wicked unbeliever. But you must have seen what a fuss there's been lately about antimony.[4] It has brought about miraculous cures which have convinced even the greatest sceptics. Only three weeks ago I saw a wonderful case with my own eyes.

DON JUAN: What was that?

SGANARELLE: There was this man who'd been at death's door for nearly a week. Nobody knew what to do for him. All remedies were useless. In the end they decided to give him this antimony emetic.

DON JUAN: And he got better, I imagine?

SGANARELLE: No, he died.

DON JUAN: Remarkably effective, I must say!

SGANARELLE: How do you mean? He'd been dying for the best part of a week and couldn't manage it by himself, and this stuff finished him off in no time. What could you want that's more effective than that?

DON JUAN: You're right.

SGANARELLE: But let's drop medicine, since you don't believe in it, and talk about something else. This get-up gives me ideas and I feel in the mood for arguing with you. You recall I'm allowed to argue so long as I don't preach at you.

DON JUAN: Very well, proceed.

SGANARELLE: I'd like to know what you truly think. Is it really the case that you don't believe in Heaven?

DON JUAN: Let's not go into that.

SGANARELLE: That means you don't. What about Hell?

DON JUAN: Pshaw!

SGANARELLE: No, again. And the Devil, if I might make so bold?

DON JUAN: Oh, absolutely.

SGANARELLE: No more than the rest. Don't you believe in a life after this?

DON JUAN: Ha ha ha!

SGANARELLE (*aside*): Here's someone who'll take a bit of converting. And just tell me this: the Bogey Man, what do you reckon to him?

DON JUAN: Too stupid for words.

SGANARELLE: Now I can't allow that. There's nothing truer than the Bogey Man – I'd go to the stake for it.[5] But a man's got to believe in something. What is it you believe?

DON JUAN: What do I believe?

SGANARELLE: Yes.

DON JUAN: I believe that two and two make four, Sganarelle, and that four and four are eight.

SGANARELLE: Now there's a fine set of beliefs! As far as I can see then, your religion is arithmetic. You must admit that men get all sorts of queer ideas into their heads. And more often than not, the more they've studied the less sense they have. Not that I've done much studying myself sir, thank God, not like you have, and nobody can boast they ever taught me anything. But using my common-sense and my own judgement, I can see things better than in books, and I know for sure that the world we see about us didn't spring up overnight, like a mushroom. I'd like to ask you who made those trees, the rocks, the earth and the sky above, or did it all come about by itself? Take yourself, for example. You're here. Are you something you made yourself, or didn't it take your father and mother to make you? Can you see all the parts of the mechanism a man is made of and not wonder at the way each component fits with the others, nerves, bones, veins, arteries . . . er . . . lungs, heart, liver and all the other bits and pieces which go . . . Oh, for goodness' sake, please interrupt me. I can't argue if people don't butt in. You're not saying anything on purpose and letting me burble on out of sheer spite.

DON JUAN: I'm waiting until you've made your point.

SGANARELLE: My point is that there's something wonderful about man, say what you like, that all your men of science can't explain. Isn't it remarkable that I'm here and that there's something in my head which can think of a hundred different things in a moment and can make my body do whatever it wants? For example, clap my hands, lift my arms, raise my eyes to Heaven, bow my head, move my feet, go to the right, to the left, forwards, backwards, turn round . . . (*As he turns he falls over.*)

DON JUAN: Good! And so your argument bites the dust.

SGANARELLE: Blast! I'm a fool to waste my time arguing with you! Believe what you like then! What's it to me if you are damned?

DON JUAN: I think we've got lost while we've been arguing. Give that man down there a shout and ask him the way.

SGANARELLE: Hello! You there! Hello! Just a word friend, if you can spare a moment.

Scene ii:

DON JUAN, SGANARELLE, *a* POOR MAN

SGANARELLE: Can you tell us which is the way to town?

POOR MAN: All you do is follow this road, your honours, and then turn right when you get to the end of the forest. But I warn you that you'd better keep your eyes open. There've been robbers around here lately.

DON JUAN: I'm obliged to you friend. Thank you very much indeed.

POOR MAN: Could you see your way, sir, to help me out with a little something?

DON JUAN: Ah! so your advice wasn't disinterested I see.

POOR MAN: I'm a poor man, sir, I've lived alone in this wood for ten years. I will not fail to pray to Heaven that you be granted all manner of blessings.

DON JUAN: Hm! You'd do better to pray Heaven to grant you a coat than concern yourself with other people's business.

SGANARELLE: My good man, you don't know my master. All he believes is that two and two make four and four and four make eight.

DON JUAN: How do you spend your time by yourself here in the forest?

POOR MAN: I spend all day praying for the prosperity of the good people who show me charity.

DON JUAN: So you must be doing very nicely?

POOR MAN: Alas, sir, I live in the greatest poverty.

DON JUAN: You can't be serious. A man who spends all day praying to God cannot fail to be pretty well off.

POOR MAN: I can assure you, sir, that more often than not I don't have a crust of bread to eat.

DON JUAN: How strange that you should be so badly rewarded for your trouble. Very well, I'll give you a gold piece here and now – provided you curse and blaspheme.

POOR MAN: Oh sir, surely you can't want me to commit a sin like that?

DON JUAN: All you have to do is make up your mind whether you want a gold piece or not. There's one here and I'll give it to you – provided you curse. Here it is: now curse.

POOR MAN: Sir . . .

DON JUAN: Unless you do, you don't get it.

SGANARELLE: Go on, just a little curse will do. There's no harm in it.

DON JUAN: Here, take it. Take it, I tell you. But you must blaspheme first.

POOR MAN: No sir, I'd rather starve to death.[6]

DON JUAN: Oh very well, I give it to you for the love of humanity. But what's going on over there? One man being set upon by three others? That isn't fair odds and I won't allow such villainy! (*He goes off towards the fight.*)

Scene iii:
DON JUAN, DON CARLOS, SGANARELLE

SGANARELLE: My master is completely mad to go rushing off looking for danger when it isn't looking for him! Upon my word though, he's tipped the scales! The two of them have seen off the other three.

DON CARLOS (*sword in hand*): You can judge by the fact that they took to their heels how crucial your help was. Allow me sir to thank you for your generous intervention and how –

DON JUAN (*returning, holding his sword*): I did nothing sir that you would not have done in my place. We are in honour bound to intervene on such occasions. The behaviour of those scoundrels was so cowardly that to have kept out would have amounted to taking their side. But through what circumstances did you fall into their clutches?

DON CARLOS: I happened by chance to become separated from my brother and the rest of our company. And as I was trying to join up with them again, I ran into those robbers. First they killed my horse and then, had it not been for your courage, they would have done the same to me.

DON JUAN: Are you intending to make for the town?

DON CARLOS: Yes, but I don't mean to go in. My brother and I are obliged to remain outside to settle one of those troublesome affairs which require gentlemen to sacrifice themselves and their families to their rigorous code of honour, since even the happiest outcome is always a disaster. If we don't lose our lives we are forced to leave the kingdom. It's this, to my way of thinking, that makes the condition of a gentleman most unfortunate: he cannot be certain, however prudently and honourably he conducts himself, that he won't get involved, as the laws of honour require, in someone else's misconduct and find that his life, his peace of mind and his property depend on the whim of the first rash fool who takes it into his head to offer him one of those insults for which a man of honour must be prepared to die.

DON JUAN: But we do have the comfort, when confronted by people who fancy their chances and insult us without a second thought, of knowing that we can make them run the same risks as we do and give them the same hard time that we go through. But would it be indiscreet of me to ask what this business of yours might be?

DON CARLOS: It's got to the point where it won't remain a secret much longer, and once the insult has become public knowledge we are not bound by honour to hide our shame, but on the contrary to proclaim our determination to be avenged and declare just how we plan to do it. Therefore sir, I do not hesitate to tell you that we seek revenge for the insult done to our sister who was seduced and abducted from a convent. The man responsible for this outrage is a certain Don Juan Tenorio, son of Don Louis Tenorio. We have been looking for him for several days and followed him this morning on information provided by a servant who told us he set out on horseback with four or five others, riding along this coast. But all our efforts have been in vain. We haven't been able to discover what's become of him.

DON JUAN: Do you know him sir, this Don Juan you speak of?

DON CARLOS: Personally, no. I've never seen him myself. I've only my brother's description of him. But by report there's little to be said in his favour. He's a man whose life –

DON JUAN: Say no more sir, if you please. He is, after a fashion, a friend of mine, and I would think it cowardice on my part to hear him ill spoken of.

DON CARLOS: Out of consideration for you, sir, I won't mention him again. The very least I owe you for saving my life is to keep silent in your presence about a man you know, for if I did speak of him I could say nothing good. But though you are his friend, I should hope you will not condone what he has done and that you will not think it strange that we seek revenge on him.

DON JUAN: On the contrary, I want to be of assistance and spare you unnecessary trouble. I am a friend of Don Juan – I can hardly help that. But it is not reasonable that he should go round insulting gentlemen and not face the consequences. I undertake to ensure that he gives you satisfaction.

DON CARLOS: But what satisfaction can he give for an outrage such as this?

DON JUAN: Anything you can in honour require. To save you the trouble of looking any further for Don Juan, I guarantee to produce him wherever and whenever you wish.

DON CARLOS: An agreeable prospect sir to any man who has been offended. But, given all I owe you, it would be very painful for me to see you dragged into this affair.

DON JUAN: My connection with Don Juan is so close that he could hardly fight unless I fought too. Indeed, I answer for him as I do for myself. You need only say when you want him to appear and give you satisfaction.

DON CARLOS: What a cruel fate is mine! Must I owe you my life and yet know that Don Juan is your friend?

Scene iv:
DON ALONZO *and three followers*, DON CARLOS,
DON JUAN, SGANARELLE

DON ALONZO: Have my horses watered and bring them along after us. I will walk a little while. Great heavens! What's this? You brother, with our mortal enemy?

DON CARLOS: Our mortal enemy?

DON JUAN (*stepping back three paces and defiantly grasping the hilt of his sword*): Yes, I am Don Juan. The advantage you have of numbers shall not make me disown my name.

DON ALONZO: Ah, villain! You must die!

DON CARLOS: Wait brother! I owe him my life. Had it not been for his help I would have been killed by robbers I encountered.

DON ALONZO: And do you intend to let this consideration stand between us and our revenge? No assistance received from the hand of an enemy can have any claim to hold us to such scruples. If the obligation is to be measured against the insult brother, your gratitude is absurd. Honour is more precious than life. We owe absolutely nothing to a man who has let us live but has robbed us of our honour.

DON CARLOS: I am aware brother of the distinction a gentleman must always make between the two, and I do not cease to resent the offence because I acknowledge the obligation. But I ask you to let me return to him what he has loaned me: to repay in full the life I owe him. Let us postpone our vengeance and allow him a few more days to enjoy the fruits of his noble action.

DON ALONZO: No no! Postponing our vengeance will jeopardize it. This opportunity for taking it might never come again. Heaven offers it to us now, and it is for us to make the most of the opportunity. When honour has been mortally offended we should not think of acting with moderation. If you feel reluctant to take a hand in this business you can simply withdraw and leave the honour of the sacrifice to me.

DON CARLOS: I beg you, brother . . .

DON ALONZO: All this talk is beside the point. He must die.

DON CARLOS: Wait I say brother. I cannot allow any attempt on his life and I swear to Heaven that I will defend him here and now against anyone who attacks him. This same life which he saved shall become a rampart that stands in front of him. If you wish to strike at him, you will first have to run me through.

DON ALONZO: What? You take the side of our enemy against me? And far from being filled with the same rage as I am at the sight of him, you treat him with the greatest forbearance?

DON CARLOS: Brother, let us show moderation in pursuing our cause which is just. In avenging our honour let us not be ruled by the fury which is written in your face. Let us be masters of our courage and demonstrate that our valour is not hot-blooded and that the course we take is dictated by reason alone, and not the promptings of blind rage. I do not mean, brother, to stand long in my enemy's debt, but my obligation to him is something which I must discharge before I do anything else. Our vengeance will not be any the less honourable for being deferred. On the contrary, it will be enhanced as a result, for to have had the opportunity and not taken it will make our revenge appear more just in the eyes of the world.

DON ALONZO: Oh! this is strange, weak and dreadfully blind! To jeopardize the demands of honour like this all because of an absurd notion of an imaginary obligation!

DON CARLOS: No brother, you need have no concern. If it turns out that I have made a mistake then I shall make amends. I accept full responsibility for defending our honour. I realize the obligation it lays upon us and the single day's grace which in my indebtedness I request on his behalf will only make me the more determined that we shall have satisfaction. Don Juan, you see I am at pains to repay what I have received from you. You can judge the rest by this and be quite clear that I always settle my debts with the same zeal and that I shall not be less prompt in repaying an insult than in returning a benefit. I will not require you to explain yourself now and I give you an opportunity to consider at leisure what decision you must take. You know the enormity of the offence you have done us: I leave you to judge for yourself what reparation it calls for. There are peaceful means of satisfying us, and others which are violent and bloody. But whatever choice you make, you have given me your word, you have promised me satisfaction, Don Juan. I beg you to see I have it and remember that from this time forward I owe nothing except to my honour.

DON JUAN: I have asked nothing of you. I shall keep to what I have promised.

DON CARLOS: Come brother. A moment's restraint will not blunt the edge of our resolution.

Scene v:
DON JUAN, SGANARELLE

DON JUAN: Hey, Sganarelle! Where are you?

SGANARELLE: You called?

DON JUAN: So villain, you run away when I am attacked?

SGANARELLE: Sorry sir. I wasn't far away. I think these doctor's clothes must have a purgative effect. Wearing them is as good as taking a dose of medicine.

DON JUAN: Confound your impudence. Can't you come up with a more decent excuse for your cowardice? Do you know who the man whose life I saved happens to be?

SGANARELLE: Me? No.

DON JUAN: One of Elvira's brothers.

SGANARELLE: One of . . .

DON JUAN: He's a very decent sort. He behaved very well. I'm sorry to have any quarrel with him.

SGANARELLE: You could settle everything easily, though.

DON JUAN: True, but my passion for Dona Elvira is spent and being entangled with her doesn't suit my present mood. I must be free to love as I choose, as you know, and I could never resign myself to locking my feelings up inside four walls. I've told you a score of times that I'm naturally inclined to follow my fancy wherever it leads. My heart belongs to all women. It's theirs to take in turn and keep for as long as they can. But what's that noble edifice I see among those trees?

SGANARELLE: You don't know?

DON JUAN: Indeed I don't.

SGANARELLE: Why, it's the tomb the Commander was having built when you killed him.

DON JUAN: You're right. I didn't know it was in these parts. Everyone tells me how wonderful it is, and the statue of the Commander too. I should like to go and see it.

SGANARELLE: Sir, don't go near it!

DON JUAN: Why not?

SGANARELLE: It's not decent, to go calling on a man you've killed.

DON JUAN: On the contrary, I wish to pay him the courtesy of a visit. If he's a gentleman he'll give me a civil welcome. Come, let's go in. *The tomb opens, revealing a superb mausoleum and the Statue of the Commander.*

SGANARELLE: Oh isn't it superb! Superb statues, superb marble, superb pillars! It's all superb! What do you say sir?

DON JUAN: I say that a dead man's ambition could hardly go much further. What I find remarkable is that a man who was happy with a modest abode when he was alive should want one quite so grandiose for the time when he would no longer have any use for it.

SGANARELLE: That's the statue of the Commander.

DON JUAN: By Jove, he looks damn silly dressed up like a Roman emperor!

SGANARELLE: I say sir, it's a handsome piece of work. You'd think he was alive and about to say something. If I was by myself I'd be scared by the way he's looking at us. I don't think he's very pleased to see us.

DON JUAN: That's very wrong of him. It's not a very polite way of receiving the honour I'm paying him. Ask him if he would like to come and sup with me.

SGANARELLE: I should think that's something he's got no need of.

DON JUAN: Ask him I tell you.

SGANARELLE: You can't mean it! I'd be an idiot to start talking to a statue.

DON JUAN: Do what I say.

SGANARELLE: This is crazy! Commander, your excellency. (*Aside*) I've got to laugh, I feel so silly, but it's the master who's making me do this. (*To the Statue*) Your excellency, my master Don Juan asks if you would do him the honour of coming to sup with him. (*The Statue nods.*) Aargh!

DON JUAN: What is it? What's wrong with you? Come on, speak won't you?

SGANARELLE (*nodding his head the way the Statue did*): The statue ...

DON JUAN: Well, what have you got to say for yourself, you rogue?

SGANARELLE: I tell you the statue ...

DON JUAN: Well, and what about the statue? I'll brain you if you don't speak.

SGANARELLE: The statue . . . it nodded its head at me.

DON JUAN: Devil take the scoundrel!

SGANARELLE: It nodded at me I tell you, true as I'm standing here. Go and talk to him yourself and you'll see. Maybe . . .

DON JUAN: Come on you ruffian, over here. I'll show you what a lily-livered coward you are. Watch me. Commander, would your excellency care to take supper with me? (*The Statue nods again.*)

SGANARELLE: I wouldn't have missed that for ten doubloons. Well sir?

DON JUAN: Come on, let's go.

SGANARELLE: That's your free-thinkers for you. They won't believe in anything!

Act IV

Scene i:

DON JUAN, SGANARELLE

DON JUAN: Whatever it was, let's leave it at that. It wasn't anything. We may have been deceived by a trick of the light or exposed to fumes of some sort which affected our eyes.

SGANARELLE: Oh sir, don't try to deny what we both saw as plain as could be. Nothing could be more unmistakable than that nod of the head. It's perfectly clear: Heaven is shocked by the way you live your life and has produced this miracle to make you change your mind and prevent you from –

DON JUAN: Listen! If you pester me any more with your stupid moralizing, if I hear one more word from you on the subject, I shall send for reinforcements, ask for a whip, have you held down by three or four large men and flog you within an inch of your life. Do I make myself clear?

SGANARELLE: Loud and clear sir, as a bell. You make your meaning very plain. That's one good thing about you sir: you don't beat about the bush. You put things with such wonderful bluntness.

DON JUAN: Come along, order my supper to be served as soon as possible. (*To a servant*) You there, bring me a chair.

Scene ii:

DON JUAN, LA VIOLETTE, SGANARELLE

LA VIOLETTE: Sir, there's a tradesman, a Monsieur Dimanche, who would like to speak to you.

SGANARELLE: How splendid! That's all we need: a visit from a creditor! What's he think he's playing at, coming here asking for money? Why didn't you tell him the Master was out?

LA VIOLETTE: I've been telling him that for the last three quarters of an hour, but he won't believe it. He's sitting outside, waiting.

SGANARELLE: He can wait as long as he likes.

DON JUAN: No, on the contrary, show him in. It's bad policy to hide from one's creditors. It's a good idea to give them something to be going on with – I know exactly how to send them away happy without parting with a penny.

Scene iii:

DON JUAN, MONSIEUR DIMANCHE, SGANARELLE
and attendants

DON JUAN (*extremely polite*): Ah! Monsieur Dimanche! Do come in. I'm delighted to see you. I'm extremely cross with my servants for not showing you in at once. I'd given orders I didn't want to speak to anyone, but that did not include you. My door should never be closed to you.

M. DIMANCHE: I am most obliged to you, sir.

DON JUAN (*to his servants*): By God you curs, I'll teach you to leave Monsieur Dimanche kicking his heels in an antechamber! I'll teach you to recognize who's who!

M. DIMANCHE: Really sir, it is of no consequence.

DON JUAN: Come now! Telling you I was not at home? Saying that to Monsieur Dimanche, the very best of my friends?

M. DIMANCHE: Your servant sir. What I came for was —

DON JUAN: Quickly now, a chair for Monsieur Dimanche.

M. DIMANCHE: I'm quite all right as I am sir.

DON JUAN: I won't hear of it. I want you to come and sit by me.

M. DIMANCHE: There is really no need sir.

DON JUAN: Remove this stool and bring an arm-chair.[7]

M. DIMANCHE: Sir, you can't mean it . . .

DON JUAN: No, no, I am quite aware of what I owe to you. I won't have them make any difference between us.

M. DIMANCHE: Sir . . .

DON JUAN: Come, sit down.

M. DIMANCHE: There's really no need sir. I only have a brief word to say to you. I was —

DON JUAN: Sit here, I say.

M. DIMANCHE: No sir, I'm quite all right as I am. I came to —

DON JUAN: No, I won't listen unless you sit down.

M. DIMANCHE: I shall do as you wish sir. I —

DON JUAN: By God Monsieur Dimanche, you're looking well!

M. DIMANCHE: Yes sir, at your service. I came —

DON JUAN: You're the picture of good health: red lips, fresh cheeks and a sparkle in your eye.

M. DIMANCHE: I'd like to —

DON JUAN: And how is your good lady, Madame Dimanche?

M. DIMANCHE: She's very well sir, thank the Lord.

DON JUAN: What a splendid woman she is!

M. DIMANCHE: She's your humble servant sir. I came —

DON JUAN: And your little girl, Claudine, how is she?

M. DIMANCHE: She's very well.

DON JUAN: Such a pretty child. I'm really fond of her.

M. DIMANCHE: You are too kind sir. I just wanted to —

DON JUAN: And little Colin? Still making that terrible racket with his drum?

M. DIMANCHE: Just the same sir. I —

DON JUAN: And your little dog, Brusquet? Does he still growl as ferociously? Does he still bite the ankles of your visitors?

M. DIMANCHE: He's worse than ever sir, we just can't break him of it.

DON JUAN: Don't be surprised if I ask for news of all the family. I take a genuine interest in all of them.

M. DIMANCHE: We are infinitely obliged to you sir.

DON JUAN (*offering his hand*): Give me your hand on it Monsieur Dimanche. Do you really feel you are one of my friends?

M. DIMANCHE: Sir, I am your most humble servant.

DON JUAN: And I, by God, am devoted to you.

M. DIMANCHE: You do me too much honour. I –

DON JUAN: There's nothing I wouldn't do for you.

M. DIMANCHE: Sir, you are really too kind.

DON JUAN: And for no other reason than the regard I have for you, believe me.

M. DIMANCHE: I have done nothing to deserve such kindness. But, sir –

DON JUAN: Oh, come now. Monsieur Dimanche, don't stand on ceremony: will you stay and sup with me?

M. DIMANCHE: No sir. I really must be getting back at once. I only came –

DON JUAN (*standing up*): Quickly there. A torch for Monsieur Dimanche. Four or five of you get your muskets and escort him home.

M. DIMANCHE (*standing*): Sir, it's not necessary. I shall be perfectly all right on my own. But – (*Sganarelle promptly removes the chairs.*)

DON JUAN: I won't hear of it. I insist that you have an escort. I'm far too concerned for your safety. I am your servant sir, and what's more, your debtor.

M. DIMANCHE: Oh sir –

DON JUAN: I make no secret of it. I tell everyone.

M. DIMANCHE: If –

DON JUAN: Would you like me to see you home myself?

M. DIMANCHE: Oh sir, you're joking sir –

DON JUAN: Well then, give me your hand if you will. And again, please think of me as a loyal friend. There's nothing in the world I wouldn't do for you. (*He goes out.*)

SGANARELLE: You must admit, the Master's a man who is genuinely fond of you.

M. DIMANCHE: True. He's so polite and civil to me that I never get round to asking for my money.

SGANARELLE: I assure you, everyone in this house would go to the stake for you. I only wish something would happen to you, someone try to beat you up say, and then you'd see how we'd all . . .

M. DIMANCHE: I don't doubt it. But Sganarelle, I'd be very grateful if you'd have a word with him about my money.

SGANARELLE: Oh, don't you worry. He'll pay you all right.

M. DIMANCHE: But you yourself Sganarelle owe me something on your own account.

SGANARELLE: Come now, let's not go into that.

M. DIMANCHE: Why not? I . . .

SGANARELLE: Do you think I don't know I owe you money?

M. DIMANCHE: Of course, but . . .

SGANARELLE: Well in that case, I'll show you out.

M. DIMANCHE: But what about my money . . .

SGANARELLE (*taking his arm*): You must be joking!

M. DIMANCHE: I want —

SGANARELLE (*pulling him*): Eh?

M. DIMANCHE: I mean —

SGANARELLE (*pushing him*): Oh nonsense!

M. DIMANCHE: But —

SGANARELLE (*pushing him*): Go on with you!

M. DIMANCHE: I —

SGANARELLE (*pushing him off the stage*): Get along with you I say!

Scene iv:

DON LOUIS, DON JUAN, LA VIOLETTE,
SGANARELLE

LA VIOLETTE: Your father is here sir.

DON JUAN: Oh splendid! A visit from him was all I needed to make me completely furious!

DON LOUIS: I see I embarrass you. No doubt you could well do without my coming here. The truth is that we are the bane of each other's lives. If you are tired of the sight of me, I am equally weary of your behaviour. Oh, how little we know what we are doing when, instead of leaving it to God to decide what is good for us, we try to be cleverer than he is and start pestering him with our blind wishes and inconsiderate demands! No man ever wanted a son more than I did. No man ever prayed for one more insistently and ardently than I. And now the son whom I got by wearying Heaven with my prayers, and thought would be the joy and consolation of my life, turns out to be a trial and a torment. Tell me, what am I to think of your roll-call of actions so dishonourable that it would be extremely difficult to put a tolerable face on their villainy for the world at large? How should I regard this never-ending succession of infamous affairs which has reduced me to wearying the king's indulgence day and night until I have exhausted the credit earned by my services to the Crown and the goodwill of my friends? What depths have you sunk to! Are you not ashamed to be so unworthy of your birth? Tell me, what right do you think you have to take pride in it? What have you ever done that entitles you to be considered a gentleman? Or do you think it is enough to have a name and bear arms to be one? that we can still deem it an honour to be born of noble blood, when we live ignoble lives? No, birth is nothing when it is not accompanied by virtue. Which is why we have no claim to share the glory of our ancestors unless we strive to be like them. The distinction which their glorious actions confers on us imposes a commitment to return the honour, to follow in the footsteps they left to guide us and, if we wish to be considered their true descendants, never to fall short of their virtues. You are no true descendant of the forefathers who gave you life – they disown you as not of their blood, and all their glorious deeds reflect no credit on you. On the contrary, their illustriousness merely serves to throw your dishonour into greater relief. Their fame is a torch which lights your shameful actions for all to see. Be advised of this: a gentleman who lives a wicked life is an offence against nature, that virtue is the essential qualification for nobility, that I have more regard for a man's deeds than for the name he signs himself with, and that I should have more respect for the son of a common porter who was an honest man than for a prince of the blood who lives as you do.

DON JUAN: You'd find speaking more comfortable if you were sitting down sir.

DON LOUIS: No, you insolent puppy, I will not sit down nor will I speak another word. I see that nothing I say makes any impression on you. But I would have you know, unworthy son that you are, that you have pushed your father's love to the limit and that I shall find a way, sooner than you think, to put an end to your scandalous conduct, to anticipate the wrath of Heaven by punishing you myself and thus wash away the disgrace of having brought you into the world. (*He goes out.*)

Scene v:
DON JUAN, SGANARELLE

DON JUAN (*to his retreating father*): Oh why don't you just die – and make it soon. Every dog has its day. I can't stand it when fathers hang around too long and are a nuisance to their sons. (*He sits in his arm-chair.*)

SGANARELLE: Oh sir, that was wrong of you.

DON JUAN: Wrong?

SGANARELLE: Sir . . .

DON JUAN (*getting up*): What do you mean, wrong?

SGANARELLE: Oh yes sir, quite wrong to let him talk like that. You should have taken him by the scruff of the neck and booted him out. Did you ever hear the like! Fancy, a father coming and remonstrating with his son, telling him to mend his ways and remember the obligations of his birth, saying he should lead a decent life and spouting a lot of other nonsense of that kind. How could you stand it, a man like yourself, who knows the ways of the world? I admire your patience. If I'd been in your shoes I'd have kicked him out. (*Aside*) Oh cursed subservience, to what depths do you reduce me?

DON JUAN: Will my supper be ready soon?

Scene vi:
DON JUAN, DONA ELVIRA *dressed in convent black,*
RAGOTIN, SGANARELLE

RAGOTIN: There's a lady sir, wearing a veil, wants to speak to you.

DON JUAN: Now who could this be?

SGANARELLE: We must see.

DONA ELVIRA: Do not be surprised, Don Juan, to see me at this hour and dressed like this. It is for an urgent reason that I am compelled to pay you this call. What I have to tell you permits of no delay. I do not come here in anger, the anger which I allowed myself to show earlier. You now see in me someone very different from the person I was this morning. I am no longer the Dona Elvira who called down the wrath of Heaven on you, whose indignant spirit spat threats and breathed only vengeance. Heaven has purged my soul of all the unworthy passion I felt for you, the stormy emotions of an illicit relationship, the shameful agitation of earthly, physical love. All it has left in my heart for you is a love cleansed of sensuality, a blessed tenderness, a love that is free of all ties, asks nothing for itself and concerns itself only with your welfare.

DON JUAN (*to Sganarelle*): You're crying, I fancy.

SGANARELLE: Excuse me.

DONA ELVIRA: It is this perfect, pure love which brings me here for your own good, to convey a warning from Heaven and pluck you from the abyss into which you are about to fall. Yes Don Juan, I am well aware of the dissoluteness of your life, but the same God who pricked my conscience and opened my eyes to the wildness of my own conduct has prompted me to seek you out and give you a warning from him that your crimes have exhausted his mercy, that His dread anger is about to fall on you, and that you may yet avoid it by immediate repentance. It may be that you have not a single day left in which to escape the most terrible of all misfortunes. I myself am freed of all earthly ties that bound me to you. I have turned my back, thanks be to Heaven, on all my foolish fancies. I have resolved to withdraw from the world and now ask for nothing more than to live long enough to expiate the sin I committed, and by strict penance to earn pardon for the blindness to which I was driven by the excesses of guilty passion. But in retiring from the world I would sincerely grieve to see someone I once loved so tenderly become an awful example of Heavenly justice. It would give me unspeakable joy could I but persuade you to parry the dreadful fate hanging over your head. I implore you Don Juan, as one last favour, grant me this sweet consolation. Do not deny me your salvation which I beg with my tears. If you are not interested in your own well-being, at least let my prayers move you and spare me the horrible spectacle of seeing you condemned to eternal torment.

SGANARELLE: Poor lady!

DONA ELVIRA: I loved you with all the tenderness at my command. You were dearer to me than all the world. For you, I forgot my duty and for you there was nothing I did not do. The only recompense I ask of you is that you mend your ways and stave off certain damnation.

Save yourself, I beseech you, whether for love of yourself or for love of me. Once more Don Juan, I ask this with my tears. And if the tears of a woman you once loved are not enough, I ask it in the name of what is most dear to you.

SGANARELLE (*aside*): Oh tiger-hearted villain!

DONA ELVIRA: I have spoken and shall now withdraw. That is all I had to say to you.

DON JUAN: Madame, it's late. Stay here tonight. You shall be given the very best lodging there is.

DONA ELVIRA: No Don Juan, do not detain me any longer.

DON JUAN: Madame, it would give me great pleasure if you would stay.

DONA ELVIRA: No I tell you. Let us waste no more time in idle conversation. Permit me to leave at once. Do not insist on escorting me. Think only of how you might take advantage of the warning I have given you.

Scene vii:
DON JUAN, SGANARELLE

DON JUAN: Would you believe it, but I again found it in my heart to experience a faint twinge of feeling for her? There was something rather agreeable in the novelty of the situation. Those dishevelled clothes, her languid air, the tears, all fanned in me the dying embers of a fire that I thought was out.

SGANARELLE: Which means that what she said had no effect on you at all?

DON JUAN: Quickly now, let's have that supper.

SGANARELLE: Very well.

DON JUAN (*sitting at the table*): All the same Sganarelle, we shall have to think about mending our ways.

SGANARELLE: We shall indeed!

DON JUAN: Upon my word, yes! We'll have to mend our ways. Another twenty or thirty years of this sort of life and then we'll start looking to ourselves.

SGANARELLE: Oh!

DON JUAN: What's that you say?

SGANARELLE: Nothing. Here comes supper. (*He takes something from one of the dishes which are brought and puts it in his mouth.*)

DON JUAN: Your cheek looks very swollen to me. What is it? Speak up! What's that you've got in your mouth?

SGANARELLE: Nothing.

DON JUAN: Let me see. Good Lord! He has a swelling in his cheek! Quick, something to lance it with. The poor lad can't stand the pain — the abscess could choke him! Steady now! See, it was ready to burst! Ah! you rogue!

SGANARELLE: No, honestly sir, I only wanted to make sure your cook hadn't put in too much salt or pepper.

DON JUAN: Come along, sit yourself down there and eat. I shall need you when I've finished. You're ravenous I see.

SGANARELLE (*sitting at the table*): I should think I am sir. I haven't eaten since this morning. Try some of this. It's excellent. (*A servant removes Sganarelle's plates as soon as he puts food on them.*) My plate! That's my plate! Just go easy, if you don't mind. Goodness me lad, you've certainly got the knack of handing out clean plates. As for you La Violette, you've got the knack of pouring out the wine at the right moment! (*While one servant fills Sganarelle's glass, another takes his plate away again.*)

DON JUAN: Who can be knocking like that?

SGANARELLE: Who the devil has come to bother us in the middle of dinner?

DON JUAN: I intend at least to finish my supper in peace. No one is to be shown in.

SGANARELLE: Leave it to me, I'll go myself.

DON JUAN: Who is it? Who's there?

SGANARELLE (*nodding his head as the Statue did*): The . . . it's come!

DON JUAN: Let's go and see. I'll show there's nothing that can unsettle me.

SGANARELLE: Poor Sganarelle, where can you go and hide?

Scene viii:

DON JUAN, *the* STATUE *of the Commander which
advances and sits at the table,* SGANARELLE *and
attendants*

DON JUAN: A chair, lay an extra place – and quick about it! (*To Sganarelle*) Come, sit down at the table.

SGANARELLE: I've lost my appetite sir.

DON JUAN: Sit down I tell you. Bring wine. I give you a toast, Sganarelle: the Commander's health. Fill his glass somebody.

SGANARELLE: I'm not thirsty sir.

DON JUAN: Drink up, and give us a song to entertain the Commander.

SGANARELLE: I've got a cold sir.

DON JUAN: Never mind about that. Right, you others, come and accompany him.

STATUE: Enough Don Juan. I invite you to come and sup with me tomorrow. Do you dare accept?

DON JUAN: Yes, I'll come – with Sganarelle and no one else.

SGANARELLE: Thank you very much, but tomorrow I'm fasting.

DON JUAN (*to Sganarelle*): Take this torch.

STATUE: There is no need for light when Heaven shows the way.

Act V

Scene i:

DON LOUIS, DON JUAN, SGANARELLE

DON LOUIS: Can this be, my boy? Is it possible that Heaven in its mercy has answered my prayers? Is what you say really true? You aren't deluding me with false hopes? Can I really trust myself to believe in this recent and surprising conversion?

DON JUAN (*playing the hypocrite*): Yes, you see before you a man who has seen the error of his ways. I am not the same as I was last night: the Lord has wrought a sudden change in me which will astonish everyone. He touched my heart and made the scales fall from my eyes. I look back with horror on the blindness in which I dwelt so long and the sinful waywardness of the life I led. When in my mind I review all the abominable actions I have committed, I am amazed that Heaven tolerated them for so long and did not unleash the sanction of its awesome justice against me a score of times. I now see what great favour it has shown me in its mercy by not punishing me for my crimes. I intend to take advantage of its forbearance, as I must, and offer the world the dramatic spectacle of the sudden change in my way of life. Thus I shall make amends for the scandalous example of my past deeds and endeavour to earn a full pardon for my sins. This is the task I have set myself and I ask you sir to assist me in this design by personally choosing for me a guide and mentor under whose direction I may safely follow the path on which I am about to set my feet.

DON LOUIS: Oh my boy! How easily can the love of a father revive and the crimes of a son be erased at the first word of repentance! I have already forgotten all the grief you have caused me: everything has been blotted from my memory by what you have just told me. I confess I am quite overcome. I weep tears of joy. All my prayers are answered and I have nothing more to ask of Heaven. Come, embrace me my son, and do not falter, I beseech you, in your laudable intentions. I must go at once and take the good news to your mother, share the relief and happiness I feel and give thanks to God for the holy purpose he has inspired in your heart. (*He goes out.*)

Scene ii:

DON JUAN, SGANARELLE

SGANARELLE: Oh sir! I can't tell you how overjoyed I am to see you converted! I've been waiting a long time for this moment and now, thanks be to God, all my wishes have been granted.

DON JUAN: A plague on the fool!

SGANARELLE: Fool? Me?

DON JUAN: What? You mean to say you've taken what I just said at its face value? You think my lips are in tune with my heart?

SGANARELLE: Then it isn't ... You're not ... You ... Oh, what a man, what a man, what a man!

DON JUAN: I have not changed at all. My sentiments are still the same.

SGANARELLE: And hasn't the amazing, miraculous, walking, talking statue made you have second thoughts?

DON JUAN: There's certainly something there I don't understand, but whatever it is it shall neither change my mind nor shake my courage. When I said I intended to mend my ways and start to lead an exemplary life it was a ploy I adopted out of sheer expediency, a useful tactic, a necessary pretence which I fully intend to maintain if I am to keep on the right side of my father, because I need him. It will also protect me against other people and all the tiresome things that may happen to me. I don't mind taking you into my confidence Sganarelle. I rather like having one witness to my real feelings and the motives which drive me to behave the way I do.

SGANARELLE: What? You don't believe in anything, but you want to set yourself up as a man of principle?

DON JUAN: And why not? There are plenty like me who ply the same trade and don the same mask to deceive other people!

SGANARELLE: Oh! what a man, what a man!

DON JUAN: There's no shame in it nowadays. Hypocrisy is a fashionable vice and all vices that are fashionable turn into virtues. These days the role of a man of principle is the pick of the parts you can play, for to profess hypocrisy is to acquire remarkable advantages. It is an art, and practising it invariably commands respect. People might see through it, but they dare not speak out. All mankind's vices are subject to criticism and anyone is free to attack them openly. But hypocrisy is a privileged vice. With a gesture of its hand, it can stop the mouths of everyone and is left in peace to enjoy unlimited immunity. With its cant and humbug it binds all those who practise it in close fellowship, and whoever clashes with one of them brings down the rest of the pack on himself. Men whom you know to be acting in good faith, men who are truly god-fearing, are always taken in by the hypocrites. The first are easily caught in the snares of the second, and give their support blindly to wicked men who do no more than mimic their own virtuous conduct. How many men do you think I know who use such clever tactics to cover up the disorderly conduct of their youth, shielding themselves by donning the cloak of religion, and then, robed in the cloth of its respectability, have everyone's permission to be as wicked as they like? People may be aware of their machinations, they may even recognize such men for what they are, but they are not held in less regard on that account. They bow their heads, heave a sigh of mortification and roll their eyes a couple of times, and that, as far as other people are concerned, makes everything they do all right again. I intend to shelter behind this friendly cover and by so doing make my position secure. I shall not abandon my pleasant ways, but I shall take care to operate in secret and amuse myself discreetly. Then if by chance I am found out, I shall simply watch without having to lift a finger myself, while the whole fraternity makes my cause its own and defends me against any and every criticism. In other words, it's the best way of getting whatever I want with impunity. I shall become a self-appointed judge of other people's behaviour, pass stern sentences on all and sundry and have a good opinion of no one – except myself. Let anyone offend me in however insignificant a way, and I shall never forgive but privately nurse an implacable hatred. I shall play the role of avenger of the word of God and use this convenient pretext to harass my enemies. I shall accuse them of irreligion and find ways of unleashing the officious zealots who will raise a public outcry against them without even knowing what they are supposed to have done, heap insults on them and damn them roundly on their own personal authority. That's how to exploit human frailty. That's how a wise man can turn the vices of his times to his own advantage.

SGANARELLE: Oh Lord! Can I believe my ears? All you needed to put the finishing touches to your character was to turn hypocrite. This is the final abomination! It's the last straw sir and I cannot stay silent any longer. You can do what you like to me: hit me, beat me senseless, kill me if you like, but I must get this off my chest and say what I have to, as a faithful servant should. You know sir, the pitcher can go to the well once too often and get broken. And like some writer or other said, who he was I don't know, men in this world are like the bird on the bough; the bough is attached to the tree and whoever clings to that tree is following good advice; good advice is better than fine words; fine words are what you get at Court; at Court you find courtiers; courtiers do whatever's in fashion; fashion is the result of imagination; the imagination is a product of the soul; the soul is what gives us life; life ends in death; death makes us think of Heaven; Heaven is above the earth; the earth's not the same as the sea; the sea is prone to storms; storms attack ships; ships need a good pilot; a good pilot needs prudence; prudence is not something you find in the young; the young should obey the old; the old like money; money makes people rich; rich people aren't poor; the poor know poverty; poverty knows no law; without law men live like brutes. Which all goes to prove that you will be damned for all eternity!

DON JUAN: Excellently argued!

SGANARELLE: If you don't admit you're wrong after all that, then on your own head be it.

Scene iii:

DON CARLOS, DON JUAN, SGANARELLE

DON CARLOS: Don Juan, this is well met. I'm glad to have an opportunity to speak to you here rather than at your house, to ask what you have decided. You know this is a matter which concerns me closely, since you were there when I took the obligation upon myself. I will not hide the fact that, for my part, I would much prefer to see things settled amicably. I would give anything to induce you to choose that alternative and see you publicly acknowledge my sister as your wife.

DON JUAN (*speaking like a hypocrite*): Alas, I wish with all my heart that I could give you the satisfaction you ask. But Heaven has set its face emphatically against it, for it has planted in my soul a determination to change the direction of my life. I have only one thought now: to renounce all earthly ties, to divest myself at once of vanity in all its forms and, by a life of austerity, to atone for all the wicked excesses into which the blindness of youth has led me.

DON CARLOS: But your decision does not contradict what I'm saying. To enjoy the companionship of a lawful wife is not incompatible with the admirable intentions which Heaven has kindled in you.

DON JUAN: That, alas, is not so. Your sister herself has taken the same decision. She has decided to withdraw to a convent. The spirit moved both of us at the identical moment.

DON CARLOS: She may take the veil, but that can in no way satisfy us, since it could be attributed to the contempt you continue to show both to her and to our family. Our honour demands that she live with you as your wife.

DON JUAN: That, I do assure you, cannot be. As far as I am concerned there once was nothing I could have wished for more. Only today I have sought the guidance of Heaven on that very subject. But after I prayed, I heard a voice which said unto me I should think no more of your sister since I should never find salvation with her.

DON CARLOS: Do you seriously think you can fool us with such lame excuses Don Juan?

DON JUAN: I must obey the voice of Heaven.

DON CARLOS: What? Do you think I will be satisfied by this sort of talk?

DON JUAN: It is Heaven that wills it so.

DON CARLOS: You think you can abduct my sister from a convent and then simply abandon her?

DON JUAN: Such is Heaven's command.

DON CARLOS: And are we to be left with this stain on our family honour?

DON JUAN: You must blame Heaven for that.

DON CARLOS: What! You persist in invoking Heaven?

DON JUAN: It is what Heaven has ordained.

DON CARLOS: Enough Don Juan! I understand you. I cannot deal with you here, this is not the place for it. But it will not be long before I come looking for you.

DON JUAN: You must do what you think best. You know I am no coward and that I can use a sword when the need arises. In a little while I shall stroll down the quiet lane which leads to the convent. But I tell you now that if we fight it will be through no wish of mine. Heaven forbids me even to think of it. But if you challenge me, we'll have to see what happens next.

DON CARLOS: We shall, we shall indeed.

Scene iv:

DON JUAN, SGANARELLE

SGANARELLE: Sir, what do you think you're playing at? This is far worse than all the rest of it. I'd much rather have you as you used to be. I always had hopes for your salvation but now I begin to despair. I cannot think that Heaven, which has tolerated you until now, can possibly overlook this last outrage.

DON JUAN: Oh, come now! Heaven is not as particular as you think. If every time a man –

SGANARELLE (*seeing the Spectre*): Ah sir! Heaven speaks here now! It has a warning for you!

DON JUAN: If Heaven wishes to give me a warning, then it should speak rather more clearly if it wants me to understand.

Scene v:
DON JUAN, *a* SPECTRE *in the form of a veiled woman*, SGANARELLE

SPECTRE: Don Juan has but a moment left to take advantage of the mercy of Heaven. If he repent not now, his end is certain.

SGANARELLE: Did you hear that sir?

DON JUAN: Who dares speak to me like this? I think I recognize that voice.

SGANARELLE: Oh sir! It's a spirit. I can tell by its walk.

DON JUAN: Spirit, phantom, devil, I insist on knowing what it is.

The Spectre alters its appearance and represents Time with a scythe in its hand.

SGANARELLE: Oh heavens! Look sir, see how it changes shape!

DON JUAN: No, there is nothing that can fill me with terror. I shall test whether it be flesh or spirit with my sword.

The Spectre disappears as Don Juan is about to strike it.

SGANARELLE: Oh sir! You must submit to the evidence of your eyes and repent at once.

DON JUAN: No, no, it shall never be said, whatever happens, that I am the repenting kind. Come, follow me.

Scene vi:
The STATUE, DON JUAN, SGANARELLE

STATUE: Stop, Don Juan! You gave me your word yesterday that you would come and sup with me.

DON JUAN: Quite so. Which way is it?

STATUE: Give me your hand.

DON JUAN: There.

STATUE: Don Juan, those who persist in their wickedness shall meet a dreadful end. Those who reject the mercy of Heaven call down its wrath.

DON JUAN: Oh God! What's happening to me? Unseen fires consume me! I cannot bear the pain! My whole body is aflame! Aaah!

Rolls of thunder and flashes of lightning envelop Don Juan. The earth opens and swallows him up. Great flames rise from the pit into which he has vanished.

SGANARELLE: My wages! What about my wages? Well, there it is. His death makes everybody happy: the Heaven he offended, the laws he violated, the girls he seduced, the families he dishonoured, the parents he outraged, the women he led astray, the husbands he drove to despair – everybody's satisfied. There's only me who's come out of it badly. After all my years of service, all the reward I get is to see my master punished for his impiety in the most dreadful way imaginable. But what about my wages? My wages! My wages!

The Miser, a Comedy

L'Avare, Comédie

Performed for the first time on 9 September 1668 at the Palais Royal by the King's Players

The first run of *The Miser* was not a success, for reasons which are unclear, for it is now regarded as one of Molière's finest high comedies. It is inventive and solidly constructed and it has the kind of denouement which, though it now appears contrived, normally delighted contemporary audiences. At the time it was said that the public did not take to the play because it was written not in verse but in prose, but this is not a totally convincing explanation. Even so, by 1672 it had been performed a respectable forty-seven times and since then only *Tartuffe* has been staged more often.

For *The Miser* Molière borrowed from a number of sources, notably Plautus's *Aulularia* and *La Belle Plaideuse* (1655) by Boisrobert. But his miser is not the two-dimensional caricatural tightwad of tradition, nor does he embody abstract Avarice. Rather he has the characteristics of three distinct literary types – miser, usurer and amorous greybeard – which merge into a fourth: Harpagon is a money-conscious Paris bourgeois with social aspirations. Though he regrets the expense, his status requires him to keep a carriage and servants, and his ambition is to see his children marry money. Extravagance such as Cléante's is an insult, and affection an irrelevance. His decision to marry Mariane has little to do with love. To complete his image he needs a pretty young wife on his arm.

Harpagon belongs in the ranks of Molière's great monomaniac fathers. Like Orgon (*Tartuffe*), Monsieur Jourdain (*The Would-Be Gentleman*) and Argan (*The Hypochondriac*), he views the marriage of his children as a way of furthering an obsession. Scenes of farce (with his servants, his repetition of 'But – no dowry!') make him a comic character, but the impact of his tunnel-vision on others has led some critics to regard the play primarily as a drama which shows how dangerous obsessions can be. Moreover, Harpagon never learns to look beyond his money-box, and because he seems trapped inside what may be regarded as a pathological state he has sometimes been seen as a tragic figure.

While at times Harpagon on the page is odious enough not to be altogether comic, it seems unlikely that Molière's own performance in the role laid much emphasis on Harpagon's sinister side. In 1668 Molière was ill and physically diminished, and it is probable that his miser was more ridiculous and less in control than other interpretations from the eighteenth century onwards have made him seem. Indeed, actions which are hard to account for become comprehensible if we think of Harpagon as a man who is afraid — of being robbed, of affection, of life itself.

This view of him becomes more plausible still when it is set against the values which Molière defends in the play. Here, in a bourgeois setting, a family is threatened by the abuse of paternal authority. The younger generation find comfort and happiness with each other, and their values are based on the love they feel. They are right and Harpagon is wrong: it is unnatural for parents to sacrifice the happiness of their children to their own. This, rather than the 'golden mean', is the common-sense of which Molière sets out to remind us. Comic servants can see what their master cannot, and brothers, sisters and lovers show how life-denying avarice can be. Far from being the study in monomania it is sometimes taken to be, *The Miser* needs its lesser parts as much as it needs Harpagon.

Characters

HARPAGON, father to Cléante and Élise, suitor for the hand of Mariane

CLÉANTE, son of Harpagon, in love with Mariane

ÉLISE, daughter of Harpagon, in love with Valère

VALÈRE, son of Anselme, in love with Élise

MARIANE, in love with Cléante, and loved by Harpagon

ANSELME, father of Valère and Mariane

FROSINE, a go-between

MAÎTRE SIMON, a broker

MAÎTRE JACQUES, cook and coachman to Harpagon

LA FLÈCHE, valet to Cléante

DAME CLAUDE ⎫
BRINDAVOINE ⎬ servants to Harpagon
LA MERLUCHE ⎭

OFFICER OF THE LAW

CONSTABLE

The scene is set in Paris.

Act I

Scene i:
VALÈRE, ÉLISE

VALÈRE: What is it dearest Élise? Why so sad when you have just given the most gratifying assurance that you love me? Here I am, the happiest of men, and I find you sighing! Tell me, is it because you regret making me happy and are having second thoughts about a promise you may feel you were forced into giving by the strength of my love?

ÉLISE: No Valère, I could never regret anything I did for you. I have a sense of being swept along by feelings too tender for that, and I would not wish what is done to be undone. But I must confess I am worried about how it will all turn out, and more than a little afraid that I love you rather more than I should.

VALÈRE: But Élise, what can you possibly have to fear from loving me?

ÉLISE: Alas, a great deal, and on many fronts: my father's anger, the reproaches of my family, what people will say. But most of all Valère, I am afraid you might have a change of heart, that you will turn cold and cruel, which is the way men always return the over-eager affections of an innocent heart.

VALÈRE: Oh do not be so unjust as to judge me by other men. Think me capable of anything Élise, but do not believe I would ever go back on my obligations to you. I love you too much and I shall go on loving you for as long as I live.

ÉLISE: Ah! Valère, you all talk like that. Men are all the same in what they say. It is only in what they do that they are different.

VALÈRE: If actions alone reveal us as we are, then at least wait and judge my love by mine. Do not look for faults that exist only in your unjustified fears and dire forebodings. I implore you, do not let the wounding effects of excessive suspicion destroy my happiness! Just give me time to convince you and you shall have all the proof you need that my love is true.

ÉLISE: Ah! how easy it is to let ourselves be convinced by those we love. Oh yes, I really think you would never deceive me Valère, and I do believe you love me truly and will be faithful. I have not the least wish to doubt you. My only concern is that everyone will say I am to blame.

VALÈRE: And why should that trouble you?

ÉLISE: I would have nothing to fear if only everyone could see you as I do. The qualities I find in you more than repay everything I do for you. My love, pleading your virtues in its defence, can also call upon the gratitude with which Heaven itself has committed me to you. For I keep remembering that moment of terrible danger when we first set eyes on each other, your amazing courage in risking your life to drag me from the fury of the waves, the gentleness and concern you showed after pulling me out of the water, and the constant proofs you have given of a sincere affection which neither time nor adversity have diminished and for the sake of which you neglect your family and your country, remain here, conceal your true rank on my account and stoop to being a servant in my father's household simply to be near me! All this has made a great impression on me Valère, and, to me, is itself enough to justify the promise I made you. But it may not be enough for others and I cannot be certain that they will view matters as I do.

VALÈRE: Of all these things you mention, only one gives me any claim on you, and that is my love. As to your scruples, surely your father has done everything he could to justify you to other people. Actually, his excessive avarice and the beggarly footing on which he lives with his children would surely justify much stranger things than that! Forgive me, dearest Élise, for speaking of him this way – as you know only too well there is not much good to be said in his favour. But if, as I hope, I can find my parents again, we shouldn't have much trouble in obtaining their consent. I'm anxious for news of them and if I don't hear soon I shall go looking for them myself.

ÉLISE: Oh no Valère! Please don't go! Stay and think only of how to gain my father's confidence.

VALÈRE: Haven't you noticed how hard I've been trying? All that simpering subservience to get taken on as a servant, the mask of fellow-feeling and conformity to his sentiments I assumed in order to ingratiate myself with him, the role I play whenever he is around just so I can gain his favour. But I'm making excellent progress. I find the best way to get on the right side of people is to pretend to fall in with their view of things, agree with their principles, encourage their foibles and applaud whatever they do. There's no fear of overdoing the grovelling and you can't be too blatant in playing them along. The cunning ones are the most vulnerable to flattery. People can be persuaded to swallow anything, however absurd and ridiculous, provided it is sufficiently seasoned with praise. True, such tactics do little for one's own sincerity, but if you need people you have to adapt to them and since there is no other way of getting their backing, well then, the blame lies not with the flatterers but with those who wish to be flattered.

ÉLISE: Why don't you try to get my brother's support too, in case the maid takes it into her head to give our secret away?

VALÈRE: No, I couldn't handle father and son at the same time. They see things so differently that it would be difficult to have the ear of both simultaneously. Do what you can with your brother. Make the most of your mutual affection to win him over to our side. He's coming. I'll leave you now. Take this opportunity to have a word with him, but tell him only so much of our affairs as you think fit.

ÉLISE: I don't know if I can bring myself to take him into my confidence.

Scene ii:
CLÉANTE, ÉLISE

CLÉANTE: I'm so glad I've got you alone sister. I've been dying for a chance to speak to you. I want to tell you something, a secret.

ÉLISE: Well Cléante, I'm all ears. What do you want to tell me?

CLÉANTE: A world of things sister, but – to sum it up in one word – I'm in love!

ÉLISE: You, in love?

CLÉANTE: Yes, in love. But before we go any further, let me say I am quite aware that I am dependent on my father, that as a son I must submit to his good pleasure, that we should never even think of marriage without first obtaining the consent of those who brought us into the world, that Heaven has made them the arbiters of our wishes, that it is our duty never to give our affections except as they may decide, that, not being misled by foolish passion, they are less likely than we are to make mistakes and much better placed to see what is good for us, that we must trust in their wisdom and prudence rather than in our own blind desires, and that the impetuosity of youth leads, as often as not, to the most terrible disasters. I mention all this Élise to save you the trouble of saying it. The fact is I'm far too much in love to listen to anything you might have to say, so please, spare me the sermons.

ÉLISE: And have you told her you are going to marry her Cléante?

CLÉANTE: Not yet. But my mind's made up, so once again I ask you not to try and talk me out of it.

ÉLISE: Am I such a strange person, brother?

CLÉANTE: No, but you're not in love. You know nothing of the power that tender passion exerts over the hearts of us lovers, and I'm afraid you may take the sensible view.

ÉLISE: Oh, don't talk to me of being sensible! Everyone ends up not acting sensibly at some time or other, and if I were to tell you everything that's in my own heart you might think I've been even less sensible than you have.

CLÉANTE: Ah! if only you were like me, if only you were in love . . .

ÉLISE: Let's deal with your problem first. Tell me who she is.

CLÉANTE: A girl who's only just come to live in the district – she's charming, to see her is to love her. Nature never made anything lovelier and I was swept off my feet the moment I set eyes on her. Her name is Mariane and she lives with her mother who is almost always ill and to whom she is utterly and quite wonderfully devoted. She fetches and carries for her, is sweet to her, and consoles her in her sufferings with the most touching devotion. She lends charm to everything she touches and grace to everything she does. She is so gentle, so kind, so modest, so . . . Oh Élise, how I wish you'd been there to see her!

ÉLISE: I can see her very clearly from your description. Anyway, the fact that you love her is enough to tell me what sort of person she is.

CLÉANTE: I have discovered, as a result of certain discreet inquiries, that they aren't very well off and that, even living modestly as they do, they're hard put to make ends meet. Imagine, Élise, the joy of being able to restore the fortunes of the one you love, or even of discreetly supplementing the modest needs of a virtuous family! And then just think how frustrated I must be because I cannot, thanks to

my father's avarice, know such joy or even offer that lovely creature
a single token of my love.

ÉLISE: Yes, I can see how galling it must be for you.

CLÉANTE: Ah sister, it's far worse than anyone could possibly imagine.
Was there ever anything more cruel than the strict penny-pinching
he forces us to live with, the unnatural parsimoniousness in which
we are made to languish? What use will money be to us if it comes
only when we are too old to enjoy it? If, to get by at all in the
meantime, I have to borrow right and left and, like you, am always
having to ask tradesmen for credit just to have something decent to
wear? Anyway, I wanted this talk with you to ask you to sound
father out about what I have in mind. If I find he's against it, I've
decided to run away somewhere with my wonderful angel and make
the best of whatever Heaven may send us. With this in mind, I'm
trying to raise money everywhere. If you're in the same boat as me
Élise, and father opposes your wishes too, we'll both leave him and
free ourselves from the yoke of tyranny his unbearable avarice has
imposed on us for so long.

ÉLISE: It's certainly true he gives us fresh cause each day to regret our
mother's death and –

CLÉANTE: That's his voice I can hear. We'd better finish discussing our
plans somewhere else, then afterwards we can join forces and mount
a combined attack on the hard-hearted fiend.

Scene iii:

HARPAGON, LA FLÈCHE

HARPAGON: Get out this minute! And no answering back! Clear out of
my house, you sworn thief, you gallows-bird you!

LA FLÈCHE (*aside*): I never came across anyone nastier than this
bad-tempered old man and, if you asked me, I'd say he's the very
devil!

HARPAGON: What are you muttering about?

LA FLÈCHE: What are you kicking me out for?

HARPAGON: It's not for you to ask me for reasons, you scoundrel! Get
out before I throw you out!

LA FLÈCHE: What did I do you didn't like?

HARPAGON: Enough for me to want you out.

LA FLÈCHE: Your son – master – told me to wait for him.

HARPAGON: Go and wait in the street then, I'll not have you in my house any more, hanging about all the time, watching everything that goes on, constantly on the look-out for whatever you can get your hands on. I don't want some infernal spy with his nose forever in my affairs, a sneaking cur with his confounded eyes on everything I do, devouring all that I own and ferreting everywhere to see if there's anything to steal.

LA FLÈCHE: And how the devil do you think anybody could ever pinch anything of yours? Is it likely you'll ever be robbed since you keep everything under lock and key and stand guard day and night?

HARPAGON: I'll lock up whatever I want to and stand guard whenever I please. I never saw such a set of prying eyes, forever snooping on everything I do! (*Aside*) I only hope he hasn't got suspicions about my money. (*To La Flèche*) You're just the sort to go spreading it around that I've got money hidden away, aren't you?

LA FLÈCHE: You've got money hidden?

HARPAGON: No you rogue, I never said that. (*Aside*) Oh, this is maddening! (*To La Flèche*) All I'm asking is that you don't go spreading malicious rumours that I have.

LA FLÈCHE: What difference is it to us whether you have or you haven't, since either way it's all the same?

HARPAGON: Are you arguing with me? I'll teach you to argue! I'll warm your ears for you! (*Raising his fist*) I told you once, clear off!

LA FLÈCHE: All right! I'm going!

HARPAGON: Wait! You're not walking off with anything of mine are you?

LA FLÈCHE: What could I be taking?

HARPAGON: Come here, let me see. Show me your hands.

LA FLÈCHE: There.

HARPAGON: Now the other ones.

LA FLÈCHE: What other ones?

HARPAGON (*pointing to his breeches*): Have you stuffed anything down there?

LA FLÈCHE: See for yourself.

HARPAGON (*feeling the bottoms of his breeches*): Baggy breeches are just the job for hiding stolen property. I'd string up the people who make the things if I had my way.

LA FLÈCHE (*aside*): Damn, it would serve a man like him right if he got exactly what he's scared might happen. If I could, I'd be happy to oblige by robbing him.

HARPAGON: Eh?

LA FLÈCHE: What?

HARPAGON: What did you say about robbing?

LA FLÈCHE: I said, 'Take a good look and make sure I'm not robbing you.'

HARPAGON: That's exactly what I intend to do. (*He feels in La Flèche's pockets.*)

LA FLÈCHE (*aside*): Devil take all misers and their miserly ways!

HARPAGON: What's that? What did you say?

LA FLÈCHE: What did I say?

HARPAGON: Yes, what did you say about misers and their miserly ways?

LA FLÈCHE: I said 'Devil take all misers and their miserly ways.'

HARPAGON: Who do you mean?

LA FLÈCHE: Misers.

HARPAGON: Who are these misers?

LA FLÈCHE: Mean, stingy old tightwads.

HARPAGON: But who exactly do you mean by that?

LA FLÈCHE: What are you getting so worked up about?

HARPAGON: I'm worked up about what I've got a right to be worked up about.

LA FLÈCHE: Did you think I meant you?

HARPAGON: I'll think what I like. But I want to know who you were talking to when you said that.

LA FLÈCHE: I was talking to . . . to my hat.

HARPAGON: Yes, and I'll talk to your thick skull.

LA FLÈCHE: Can't I say what I like about misers?

HARPAGON: Yes, you can if you like, but I can put a stop to your impudent nonsense. Hold your tongue!

LA FLÈCHE: I mentioned no names.

HARPAGON: Another word and I'll give you a good hiding!

LA FLÈCHE: If the cap fits, say I —

HARPAGON: Will you be quiet!

LA FLÈCHE: Yes, if I must.

HARPAGON: Oh, you . . .

LA FLÈCHE (*pointing to a pocket in his jerkin*): Look, here's another pocket! Satisfied now?

HARPAGON: Come on, just hand it over so I don't have to search you.

LA FLÈCHE: Hand what over?

HARPAGON: Whatever it was you took.

LA FLÈCHE: I didn't take anything!

HARPAGON: Sure?

LA FLÈCHE: Certain!

HARPAGON: Be off then, and go to the devil!

LA FLÈCHE: That's a nice way of getting my marching orders!

HARPAGON: I'll leave you to your conscience. (*La Flèche goes out.*) That blasted valet of mine is a confounded nuisance! I can't stand the sight of the limping cur![1]

Scene iv:
HARPAGON *alone, then* ÉLISE *and* CLÉANTE

HARPAGON: It's a terrible worry having such a large sum of money in the house. Much better to have it soundly invested and just keep what's needed for day-to-day expenses. It's difficult finding a safe hiding-place anywhere in this house. I don't trust strong-boxes. Won't have anything to do with them. They're an invitation to thieves, I always think – the first thing they go for. All the same, I'm not sure it was very wise to bury in the garden the ten thousand crowns I was paid yesterday. Ten thousand in gold is a tidy sum and . . . (*Enter Élise and Cléante whispering to each other.*) Damn! I've let the cat out of the bag! I was so anxious, I let myself be carried away. I do believe I was talking to myself. (*To Cléante*) What is it now?

CLÉANTE: Nothing father.

HARPAGON: Have you been there long?

ÉLISE: No, we've just arrived.

HARPAGON: Did you hear . . . er . . .

CLÉANTE: Hear what, father?

HARPAGON: Just then.

ÉLISE: What do you mean?

HARPAGON: What I was saying.

CLÉANTE: No.

HARPAGON: You did, you did!

ÉLISE: Sorry, but we didn't hear anything.

HARPAGON: I can tell you clearly heard something. The fact is I was just remarking to myself how difficult it is nowadays to get hold of money and saying how lucky you are if you've got ten thousand crowns ready to hand.

CLÉANTE: We hesitated to say anything in case we disturbed you.

HARPAGON: I'm very glad of the chance to explain, so you don't get the wrong idea and start imagining I was saying it was me who had ten thousand crowns.

CLÉANTE: We don't concern ourselves with what's your business.

HARPAGON: I only wish I had ten thousand crowns!

CLÉANTE: I don't believe –

HARPAGON: It would be a good thing for me if I had.

ÉLISE: Such things are –

HARPAGON: I could do with the money.

CLÉANTE: I think –

HARPAGON: It would come in very useful.

ÉLISE: You are –

HARPAGON: Then I should have less cause to complain about hard times than I have.

CLÉANTE: Good God father! You've got no cause to complain. Everyone knows you are well enough off.

HARPAGON: Me! Well off? Anyone who says that is a liar. Nothing could be further from the truth! People who go around spreading tales like that are rogues!

ÉLISE: Don't lose your temper.

HARPAGON: Matters have come to a pretty pass when my own children let me down and turn against me.

CLÉANTE: Is it turning against you to say that you are well-off?

HARPAGON: Yes. What with talk like that and your extravagance, someone will turn up one of these days and slit my throat because they think I've got money coming out of my ears!

CLÉANTE: In what way am I extravagant?

HARPAGON: I'll tell you in what way! The expensive clothes you flaunt around town – it's an absolute disgrace! I told your sister off for the same thing only yesterday, but you're much worse. It's a crying scandal! Just look at you, dressed up from head to foot – that little outfit would add up to a tidy income if it was invested. I've told you a score of times my lad that I don't like the way you carry on one bit. All this aping of the nobility and going about dressed up like this can only make me suspect that you must be robbing me somehow.

CLÉANTE: And how am I supposed to be robbing you?

HARPAGON: Don't ask me. But how otherwise would you find the money to keep yourself in fancy clothes the way you do?

CLÉANTE: How do I find the money father? Gambling, that's how, and, being lucky at cards, I always wear my winnings on my back.

HARPAGON: That's no way to go on! If you're lucky at cards, you should make the most of it and invest your winnings in something sound. That way you can still get your hands on it when you want it. But what I'd like to know, leaving the rest of your outfit to one side, is what's the point of all those ribbons you're festooned with from head to foot? Wouldn't half a dozen hooks and eyes do to fasten your breeches to your doublet? And why spend money on wigs when you can wear your own hair which doesn't cost a penny? I'm willing to bet that your wigs and ribbons cost you at least twenty pistoles, and twenty pistoles, even if you only got eight per cent, would bring a return of eighteen livres, six sous and eight deniers per annum.[2]

CLÉANTE: That's true.

HARPAGON: But let's drop that and come to something else – eh? (*Aside*) They're signalling to each other: I do believe they intend to steal my wallet. (*Aloud*) What's the meaning of these gesticulations?

ÉLISE: We're trying to decide who should speak first. We've both got something to tell you.

HARPAGON: And I have something to tell both of you.

CLÉANTE: What we want to talk to you about, father, is marriage.

HARPAGON: And marriage is also what I want to talk to you about.

ÉLISE: Oh father!

HARPAGON: Why 'Oh father'? Is it the word marriage that scares you or the idea of getting married yourself?

CLÉANTE: The word marriage might well alarm both of us. It all depends on what you understand by it. We're afraid that what we mean by it may not agree with what you mean by it.

HARPAGON: Just be patient. There's no need to be alarmed. I know what's good for you both and neither of you will have reason to complain about what I propose to do. Now to begin with, tell me: have you noticed a young woman named Mariane who lives not far from here?

CLÉANTE: Yes father I have.

HARPAGON (to Élise): How about you?

ÉLISE: I've heard of her.

HARPAGON: Tell me my boy, what do you think of her?

CLÉANTE: She's utterly delightful.

HARPAGON: Her face?

CLÉANTE: Frank and intelligent.

HARPAGON: The way she looks and behaves?

CLÉANTE: Wonderful, no question about it.

HARPAGON: You think a girl like that would be worth considering seriously?

CLÉANTE: Oh yes father.

HARPAGON: That she would be an eligible match?

CLÉANTE: Very eligible.

HARPAGON: That she looks as if she would turn out to be very good at house-keeping?

CLÉANTE: No question.

HARPAGON: And whoever married her could consider himself a lucky man, eh?

CLÉANTE: Very lucky.

HARPAGON: There's just one little difficulty. I'm afraid she might not bring as much money with her as could be wished.

CLÉANTE: What does money matter father, when it is a question of marrying a good woman?

HARPAGON: Oh no, I don't go along with that. But what I *will* say is that if she doesn't have as much money as would be desirable, there may be another way of making up for it.

CLÉANTE: Naturally.

HARPAGON: Well, I'm very pleased to see that you agree with me, because her modest ways and sweet nature have quite won my heart. Provided I find that she has something of a dowry I have made up my mind to marry her myself.

CLÉANTE: What?

HARPAGON: What does 'what?' mean?

CLÉANTE: You say you've made up your mind –

HARPAGON: To marry Mariane.

CLÉANTE: You mean – you? Yourself?

HARPAGON: Yes, me! Me! Myself! What's the matter with you?

CLÉANTE: I feel faint all of a sudden. I must get out of here.

HARPAGON: It'll pass off. Go to the kitchen and get yourself a good drink – there's plenty of cold water. (*Cléante goes out.*) That's your soft young man for you. There's more go in a chicken. So there it is my girl, that's what I've decided for myself. I have a certain widow in mind for your brother: someone was here this morning to have a word with me about her. And for you – I've chosen Seigneur Anselme.

ÉLISE: Seigneur Anselme?

HARPAGON: Yes. He's a man of experience, careful and sober, no more than fifty and said to be extremely rich.

ÉLISE (*curtseying*): If you please father, I have no inclination to be married.

HARPAGON (*imitating her*): And if my little girl, my precious, pleases, I have an inclination that she *shall* be married.

ÉLISE: I'm sorry father . . .

HARPAGON: No, *I'm* sorry, daughter.

ÉLISE: I am Seigneur Anselme's most humble servant but, if you don't mind, I shan't marry him.

HARPAGON: I am your most humble servant. But, if you don't mind, you shall marry him, and do it tonight too.

ÉLISE: Tonight?

HARPAGON: This very night.

ÉLISE: Father, I won't do it.

HARPAGON: You will.

ÉLISE: No!

HARPAGON: Yes!

ÉLISE: I tell you I won't!

HARPAGON: And I say you will!

ÉLISE: You can't make me!

HARPAGON: I can make you all right!

ÉLISE: I'll kill myself rather than marry a man like that!

HARPAGON: You won't kill yourself and you *shall* marry him. The impertinence! Whoever heard of a daughter talking to her father like this?

ÉLISE: Whoever heard of a father forcing his daughter to marry like this?

HARPAGON: It is an eminently suitable match. I'd give odds that anyone you ask would say so.

ÉLISE: And I'd give odds that no reasonable person would say any such thing.

HARPAGON: Ah, here's Valère. Will you agree to let him decide this matter for us?

ÉLISE: Yes, I agree.

HARPAGON: And you'll accept his verdict?

ÉLISE: I'll go along with whatever he says.

HARPAGON: That's settled then.

Scene v:
VALÈRE, HARPAGON, ÉLISE

HARPAGON: Come here Valère, we want you to tell us which of us is in the right, my daughter here or me.

VALÈRE: Oh you sir. No question of it.

HARPAGON: But you don't know what we're talking about.

VALÈRE: True, but you can't possibly be wrong. You're always right.

HARPAGON: I mean this very night to give her hand in marriage to a man who is both wealthy and wise, and the silly girl tells me to my face that she won't have him at any price. What do you say to that?

VALÈRE: What do I say to that?

HARPAGON: Yes.

VALÈRE: Ah . . . er . . .

HARPAGON: Out with it!

VALÈRE: What I say is that basically I agree with you, because it goes without saying that you cannot not be right. On the other hand, she isn't entirely wrong either and –

HARPAGON: Come now! Seigneur Anselme is a very eligible match, he has a title – and a proper one too, sedate, staid, very sound and extremely well-off, with no children from his first marriage. Could she possibly do any better for herself?

VALÈRE: That's true – though she might say you're rather hurrying things and that she at least ought to have a little time to see if temperamentally she is compatible with –

HARPAGON: No, no, this is an opportunity to be seized – or missed. You see, there's a special advantage to consider which won't come round again. He's willing to marry her without a dowry!

VALÈRE: Without a dowry?

HARPAGON: Yes.

VALÈRE: In that case, there's no more to be said. It's an absolutely unanswerable reason. You can't argue with that.

HARPAGON: It means a considerable saving for me.

VALÈRE: Very true, that goes without saying. Of course your daughter might say that marriage is more important than people realize, that a lifetime's happiness or unhappiness can depend on it and that no one should enter into a commitment for life without thinking about it very seriously.

HARPAGON: But – no dowry!

VALÈRE: You're right. That's the clincher, of course it is, although there are people who might say that in a case like this your daughter's feelings should be taken into account and that where there is such a wide difference in age, temperament and outlook, there is a great risk that the marriage might turn out badly.

HARPAGON: But – no dowry!

VALÈRE: Oh, absolutely. No one's got an answer to that. What could they possibly say against it? Not that there aren't a lot of fathers who would much prefer putting their daughters' feelings before the cash they have to part with and would never sacrifice their happiness to monetary considerations. They would rather try to ensure above all else that the marriage was founded on mutual affection which is the permanent basis for conjugal trust, peace and contentment, and moreover –

HARPAGON: But – no dowry!

VALÈRE: True. It's unanswerable. No dowry! How could anyone argue their way round that?

HARPAGON (*aside, looking towards the garden*): Hello, can I hear a dog barking? Could it be somebody's after my money? (*To Valère*) Don't go away, I'll be back in a moment. (*He goes out.*)

ÉLISE: What are you up to Valère, talking to him like that?

VALÈRE: If we're to get what we want we mustn't rub him up the wrong way. Arguing with him would be the quickest way to ruin everything. There are some people you can't deal with except by approaching them obliquely. Temperamentally intolerant of opposition and contrary by nature, they shy away from the truth and refuse to have anything to do with plain common-sense. The only way to lead them is to point them in the direction you want them to go. So pretend to go along with what he wants and you'll find it's the best way of getting what you want.

ÉLISE: But what about this marriage Valère?

VALÈRE: We'll look for some way of stopping it.

ÉLISE: But what way is there? It's planned for tonight.

VALÈRE: You'll have to pretend to be ill and have it postponed.

ÉLISE: But they'll discover the truth if they call a doctor.

VALÈRE: You must be joking. You know what doctors are like. It's easy: have whatever illness you like and all they'll tell you is how you got it.

HARPAGON (*returning and speaking to himself*): False alarm, thank God.

VALÈRE: If the worst comes to the worst, we can always run away and be safe – if, that is, dearest Élise, you love me enough . . . (*Seeing Harpagon*) Oh yes, a daughter must always do what her father tells her. It's not her business to worry about what her husband looks like. And when she comes up against the unanswerable 'No Dowry' argument, she must be ready to take whatever she's given.

HARPAGON: Good! That's the way to talk!

VALÈRE: Forgive me, sir, for letting my feelings run away with me and for taking the liberty of speaking to her like that.

HARPAGON: Not at all, I'm delighted. I give you a free hand with her. (*To Élise*) It's no good trying to run away. I am giving him full parental authority over you. I want you to do whatever he says.

VALÈRE (*to Élise*): Now you'll have to listen when I remind you of your duty! (*To Harpagon*) I'll follow her around sir and continue the lecture I was giving her.

HARPAGON: Do. Indeed I'd be most grateful.

VALÈRE: It would be as well to keep her on a tight rein.

HARPAGON: Quite right. We should –

VALÈRE: Don't worry. I think I can deal with her.

HARPAGON: Do so, by all means. I'm going to take a stroll in town now – I shan't be long.

VALÈRE: It's true: money is the most precious thing in all the world. You should go down on bended knee and thank Heaven for giving you such a good father. He knows what life's all about. When a man offers to marry a girl with no dowry, there's no point in looking any further. It's what it's all about. 'No dowry.' Why, it's worth more than looks, youth, birth, honour, good name and principles all rolled into one. (*They go out together.*)

HARPAGON: Good lad! Spoken like an oracle! I'm lucky to have a man like him in my service.

Act II

Scene i:

CLÉANTE, LA FLÈCHE

CLÉANTE: Now you ruffian, where have you been hiding yourself? Didn't I tell you to –

LA FLÈCHE: Oh yes sir, and I came here fully intending to wait for you all day. But your father, a very awkward customer, told me to get out, though I tried to explain. I very nearly got myself a good hiding.

CLÉANTE: How is our business progressing? Matters have become even more urgent now than before. Since I saw you last I've found out that my father is my rival.

LA FLÈCHE: Your father's in love?

CLÉANTE: Yes! And I've had a terrible time hiding the effect the news has had on me.

LA FLÈCHE: Fancy, him in love! What the devil's he think he's playing at? Is it a joke? Love wasn't intended for people who look like him.

CLÉANTE: Maybe, but for my sins he's gone and got it into his head that he's in love.

LA FLÈCHE: So why make such a secret of how you feel?

CLÉANTE: To give him less cause to be suspicious and to ensure I have room to manoeuvre to stop this marriage of his if it comes to that. What sort of answer did you get?

LA FLÈCHE: I tell you straight sir, trying to borrow money is a sorry business. People who are reduced to putting themselves in the hands of the money-lenders, like yourself, have to put up with some very peculiar goings-on.

CLÉANTE: So nothing will come of it?

LA FLÈCHE: Hear me out. Maître Simon, the broker we've been put in touch with, and very keen and business-like he is too, reckons he's been moving heaven and earth for you. He likes your face and says he's taken a fancy to you.

CLÉANTE: So shall I get the fifteen thousand francs I'm asking for?

LA FLÈCHE: Yes – subject to a few minor conditions you'll have to agree to if you want to go through with it.

CLÉANTE: Did he let you speak to the actual lender?

LA FLÈCHE: Really sir, that's not the way these things are done! He's even more anxious to hide his identity than you are, for there's more secrecy involved in this sort of business than you think. They refused point blank to give his name but they did arrange for him and you to meet today in a house hired for the purpose so that he can find out from you personally all about your means and your family background. I'm pretty sure that the mere mention of your father's name will make things go smoothly.

CLÉANTE: Especially as my mother is dead and no one can stop her money coming to me.[3]

LA FLÈCHE: These are the minor conditions he himself dictated to our go-between, which you have to see before he goes any further. (*Reads*) 'Assuming that the lender is satisfied by the securities offered, and provided the borrower is of age and of a family with property adequate, substantial, and secure, clear and free of encumbrance, a proper and exact bond shall be drawn up before a notary of known probity who, to this end, shall be nominated by the lender inasmuch as he is the more concerned that the instrument be executed in due form.'

CLÉANTE: I've got nothing to say against that.

LA FLÈCHE (*reads*): 'The lender, so that his conscience may be free from all reproach, undertakes to advance his monies at a rate of five and a half per centum only.'

CLÉANTE: Five and a half per cent? I say, that's very reasonable! Can't complain there!

LA FLÈCHE: You're right. (*Reads*) 'But, insofar as the lender aforesaid does not have the sum in question to hand, and in order to accommodate the borrower, he is himself obliged to borrow the said sum elsewhere at the rate of twenty per centum, the aforesaid borrower shall agree to pay this interest without prejudice to the five and a half per centum, in consideration of the fact that it is to oblige the above-named borrower that the aforesaid lender undertakes to borrow the sum heretoforementioned.'

CLÉANTE: What the devil? What sort of Jew or Arab are we dealing with here? That makes more than twenty-five per cent!

LA FLÈCHE: Yes. That's what I said. You'd better think it over.

CLÉANTE: Think what over? I've got to have the money, so I have no choice but to agree to everything.

LA FLÈCHE: That's what I told them.

CLÉANTE: Is there anything else?

LA FLÈCHE: Just one small clause. (*Reads*) 'Of the fifteen thousand francs requested, the lender is able to advance only twelve thousand livres in cash. For the remaining three thousand, the borrower shall take household effects, clothes and miscellaneous items, as per the schedule attached, fairly priced by the aforementioned lender at the most moderate valuation possible.'

CLÉANTE: What does that mean?

LA FLÈCHE: I'll read you the schedule. 'Item: one four-poster bed complete with hangings of Hungarian lace, very tastefully worked on olive-coloured material, together with six chairs and counterpane to match, all in good condition and lined in red and blue shot silk. Item: one bed canopy with hangings of good Aumale serge in dusty pink with silk fringes and valance.'

CLÉANTE: What does he expect me to do with that?

LA FLÈCHE: Wait. (*Reads*) 'Item: one tapestry wall-hanging depicting the loves of Gombaud and Macaea.[4] Item: one large table in solid walnut with twelve pedestal or turned legs and extending leaves, and fitted underneath with a set of six matching stools.'

CLÉANTE: Damn it all, what good's all that to me?

LA FLÈCHE: Do be patient. (*Reads*) 'Item: three large muskets inlaid with mother-of-pearl, with three suitable forked rests. Item: one brick furnace, with two retorts and three flasks, ideal for the home-distiller.'

CLÉANTE: This is infuriating!

LA FLÈCHE: Keep calm. (*Reads*) 'Item: one Bologna lute, complete with strings, or very nearly. Item: one table for the game of Pigeon-Holes,[5] one draughts board and a set of snakes and ladders, as improved from the Greek model, very useful for passing the time if you have nothing else to do. Item: one crocodile skin, three feet six inches in length and stuffed with straw, an amusing curio for hanging from a bedroom ceiling. All the aforementioned articles independently valued at more than four thousand five hundred francs and reduced to three thousand at the discretion of the lender.'

CLÉANTE: The devil take him and his discretion! What a rogue! What a swindler! Did you ever hear of such usury? Not content with charging extortionate interest, he also wants to make me pay three thousand francs for a heap of old junk he's picked up here and there. I wouldn't get six hundred for the lot. But I suppose I'll just have to agree to his conditions: he's in a position to make me agree to anything. The swine's holding a dagger to my throat!

LA FLÈCHE: The way I see it sir, if you don't mind my saying so, you're rushing down the same road to ruin as Panurge, taking money in advance, buying dear, selling cheap and eating your seedcorn.[6]

CLÉANTE: What else can I do? This is what young men are reduced to by the damned stinginess of their fathers. Can anyone wonder if their sons want them dead?

LA FLÈCHE: I'll admit your father's meanness would try the patience of the most easy-going man alive. Now I have no particular hankering to get myself hung, thank God, and when I see some of my acquaintances getting mixed up in funny goings-on I know when to get out sharpish and steer well clear of any kind of business which has a whiff of the gallows about it. But I'm bound to say, the way he carries on almost makes me want to rob him rotten. If I did rob him, I'd even believe I'd done something creditable.

CLÉANTE: Give me that schedule. I want to take another look at it.

Scene ii:

MAÎTRE SIMON, HARPAGON, CLÉANTE,
LA FLÈCHE

MAÎTRE SIMON: Yes sir, it's a young man who needs money. His affairs are such that he has to have it urgently and he'll agree to any conditions you care to make.

HARPAGON: And you are absolutely sure Maître Simon that there's no risk involved? Do you know your client's name, financial standing and family background?

MAÎTRE SIMON: No, I can't tell you exactly. It was only by chance that I was put in touch with him. But you'll hear it all from himself, and his servant assures me that you'll be completely satisfied when you meet him. All I can tell you is that his family is very rich, his mother is already dead and he'll guarantee, if you insist on it, that his father will die within eight months.

HARPAGON: Well, that's good to know. Charity, Maître Simon, requires us to help others whenever we can.

MAÎTRE SIMON: Of course it does.

LA FLÈCHE (*to Cléante in a whisper*): What's going on? Why is our Maître Simon talking to your father?

CLÉANTE (*to La Flèche in a whisper*): Do you think somebody's told him who I am? It wouldn't be you who gave me away, would it?

MAÎTRE SIMON: Hey you! You're in a hurry! Who told you we were meeting here? (*To Harpagon*) It wasn't me who gave them your name and address sir, though I don't think there's much harm done. They are very discreet and you can discuss things perfectly well here.

HARPAGON: What's this?

MAÎTRE SIMON: This is the gentleman who wants to borrow the fifteen thousand francs I mentioned to you.

HARPAGON: So it's you is it, you villain, who have sunk to these evil depths!

CLÉANTE: So it's you is it, father, who have sunk to this disgraceful traffic! (*Maître Simon and La Flèche go out.*)

HARPAGON: So you're the man who wishes to ruin himself with such disgraceful borrowing?

CLÉANTE: And you're the man who wants to get rich by such criminal usury?

HARPAGON: How can you dare to face me after this?

CLÉANTE: How will you ever dare to face anyone at all after this?

HARPAGON: Aren't you ashamed of stooping to such excesses, of rushing into such appalling expense, of squandering in this disgraceful manner the money your parents have sweated to scrape together for you?

CLÉANTE: Aren't you ashamed of disgracing your position by transactions of this kind, of sacrificing honour and reputation to your insatiable thirst for piling coin upon coin and outdoing anything the most notorious usurers ever dreamed up in the way of extortionate rates of interest?

HARPAGON: Out of my sight you blackguard! Get out of my sight!

CLÉANTE: Who is guiltier, in your opinion: the man who borrows because he needs the money, or the man who extorts money he does not need?

HARPAGON: Get out I tell you, you're making my blood boil! (*Cléante goes out.*) I'm not sorry this has happened. It's a warning to me to keep an even stricter eye on what he does in future.

Scene iii:
FROSINE, HARPAGON

FROSINE: Sir . . .

HARPAGON: Just a moment. I'll be back in a minute. I'll speak to you then. (*Aside, as he goes out*) It's high time I had another look at my money.

Scene iv:
LA FLÈCHE, FROSINE

LA FLÈCHE (*not seeing Frosine*): The whole thing is very odd. He must have a large junk store somewhere. Neither of us recognized any of the items listed in the schedule.

FROSINE: Why, it's poor old La Flèche. Fancy meeting you like this!

LA FLÈCHE: Oh it's you Frosine. What are you doing here?

FROSINE: Same as I do everywhere – acting as go-between, making myself useful to people and picking up what I can from such small talents as I may have. You know, in this life you have to learn to get by on your wits and those of us who have no other capital have to depend on our natural talent for plotting and scheming.

LA FLÈCHE: Have you got some business with the master?

FROSINE: Yes, I'm handling a little transaction for him and hoping I'll get something for my trouble.

LA FLÈCHE: From him? By heaven, you'll be the clever one if you get anything out of him. Money is hard to come by in this house, I warn you.

FROSINE: But there are certain services which are wonderfully effective in loosening purse-strings.

LA FLÈCHE: I dare say you're right, but you don't know our Mr Harpagon yet. Of all human beings, our Mr Harpagon is the least human human being of the lot. Of all mortal men he's the hardest, the tightest-fisted mortal man there is. There's no service you can do that would make him grateful enough to put his hand in his pocket. Praise, compliments, kindly cordial words, yes: plenty of those. But money? Forget it! You can gain his approval, be in his good books, but you'll get nothing out of that dry old stick. He hates the word 'giving' so much that he won't even give you a 'good-morning'.

FROSINE: Good Lord! As if I don't know how to twist men round my little finger! Why, I know all there is to know about rubbing them up the right way, arousing their sympathies and finding their soft spots.

LA FLÈCHE: None of that will work here. If there's money involved, I defy you to make any impression on our man. On that score he's such a brute – it's enough to drive you to despair. You could be at death's door and he wouldn't budge, not him. In other words, he puts money before reputation, honour and virtue, and the sight of anyone asking him for anything is enough to give him a fit. It's like wounding him in some vital spot, stabbing him through the heart, tearing out his entrails, and if ... He's coming back. I must be off.

Scene v:
HARPAGON, FROSINE

HARPAGON (*to himself*): Everything's just as it should be. (*To Frosine*) Well Frosine, what is it?

FROSINE: Goodness me, how well you're looking – the picture of health!

HARPAGON: Who do you mean? Me?

FROSINE: I've never seen you looking as hale and hearty.

HARPAGON: Really?

FROSINE: Why, you've never looked younger in your whole life than now. I know plenty of twenty-five year olds who look a lot older than you do.

HARPAGON: Still Frosine, I'm well over sixty.

FROSINE: Well, what's sixty? It's nothing. It's the prime of life, you're just approaching your peak.

HARPAGON: True, but I reckon being twenty years younger wouldn't do me any harm.

FROSINE: Don't make me laugh! You don't need to wish any such thing. You've got the sort of constitution that means you'll live to be a hundred.

HARPAGON: You think so?

FROSINE: Certain. You've got all the hallmarks. Keep still a second. Yes, there, the line between the eyes, that's a sign of longevity!

HARPAGON: You know about these things?

FROSINE: Of course. Show me your hand. My God! What a life-line!

HARPAGON: A what?

FROSINE: Can't you see how far that line there extends?

HARPAGON: So? What does it mean?

FROSINE: My word! Did I say a hundred? You'll live to be more than a hundred and twenty!

HARPAGON: No! Is it possible?

FROSINE: You'll have to be put down, I tell you. You'll bury your children and your children's children.

HARPAGON: Well, that's good to know! Now, how is our little business getting on?

FROSINE: Need you ask? Do I ever start anything I can't finish? I really have this amazing gift for arranging marriages. There aren't two people in the world I couldn't have marching up the aisle in next to no time. I do believe that if I put my mind to it I could marry off the Grand Turk to the Republic of Venice![7] Not that your little business has been anything like as difficult. As I know both ladies, I've been able to talk about you to them at length and I've told the mother about what you've got in mind for Mariane as a result of seeing her walking down the street and taking the air at her window.

HARPAGON: And she said?

FROSINE: She was delighted by the proposal. And when I explained that you'd like her daughter to be present tonight at the signing of your own daughter's marriage contract, she agreed at once and put her in my charge.

HARPAGON: The fact is Frosine, I'm committed to giving a dinner for Seigneur Anselme, and I'd be very pleased if she could join the party too.

FROSINE: Good idea. She's due to call on your daughter after lunch and then intends to go on to have a look at the fair.[8] She could come straight back from there for dinner.

HARPAGON: Capital! I'll lend them my carriage and they can go together.

FROSINE: That'll suit her very nicely.

HARPAGON: But tell me Frosine, did you have a word with the mother about what sort of dowry she can give her daughter? Did you explain that she's got to lend a hand, make every effort and scrape together whatever she can for an opportunity like this? After all, nobody's going to marry a girl unless she brings something with her.

FROSINE: Why, this one will bring you twelve thousand a year!

HARPAGON: Twelve thousand? A year?

FROSINE: Why yes. To begin with, she's been brought up on a very economical diet. Here's a girl used to living on salad and milk, apples and cheese, so she won't need expensive feeding, none of your fancy soups and everlasting barley concoctions[9] nor any of the delicacies other women would insist on having – and that's no small item. It could well run to three thousand francs a year at least. Moreover, she's not very demanding and her tastes are very simple – she doesn't hanker after the expensive dresses, costly jewellery and lavish furnishings that girls of her sort are usually so fond of. That item is worth more than four thousand a year. Furthermore, she has strong views on gambling, and that's very unusual in a woman nowadays: I know one in the street where I live who has lost twenty thousand francs this year at cards. Suppose we reckon only a quarter of that. Five thousand a year saved on cards and four thousand on clothes and jewellery, that makes nine thousand, plus the three thousand for food: I think that makes your twelve thousand francs a year, doesn't it?

HARPAGON: Yes, it's not bad, but all these calculations don't add up to anything solid.

FROSINE: That's where you're wrong. Do you mean to say that when a woman brings a husband a modest appetite, a legacy of simple tastes and a lump sum of loathing for the card-table, that it doesn't add up to anything solid?

HARPAGON: It's nonsense to try and make a dowry out of the expense she won't put me to. I'll not accept terms which mean I don't get anything. I must have something I can get my hands on.

FROSINE: Heavens, man! You'll get your hands on plenty! They told me they've got money somewhere abroad. That'll come to you.

HARPAGON: We'll have to look into that. But there's one other thing that worries me Frosine. The girl is young, as you know, and young people generally prefer those of their own age and don't go much for older company. I'm afraid she mightn't take to a man of my age, and that might lead to certain domestic complications which I wouldn't like at all.

FROSINE: You don't know her very well! That's something else I wanted to tell you. She positively hates boys and only cares for the maturer man.

HARPAGON: Is that so?

FROSINE: Absolutely. I only wish you could have heard her on the subject. She can't bear the sight of a young man. She declares that nothing gives her more pleasure than seeing an old man with a distinguished beard. The older they are, the better she likes them, so don't try to make yourself look younger than you are. She wants someone who's at least in his sixties. It's not four months since she was on the point of being married but broke it off because the man let on that he was only fifty-six and didn't need to wear glasses to sign the marriage contract.

HARPAGON: Was that the only reason?

FROSINE: Yes. She said that fifty-six wasn't old enough for her and that she prefers noses that have glasses on them.

HARPAGON: Well, this is all news to me.

FROSINE: You wouldn't believe how far she takes it. She's got pictures and engravings hanging in her room, and of what, do you think? Adonis? Cephalus? Paris? Apollo? No! Pictures of Saturn, King Priam, the aged Nestor and old Anchises[10] being carried on the shoulders of his son!

HARPAGON: But that's splendid! I'd never have thought it and I'm delighted to know she is that way inclined. To tell the truth, if I'd been born a woman, I'd never have fancied young men.

FROSINE: I can well believe it. What poor stuff young men are for anyone to fall in love with. Who'd want anything to do with those youths with runny noses and fops with pretty faces? I'd like to know what anybody sees in them.

HARPAGON: I don't understand it myself and can't think for the life of me why women are so attracted to them.

FROSINE: They must be completely mad. How could anyone find young men attractive. It doesn't make any sense. Those young bucks aren't men! How can anyone take a fancy to such creatures?

HARPAGON: That's what I'm always saying. Them and their flutey voices, the two or three little wisps of beard turned up at the ends like a cat's whiskers, the albino wigs, great baggy breeches and waistcoats left unbuttoned!

FROSINE: Yes, and they make a poor show compared with a man such as yourself. Now you're more my idea of a proper man, something worth looking at. You've got exactly the sort of figure women fall in love with, and you dress the part too.

HARPAGON: You think I'm attractive?

FROSINE: I'll say! You're irresistible. Your face is a picture. Give us a little twirl would you? What could be handsomer? Let me see you walk. There's a fine figure of a man, as lithe and graceful as could be. Not a thing wrong with you!

HARPAGON: Nothing serious anyway, thank God! There's just my catarrh that plays up now and again.

FROSINE: That's nothing. Catarrh suits you. You have a very stylish cough.

HARPAGON: Tell me, has Mariane ever set eyes on me? Has she noticed me as I walked down her street?

FROSINE: No, but we've talked about you a lot. I described what you looked like and I didn't fail to sing your praises and tell her how lucky she'd be to have a husband like you.

HARPAGON: You've done well Frosine. I thank you.

FROSINE: But, sir, there is one small thing I'd like to ask of you. (*Harpagon looks stern.*) I'm involved in a lawsuit and about to lose it because I'm short of a little money. You could easily make sure I won my case if you could only see your way to helping me out. You've no idea how pleased she'll be to meet you face to face. (*Harpagon brightens again.*) Oh, she'll be delighted! She'll adore that old-fashioned ruff of yours! And she won't be able to get over your way of wearing your breeches fastened to your doublet with hooks and eyes. She'll be mad about you. A lover who wears hooks and eyes will be a wonderful novelty for her.

HARPAGON: Really, I'm delighted to hear it.

FROSINE: To be honest sir, this lawsuit is a very serious matter for me . . . (*Harpagon looks stern again.*) If I lose I'm ruined, but just a little help would save the situation. I only wish you could have been there to see her listening to me in raptures when I was talking about you. (*Harpagon brightens again.*) As I ran through your many qualities her eyes filled with pleasure, and in the end I made her terribly impatient for the marriage to be all settled.

HARPAGON: You've done me a very good turn Frosine, and I confess I am very much in your debt.

FROSINE: Please sir, will you help me out as I asked? (*Harpagon looks stern again.*) It would put me on my feet again and I'd be eternally grateful to you.

HARPAGON: Goodbye. I've some correspondence to see to.

FROSINE: I do assure you sir, I'm in the most urgent need of your help.

HARPAGON: I'll go and give instructions for my carriage to be got ready to take you all to the fair.

FROSINE: I wouldn't insist if I wasn't absolutely forced to.

HARPAGON: And I'll see that dinner is ready early so that none of you gets an upset stomach.

FROSINE: Please don't refuse the favour I'm asking. You have no idea sir, how grateful . . .

HARPAGON: I'm off. There's somebody calling me. I'll see you later. (*He goes out.*)

FROSINE: May you rot, you tight-fisted hound! Devil take the skinflint! He withstood all my best efforts. But I won't give up on him. Still, whatever happens, there's always the other party and I'm pretty sure I can wangle something lavish out of them.

Act III

Scene i:

HARPAGON, CLÉANTE, ÉLISE, VALÈRE, DAME
CLAUDE, MAÎTRE JACQUES, BRINDAVOINE,
LA MERLUCHE

HARPAGON: Come along. Let's have you all in here. I want to give you your instructions and make sure each of you knows what to do. Over here Dame Claude, we'll start with you. (*She carries a broom.*) Good, I see you're ready for the fray. Your job is to clean everywhere, but take care not to polish the furniture too hard in case you wear it out. In addition, I am putting you in charge of the bottles during dinner. If a single one goes astray or if anything gets broken, I'll hold you responsible and take it out of your wages.

MAÎTRE JACQUES (*aside*): Now that's a cunning tactic!

HARPAGON: Off you go. (*She goes.*) You Brindavoine, and you La Merluche, I'm giving you the job of washing the glasses and serving the wine – but mind, only when people are thirsty. Don't do what some impudent footmen do and encourage the guests to drink, putting the idea into their heads when they would never have thought of it for themselves. Wait to be asked more than once and remember to put plenty of water with it.

MAÎTRE JACQUES: That's right. Wine without water goes to your head.

LA MERLUCHE: Have we to take our aprons off sir?

HARPAGON: Yes, when you see the guests arriving. And be careful not to get your clothes dirty.

BRINDAVOINE: You know sir as how me doublet's got a great streak of lamp-oil all down one side.

LA MERLUCHE: And me sir, my breeches is that torn in the behind that, saving your presence, they'll see my –

HARPAGON: That's enough! Stand so you keep your back to the wall and face the company at all times. And you, when you're serving, hold your hat in front of you all the time, like this. (*Harpagon holds his hat in front of his own doublet to show Brindavoine how to hide the oil-stain.*) As for you my girl (*to Élise*), you're to keep an eye on what's cleared away and see to it that nothing gets wasted. That's a proper job for a daughter. But meantime, get ready to receive my intended. She's coming to call on you and take you to the fair. Do you hear what I'm saying?

ÉLISE: Yes father.

HARPAGON: And you my lad, my pretty dandy, I'm willing to forgive you for what happened just now, but don't you go pulling a sour face when she comes.

CLÉANTE: Me, pull a sour face? Whatever for?

HARPAGON: Come now, we all know what a carry-on there is with children when their fathers marry again and what their usual reaction is to what's called a stepmother. But if you want me to forget that last little escapade of yours, I'd advise you to put on a cheerful face for the young lady and give her as warm a welcome as you can manage.

CLÉANTE: To be honest father, I can't promise that I'm altogether glad that she's to be my stepmother. I'd be lying if I said so. But I can promise to obey you to the letter in putting on a cheerful face and a warm welcome.

HARPAGON: Well, mind that you do.

CLÉANTE: You'll see, you'll have no cause to complain on that score.

HARPAGON: I should think so. (*Cléante goes out.*) Valère, I want your help with this. Now then Maître Jacques, come here. I've left you until the last.

MAÎTRE JACQUES: Is it your coachman or your cook you want to have a word with sir? I'm both.

HARPAGON: Both.

MAÎTRE JACQUES: But which do you want first?

HARPAGON: The cook.

MAÎTRE JACQUES: Just a minute, if you don't mind. (*He removes his coachman's greatcoat and under it he is dressed as a cook.*)

HARPAGON: What the devil's the meaning of this tomfoolery?

MAÎTRE JACQUES: You can carry on now.

HARPAGON: Maître Jacques, I've invited some people to dinner tonight.

MAÎTRE JACQUES: Wonders will never cease!

HARPAGON: Tell me, can you lay on something good?

MAÎTRE JACQUES: Yes, if you give me lots of money.

HARPAGON: Devil take it! It's always money! That's all they ever seem to talk about – money, money, money! It's the only word they know

– money! They're forever going on about money! They can't put one foot in front of the other without money!

VALÈRE: I never heard a more impudent answer in my life. As if there's anything very clever about laying on a good spread if you've got lots of money! It's the easiest thing in the world. Any fool could do it. Now a man who's really good at the job would be talking about putting on something good without spending much money.

MAÎTRE JACQUES: Put on something good without spending much money?

VALÈRE: That's right.

MAÎTRE JACQUES: By Jove, you are steward here, so do us all a favour and let us in on the secret. And while you're on, you might as well take over my job as cook since it looks as if you want to be in charge of everything.

HARPAGON: That's enough! Just tell us what we'll need.

MAÎTRE JACQUES: Ask the steward there. He's the one who can put on something good without spending money.

HARPAGON: Look here, I want an answer from you.

MAÎTRE JACQUES: How many will you be for dinner?

HARPAGON: There'll be eight or ten of us, but best reckon on eight. If you cater for eight, there'll be enough for ten.

VALÈRE: Obviously.

MAÎTRE JACQUES: In that case, we'll need four sorts of soup and five main courses.[11] So soups: bisque, partridge with green cabbage, a light broth and duck and turnip. For your entrées: chicken fricassee, pigeon pie, sweetbreads, white pudding and mushroom.

HARPAGON: Good God, that's enough to feed a whole town!

MAÎTRE JACQUES: For the roast we'll use the biggest pan we've got and serve in a pyramid: a large loin of best veal, three pheasants, three broiled hens, a dozen pigeons fresh from the coop, a dozen corn-fed chickens, six wild rabbits, a dozen partridge, two dozen quail, three dozen ortolans –

HARPAGON (*putting his hand over Maître Jacques's mouth*): Stop! Ah, you blackguard! You'll eat me out of house and home!

MAÎTRE JACQUES: Then to follow . . .

HARPAGON: Aren't you done yet?

VALÈRE: Do you want everyone to burst? Surely you don't think the master has invited people here to murder them by cramming food

down their throats? Why don't you go and read up on the rules for
healthy living! Ask the doctor if there's anything that does people
more harm than over-eating.

HARPAGON: He's right.

VALÈRE: Listen Maître Jacques, you and your ilk should realize that an
overloaded table is a death-trap. Anyone who really cares about his
guests should ensure that the dinner he sets before them is notable
for its frugality. As the ancient philosopher has it, 'You should eat
to live, not live to eat!'

HARPAGON: Oh, well said! Come, let me embrace you for that. It's the
finest thing I ever heard in my life. 'You should live to eat, not eat
to . . .' No, that's not it. How does it go again?

VALÈRE: 'You should eat to live, not live to eat'.

HARPAGON: That's it! (*To Maître Jacques*) Did you hear? (*To Valère*)
Who was the great man who said that?

VALÈRE: I don't recall his name for the moment.

HARPAGON: Be sure to remember to write it down for me. I'll have it
engraved in gold letters over the chimney-piece in the dining-room.

VALÈRE: I won't forget. As for dinner, why don't you just leave it all
to me? I'll see that everything is as it should be.

HARPAGON: Yes, do.

MAÎTRE JACQUES: No skin off my nose. It'll be one job less for me.

HARPAGON: There must be things people can't eat much of, things that
fill them up quickly, like a good thick mutton stew with dumplings
and lots of chestnuts. Have plenty of that.

VALÈRE: You can rely on me.

HARPAGON: And now Maître Jacques, I'll need the carriage cleaned.

MAÎTRE JACQUES: Half a mo'. This is a job for the coachman. (*He puts
his greatcoat back on.*) You were saying?

HARPAGON: I'll need you to clean the carriage and harness the horses
ready to go to the fair.

MAÎTRE JACQUES: What horses? Yours aren't in a fit state to go anywhere.
I can't say the poor beasts can't get up off their straw, 'cos they don't
have any, and it would be wrong to say they did. You keep them
on such a strict diet they look unreal – ghostly, like phantom horses.

HARPAGON: They seem in a bad way. But they never do anything.

MAÎTRE JACQUES: Just because they don't do anything don't mean they
should get nothing to eat. The poor dumb animals would be better

off working hard and eating likewise. It fair breaks my heart to see them so thin, for the fact is I'm so fond of my horses that I suffer myself when I see them suffering. Not a day passes but I go short myself to feed them. A man must be very hard-hearted sir if he don't feel some pity for his fellow creatures.

HARPAGON: It's no great effort to go as far as the fair.

MAÎTRE JACQUES: No sir. I haven't the heart to drive them. It would go against my conscience to lay a whip on them the state they're in. How do you expect them to pull a coach when they can hardly drag themselves along?

VALÈRE: Sir, I'll get Le Picard next door to drive them. We'll also need him to lend a hand to get the dinner ready.

MAÎTRE JACQUES: Right. I'd far rather they died in someone else's charge and not mine.

VALÈRE: You're a great one for arguing, Maître Jacques.

MAÎTRE JACQUES: And you, Mr Steward, are a great one for trying to make yourself indispensable.

HARPAGON: Be quiet!

MAÎTRE JACQUES: I can't abide flatterers sir, and I can see what he's up to with his everlasting checking up on the bread and the wine and the firewood and the salt and the candles. Nothing but back-scratching, that's what it is, all done to get into your good books. I get mad about the way he carries on. And on top of that I have to put up with hearing what people say about you all the time, because when all is said and done, I still have a soft spot for you sir. Next to my horses I think more of you than anybody else.

HARPAGON: Would you mind telling me Maître Jacques, what people say about me?

MAÎTRE JACQUES: Yes, sir – if I was sure it wouldn't make you angry.

HARPAGON: It won't.

MAÎTRE JACQUES: Excuse me, but I know sure as eggs that I'll make you see red.

HARPAGON: No you won't. On the contrary, you'd be doing me a good turn. I'd be happy to know what it is say about me.

MAÎTRE JACQUES: Since you will have it sir, I'll tell you straight – you're a laughing stock everywhere. We get bombarded on all sides with jokes about you. There's nothing makes people happier than laying into you and telling stories about how mean you are. According to one tale, you have special calendars printed with twice the number of fast days and vigils on them so you can save money by making everybody in your house abstain more often. Another says you'll always have a quarrel ready to pick with your servants on quarter-days or when they're leaving your service, just so you can have an excuse for not giving them anything. According to one chap, you once had the law on a neighbour's cat for eating up the leftovers from a leg of mutton. Another reckons you were caught one night stealing oats from your own horses and says that your coachman, the one before me, gave you a damn good hiding in the dark that you never said anything about. What more can I say? We can't poke our nose out of doors without hearing you being put through the mincer. You're a figure of fun, a bye-word for everybody and no one refers to you by your name: they all call you a miser, a cheap skate, a skinflint, a tight-fisted old shark.

HARPAGON (*hitting him*): And you are a fool, a lout, a scoundrel, an insolent ruffian!

MAÎTRE JACQUES: I was right! I knew this would happen but you wouldn't believe me. I said you'd see red if I told you the truth.

HARPAGON (*going*): That'll teach you to mind your lip!

Scene ii:
MAÎTRE JACQUES, VALÈRE

VALÈRE: From what I see of it Maître Jacques, your frankness is not appreciated.

MAÎTRE JACQUES: Listen, you're mighty self-important but you've only been steward here two minutes, so this is none of your business. Keep the jokes for when it's your turn to get a good hiding and don't start laughing when it's mine.

VALÈRE: Please, my dear Maître Jacques, don't be angry . . .

MAÎTRE JACQUES (*aside*): He's backing down. I'll come on tough and if he's fool enough to be frightened, I'll give him what for. (*To Valère*) Listen, you may laugh, but I'm not laughing! And if you make me lose my temper I'll make you laugh on the other side of your face! (*He drives Valère across stage, threatening him.*)

VALÈRE: Take it easy!

MAÎTRE JACQUES: What do you mean, take it easy? Suppose I don't want to take it easy?

VALÈRE: Please!

MAÎTRE JACQUES: You've got a nerve!

VALÈRE: My dear Maître Jacques!

MAÎTRE JACQUES: Don't you dear Maître Jacques me! I don't care tuppence for it! If I took a stick to you, I'd tan your hide!

VALÈRE (*driving him back in turn*): A stick? What stick?

MAÎTRE JACQUES: Er, I didn't mean . . .

VALÈRE: Just understand, you numskull, that if anybody's hide is going to be tanned, then I'm the one who'll be doing the tanning!

MAÎTRE JACQUES: I don't doubt it.

VALÈRE: That the fact is you're only a good-for-nothing cook!

MAÎTRE JACQUES: I know, I know!

VALÈRE: That you don't know me yet.

MAÎTRE JACQUES: I'm sorry.

VALÈRE: You'll tan my hide, you say?

MAÎTRE JACQUES: I just said it as a joke.

VALÈRE: Well, I don't care for your jokes. (*He beats him.*) Let this be a lesson to you. You tell very poor jokes. (*He goes out.*)

MAÎTRE JACQUES: Damn sincerity! It's a poor line of business to be in. From now on I've done with it. No more telling the truth. I can take it from the master, he's entitled to thrash me. But as for this high and mighty steward, I'll get my own back on him if I can.

Scene iii:
FROSINE, MARIANE, MAÎTRE JACQUES

FROSINE: Maître Jacques, do you know if your master is at home?

MAÎTRE JACQUES: Oh yes, he's in all right. Don't I know it!

FROSINE: Then would you please tell him we're here? (*Maître Jacques goes out.*)

Scene iv:

MARIANE, FROSINE

MARIANE: Oh Frosine, this is a peculiar position to be in. If you want to know how I feel, I'm dreading this meeting.

FROSINE: Why? What have you got to worry about?

MARIANE: Oh, how can you ask? Can't you imagine what a girl feels when she is about to be confronted with the horrible fate that's been chosen for her?

FROSINE: Harpagon isn't the fate you'd choose if you wanted a pleasant death, I grant you, and I can guess from the look on your face that your mind's still taken up with that young man you were telling me about.

MARIANE: True Frosine, and I have no intention of denying it. He was so respectful when he came to visit us at home and I admit he made quite an impression on me.

FROSINE: Have you found out who he is?

MARIANE: No, I have no idea. But this I do know: he's handsome enough to fall in love with and, if I were free to choose, I'd rather have him than anybody else. Indeed, he has a lot to do with making me feel horror and loathing for this husband they've picked for me.

FROSINE: Heavens above, all these young men are handsome enough and they have a good line in chat, but most of them are poor as church-mice. You'd be far better off marrying an old man with lots of money. I grant you sentiment doesn't come out of it too well if you go down the road I mean, and there may be some distasteful moments to put up with from the kind of husband I'm talking about. But then it won't last for ever and after he's dead you'll be left in a position to choose someone you like better, who'll make up for everything.

MARIANE: But good heavens Frosine, it doesn't seem right that a person's happiness should involve hoping or waiting for someone to die. Anyway, death doesn't always fit in with our plans.

FROSINE: Don't be silly! You'll be marrying him only on the strict understanding that he leaves you a widow before long. We'll have to write it into the marriage contract. It would be most inconsiderate of him not to die within three months! But here comes the man himself.

MARIANE: Oh Frosine! What a face!

Scene v:

HARPAGON, MARIANE, FROSINE

HARPAGON: Don't be offended, my dear, if I come to meet you with my glasses on my nose. I know your beauty catches the eye at once and, being more than visible, does not need glasses to be seen. But it is through glass that we look at the stars and I declare, nay I affirm, that you are a star, a shining star, the loveliest star there is in the whole company of stars! Frosine, she's not saying anything and I don't get the feeling that she's very pleased to see me.

FROSINE: She's a little overcome. Young girls are always shy at first of showing their feelings.

HARPAGON: No doubt that's it. (*To Mariane*) Now my pretty, here's my daughter. She's come to welcome you.

Scene vi:

ÉLISE, HARPAGON, MARIANE, FROSINE

MARIANE: I'm afraid I'm rather late in paying my respects.

ÉLISE: On the contrary, you have done what I should have. I ought to have been here to greet you.

HARPAGON: See what a big girl she is! But there, you can't stop weeds growing!

MARIANE (*aside to Frosine*): What a horrible man!

HARPAGON: What did my pretty one say?

FROSINE: She said she thinks you're wonderful.

HARPAGON: That's too kind of you, you sweet little thing!

MARIANE (*aside*): What a beast!

HARPAGON: Very gratifying sentiments, indeed!

MARIANE (*aside*): I can't stand any more of this!

HARPAGON (*as Cléante enters*): And this is my son. He's come to pay his respects too.

MARIANE (*aside to Frosine*): Oh Frosine! Fancy meeting him here! It's the one I was telling you about.

FROSINE (*to Mariane*): What an extraordinary coincidence.

HARPAGON: I can see you are surprised to see I have grown-up children. But I'll be shot of both of them before long.

Scene vii:
CLÉANTE, HARPAGON, ÉLISE, MARIANE, FROSINE

CLÉANTE (*to Mariane*): To be perfectly frank, meeting you is the last thing I was expecting, for I was completely taken aback when my father told me earlier of his intentions.

MARIANE (*to Cléante*): I could say the same. Our meeting is as much a surprise to me as it is to you, and I wasn't prepared for such an eventuality.

CLÉANTE: Truly Madame, my father could not have made a better choice and it is a real pleasure to meet you. All the same, I cannot bring myself to say that I am overjoyed at the prospect that you might be thinking of becoming my stepmother. I must admit that it is a compliment I find hard to appreciate and, if I may say so, it is the last title I would wish you to have. What I'm saying might seem rude to some people, but I'm sure that you will know in what sense to take it. This, Madame, is a marriage for which as you might easily imagine I have no liking at all. You must be aware, knowing my situation, how much it harms my interests. In short, I hope you will allow me to say, with my father's kind permission, that if I had my way this marriage would not take place.

HARPAGON: That's a fine way to pay your respects! What a tale to tell the lady!

MARIANE: My answer is that I feel the way you do. If you are not keen to see me as your stepmother, I am no less loath to see you as my stepson. Please don't think that it is by any wish of mine that you are placed in this awkward position. I would be very sorry to upset you in any way, and, unless I am forced into it by circumstance beyond my control, I give you my word that I will never consent to a marriage which would cause you distress.

HARPAGON: She's quite right. Answer a fool according to his folly. I must apologize my dear for my son's rudeness. He's a young puppy who's not old enough to understand what he's saying.

MARIANE: I can assure you that I am not the least offended by what he said. On the contrary, it has been a pleasure to hear your son express his feelings so frankly. I value the admission coming, as it does, from him. If he'd spoken in any other way, I should have less respect for him.

HARPAGON: It's very good of you to overlook his faults. He'll get more sense as he grows older and you'll find his feelings will change.

CLÉANTE: Never father, it's not in me to change. I ask the lady to believe it.

HARPAGON: Did you ever hear such preposterous nonsense! He gets worse and worse!

CLÉANTE: Do you want me to be untrue to what's in my heart?

HARPAGON: Not done yet? Why don't you try changing your tune?

CLÉANTE: Very well, since you want me to speak in a different vein – permit me, Madame, to put myself in my father's place and let me assure you that you are the most charming person I ever saw, that the greatest happiness I can imagine would be to be loved by you, that I would rather be your husband than the greatest king on earth. Yes Madame, to be loved by you would be for me the height of felicity and that is indeed my only ambition. There is nothing I would not do to win a heart as precious as yours, and whatever obstacles may –

HARPAGON: Steady on lad, if you don't mind.

CLÉANTE: I'm addressing the lady on your behalf.

HARPAGON: Good Lord, I've a tongue of my own. I don't need someone like you to put my case for me. Here, bring some chairs.

FROSINE: No, I think it would be better if we set out for the fair now so that we can be back early and have plenty of time to talk to you then.

HARPAGON: Best have the horses harnessed to the coach then. Please forgive me my dear for not having thought of offering some refreshment before you went.

CLÉANTE: I've seen to it father. I told them to bring a couple of baskets of Chinese oranges, ripe lemons and sweetmeats. I told them to charge it all to you.

HARPAGON (*in a whisper*): Valère!

VALÈRE (*to Harpagon*): He's gone mad!

CLÉANTE: Don't you think there's enough father? Perhaps the lady will kindly excuse any shortcomings?

MARIANE: There was really no need to go to such trouble.

CLÉANTE: Madame, did you ever see a finer diamond than the one my father has on his finger?

MARIANE: It certainly sparkles!

CLÉANTE (*removing it from his father's finger and giving it to Mariane*): You need to see it close up.

MARIANE: Really, it's very lovely, so full of fire.

CLÉANTE (*standing in front of Mariane who tries to give it back*): No, no Madame! It's in such lovely hands. It's a present from my father.

HARPAGON: A what?

CLÉANTE: You do intend that Madame should keep it, don't you father, for your sake?

HARPAGON (*whispers to Cléante*): What are you playing at?

CLÉANTE (*aside*): He might well ask! (*To Mariane*) He means that I am to make you accept it.

MARIANE: But I have no wish –

CLÉANTE: You mustn't say that! He wouldn't dream of taking it back.

HARPAGON (*aside*): This is intolerable!

MARIANE: It would be –

CLÉANTE (*still preventing Mariane from returning the ring*): No, I assure you, you would offend him.

MARIANE: Please –

CLÉANTE: Oh no.

HARPAGON (*aside*): Damnation!

CLÉANTE: You see how shocked he is by your refusal.

HARPAGON (*whispers to Cléante*): Back-stabber!

CLÉANTE: See? He's running out of patience.

HARPAGON (*in a threatening whisper to Cléante*): Cut-throat!

CLÉANTE: It's not my fault father. I'm doing everything I can to get her to keep it but she is very obstinate.

HARPAGON (*whispering to Cléante, almost losing his temper*): You villain!

CLÉANTE: My father's getting angry with me Madame, and it's your fault.

HARPAGON (*whispering to Cléante, as before*): You blackguard!

CLÉANTE: You'll make him ill. Please Madame, don't keep saying no.

FROSINE: Good gracious, what a fuss! Keep the ring, since that's what the gentleman wants.

MARIANE: Rather than make you lose your temper, I shall keep it for now, but I will find another time when I can return it to you.

Scene viii:

BRINDAVOINE, CLÉANTE, HARPAGON, ÉLISE, MARIANE, FROSINE

BRINDAVOINE: Sir, there's a man here wants to have a word with you.

HARPAGON: Tell him I'm busy. Tell him to come back another time.

BRINDAVOINE: He says he has some money for you.

HARPAGON: Excuse me. I won't be long.

Scene ix:

LA MERLUCHE, CLÉANTE, HARPAGON, ÉLISE, MARIANE, FROSINE

LA MERLUCHE (*enters running and knocks Harpagon over*): Sir!

HARPAGON: Ah! I'm done for!

CLÉANTE: What is it father. Are you hurt?

HARPAGON: The swine's obviously been paid by people who owe me money to make me break my neck.

VALÈRE: It's nothing serious.

LA MERLUCHE: I'm sorry sir but I thought I was doing right to come running.

HARPAGON: What did you come for, you ruffian?

LA MERLUCHE: To tell you that both your horses have cast their shoes.

HARPAGON: Have them taken to the smith this minute.

CLÉANTE: And while we're waiting for them to be shod father I shall do the honours of your house for you, and show Madame the garden. I'll have the refreshments sent out there.

HARPAGON: Valère, go and keep an eye on what's being served and

please save as much of it as you can so that it can go back to the
caterers.

VALÈRE: Say no more.

HARPAGON (*alone*): I've a scoundrel for a son! He wants to ruin me!

Act IV

Scene i:
CLÉANTE, MARIANE, ÉLISE, FROSINE, *returning*
from the garden

CLÉANTE: Let's go in this way, we'll be better off indoors. There's
nobody about to spy on us, so we can speak freely.

ÉLISE (*to Mariane*): My brother has told me how he feels about
you. I know how difficult and distressing times like these can be
and I assure you that I take the warmest interest in your predicament.

MARIANE: It's a great comfort to have someone like you on my side.
Oh, I do hope you'll always have the same generous feelings for me.
It is such a consolation in times of trouble.

FROSINE: Honestly, you're a fine pair, the both of you, not to have
thought of letting me into your little secrets before this! I could have
saved you all this worry. I'd never have let matters go the way they
have.

CLÉANTE: What's the use? It's my bad luck: it had to happen. What
decision have you come to, dear Mariane?

MARIANE: Alas! How can I come to any decisions? Dependent as I am
on other people, what more can I do but hope for the best?

CLÉANTE: Is hoping for the best all the encouragement I can expect to
receive from your heart? No tender support? No helping hand? No
active affection?

MARIANE: What can I say? Put yourself in my place and tell me what
I should do! Advise me! Command me! I'll go along with whatever
you say. I know you are much too fair-minded to ask me to do
anything that would not be right and proper.

CLÉANTE: But what room for manoeuvre have I got left if you want me to stay inside the strict limits of that which is scrupulously right and proper?

MARIANE: So what do you expect me to do? Even if I could disregard all the many conventions women are supposed to follow, I still have my mother to consider. She brought me up with love and affection and I could never bring myself to do anything that would hurt her. Go and see her, persuade her, do everything you can to get her approval. You can say and do whatever you like: you have my permission. And if it comes to the point where all I have to do is decide in your favour, then I'll be only too willing to tell her exactly how I feel about you.

CLÉANTE: Frosine, dear Frosine, won't you help us?

FROSINE: Heavens! There's no need to ask – I'd love to, there's nothing I'd like better! You know deep-down I'm really a very decent sort. I wasn't born with a heart of stone and I'm always ready to lend a helping hand when I see people who are truly in love. The question is, what can we do?

CLÉANTE: Please, try and come up with something.

MARIANE: Tell us what you think.

ÉLISE: Find some way of undoing what you've done.

FROSINE: It's not so easy. (*To Mariane*) As far as your mother's concerned, she's not altogether unreasonable and we might get round her and persuade her to transfer to the son what she intended for the father. (*To Cléante*) The real difficulty, as I see it, is that your father's your father.

CLÉANTE: Exactly!

FROSINE: By that I mean that he'll turn all resentful if I let him know to his face that he's going to be refused. He'll then be in no mood to consent to your marriage. What we really need is to arrange things so that he turns *you* down, and for that to happen we need to find a way of making him take a dislike to you Mariane.

CLÉANTE: You're right!

FROSINE: Of course I'm right, I don't need to be told. So that's what we've got to do. The problem is: how the devil are we to manage it? Wait a minute! If we could come up with some woman, getting on a bit, who had a touch of my talent and could play the part of a lady of quality, with the help of a set of improvised retainers and some fancy title or other – a marchioness or viscountess from Lower Brittany shall we say – I think I could manage to persuade your father that she was a wealthy woman with a hundred thousand crowns in ready money and landed property as well, and that she was head-over-heels in love with him – so keen to marry him in fact that she'd be willing to hand over everything she possessed and sign a marriage contract to that effect. I'm absolutely certain he'd agree to the proposition because (*to Mariane*) although I know he loves you very much, he loves money more. Once he's swallowed the bait and agreed to everything you want, it wouldn't matter if he found out the truth when he came to look into our marchioness's fortune more closely!

CLÉANTE: That's very ingenious!

FROSINE: Leave it all to me. I've just thought of a friend of mine who'll fit the bill.

CLÉANTE: Frosine, if you carry this off you can count on my gratitude. In the meantime, dear Mariane, let's make a start by trying to convince your mother. It would be a good step on the way if we could break off your marriage. Please do absolutely everything you can in that direction. Make the most of the tenderness she feels for you. Use all the powers of persuasion, the grace and charm that Heaven has placed in your eyes and upon your lips. Use every last one of your tender words, gentle persuasions and soft entreaties and they will, I'm certain, prove irresistible.

MARIANE: I'll do everything I can. I won't forget anything you've told me.

Scene ii:

HARPAGON, CLÉANTE, MARIANE, ÉLISE, FROSINE

HARPAGON (*aside, as he enters*): What's this? My son kissing the hand of his stepmother-to-be! And the stepmother-to-be is not putting up much resistance? Is there something fishy going on here?

ÉLISE: Here comes father.

HARPAGON: The coach is all ready. You can set off whenever you like.

CLÉANTE: Since you're not going yourself father, I'll go with them.

HARPAGON: No, you stay. They can manage very well by themselves, and I need you here.

Scene iii:
HARPAGON, CLÉANTE

HARPAGON: Tell me, leaving aside this stepmother nonsense, what do you make of her?

CLÉANTE: What do I make of her?

HARPAGON: Yes, her looks, her manner, her figure, her intelligence.

CLÉANTE: Oh – so-so.

HARPAGON: Is that all you can say?

CLÉANTE: To be perfectly frank with you, she doesn't live up to what I was expecting. She has a flighty way with her. Her figure isn't particularly good, her looks are fair to average and she isn't very bright. Don't think I'm trying to put you off father. As stepmothers go, I'd as well have her as another.

HARPAGON: But before, you were telling her –

CLÉANTE: Just a few flattering remarks on your behalf. I only did it to please you.

HARPAGON: So you wouldn't fancy her for yourself then?

CLÉANTE: Me? Not at all.

HARPAGON: Pity. It puts paid to an idea that was running through my mind. Seeing her here just now, I began to reflect about my age and wondered what people would say if I married a girl so young. Thinking along those lines, I was on the point of giving up the idea, but since I'd already asked for her hand and given her my word I would have let you have her, only now you say you've taken a dislike to her.

CLÉANTE: Let me have her?

HARPAGON: Yes, you.

CLÉANTE: In marriage?

HARPAGON: In marriage.

CLÉANTE: Listen. It's true that she doesn't suit my taste exactly, but if it makes you happy father, I'm prepared to marry her if you really want me to.

HARPAGON: Oh no, I'm not so unreasonable as you think. I have no wish to push you into marriage against your wishes.

CLÉANTE: Excuse me, but I'm willing to make an effort for your sake.

HARPAGON: No no. There's no happiness in marriage without love.

CLÉANTE: Well, perhaps that will come in time. People say that love often comes after marriage.

HARPAGON: No, as far as the marrying man is concerned I'm against taking chances. I don't want to run any risk that things might turn out badly. Now if you'd only felt something for her, that would have been fine, and I'd have arranged for you to marry her instead of me. But seeing you don't, I'll stick to my original plan and marry her myself.

CLÉANTE: Listen father, since that's how things stand, I must tell you how I really feel and let you into our secret. The truth is that I've loved her from the first day I saw her out walking. I was intending just now to ask your permission to marry her. It was only when you revealed your own feelings, and the fear of offending you, that prevented me from doing so.

HARPAGON: Have you visited her at home?

CLÉANTE: Yes father.

HARPAGON: Often?

CLÉANTE: Fairly often, given that we've not known each other very long.

HARPAGON: Were you made welcome?

CLÉANTE: Very, though they had no idea who I was, which explains why Mariane was so surprised when we met just now.

HARPAGON: Did you tell her you loved her and were intending to marry her?

CLÉANTE: Yes, and I even raised the issue with her mother.

HARPAGON: And did she entertain your proposal on her daughter's behalf?

CLÉANTE: Yes, she was very civil.

HARPAGON: And did the daughter return your affection?

CLÉANTE: In so far as I can judge by appearances, I do believe father that she does not dislike me.

HARPAGON (*aside*): I'm glad I've got to the bottom of all this. That's what I wanted to know. (*To Cléante*) Right my lad, you want to know how things stand? I'll tell you. You had better forget about

being in love, if you don't mind. And you can stop pestering the
lady whom I have every intention of marrying myself, and start
thinking about marrying the bride I picked for you – and sharp about
it.

CLÉANTE: So that was your game father! Very well, since that's what
things have come to, I'll say this: I shall never stop loving Mariane
and I'll do anything to prevent you from having her. You may have
her mother's consent, but I might just be able to count on help from
other quarters to fight on my side.

HARPAGON: What, you puppy! You have the audacity to trespass on
my territory!

CLÉANTE: It's you who are trespassing on mine. I was there first.

HARPAGON: I'm your father, aren't I? Shouldn't you be showing more
respect?

CLÉANTE: This isn't a matter where a son must respect his father's
wishes. Love is no respecter of persons.

HARPAGON: I'll give you a good hiding! I'll teach you to respect me!

CLÉANTE: Your threats will get you nowhere.

HARPAGON: You will give up Mariane!

CLÉANTE: Never!

HARPAGON: Bring me a stick – now!

Scene iv:
MAÎTRE JACQUES, HARPAGON, CLÉANTE

MAÎTRE JACQUES: Now now gentlemen, what's all this? What on earth
are you playing at?

CLÉANTE: I'm past caring!

MAÎTRE JACQUES (*to Cléante*): Steady on sir!

HARPAGON: Talking to me like that! The impudence!

MAÎTRE JACQUES (*to Harpagon*): Come sir, please!

CLÉANTE: I won't give him an inch.

MAÎTRE JACQUES (*to Cléante*): Who? Your father?

HARPAGON: Let me get my hands on him!

MAÎTRE JACQUES (*to Harpagon*): Who? Your son? I hope you don't
mean me!

HARPAGON: I want you to be the judge of this Maître Jacques, and prove that I'm right.

MAÎTRE JACQUES: Agreed. (*To Cléante*) Go and stand a bit further along.

HARPAGON: I'm in love and fully intend to marry the girl. And this scoundrel has had the nerve to fall in love with her too and now wants to marry her, although I've told him he can't.

MAÎTRE JACQUES: Oh! That's wrong of him.

HARPAGON: Don't you think it's appalling for a son to try and compete with his father? Isn't he duty bound not to want to interfere with my wishes?

MAÎTRE JACQUES: You're right. Let me have a word with him. You stay here. (*He crosses the stage to Cléante.*)

CLÉANTE: Well now, since he insists on letting you be the judge, I shan't raise any objection. I don't care who it is. I'm quite willing too for you to settle our differences Maître Jacques.

MAÎTRE JACQUES: Honoured, I'm sure.

CLÉANTE: I fall madly in love with a young lady. She feels as I do and is more than sympathetic when I ask her to marry me. And then my father takes it into his head to come along and upset everything by deciding to marry her himself.

MAÎTRE JACQUES: That's quite wrong of him.

CLÉANTE: Shouldn't he be ashamed to be thinking of getting married at his age? Is it right for him to go falling in love? Don't you think he should leave that sort of thing to younger men?

MAÎTRE JACQUES: You're right. He can't be serious. Just let me have a word with him. (*Returning to Harpagon*) Well now, the boy isn't as bad as you make out. He's ready to listen to reason. He says he knows he owes you respect – that he got carried away in the heat of the moment and that he won't say no to whatever you suggest, provided you start treating him better than you have in the past and arrange for to him to marry someone to his liking.

HARPAGON: Very well Maître Jacques, you can tell him, on that under-standing, that he can count on me absolutely. Say I leave him a free hand to choose whatever wife he fancies – except Mariane.

MAÎTRE JACQUES: Leave it to me. (*Crossing to Cléante*) Well now, your father isn't as unreasonable as you make out. He gave me to understand that he only got angry because you lost your temper – that all he took exception to was your way of going about things and he'd be happy to let you do whatever you ask, provided you go about it calmly and show him all the respect, deference and obedience that a son owes his father.

CLÉANTE: Oh Maître Jacques, you can assure him that if he lets me marry Mariane he'll find me the most respectful of sons and from now on I'll never do anything he doesn't want me to.

MAÎTRE JACQUES (*to Harpagon*): It's all settled. He agrees to everything you said.

HARPAGON: That's splendid!

MAÎTRE JACQUES (*to Cléante*): It's all over. He's happy with your promises.

CLÉANTE: Thank heaven for that!

MAÎTRE JACQUES: Gentlemen, it only remains for you to put your heads together. You are now in complete agreement. If you were at daggers drawn, it was all because you were failing to understand each other.

CLÉANTE: Dear Maître Jacques, how ever can I thank you?

MAÎTRE JACQUES: Don't mention it sir.

HARPAGON: You have done me a good turn Maître Jacques, and you deserve a reward. (*He takes his handkerchief from his pocket, which makes Maître Jacques think he is about to give him something.*) Now be off with you. But I'll not forget this, you just see if I don't.

MAÎTRE JACQUES: Thank you kindly sir. (*He goes out.*)

Scene v:

CLÉANTE, HARPAGON

CLÉANTE: Father, I ask you to forgive me for having been so angry.

HARPAGON: Think nothing of it.

CLÉANTE: I do assure you: I am really extremely sorry.

HARPAGON: And I for my part am extremely pleased to find you so reasonable.

CLÉANTE: It's very good of you to forgive me so quickly.

HARPAGON: A father can always forgive his children's faults when they remember their duty.

CLÉANTE: What! You mean you really don't hold my outrageous behaviour against me?

HARPAGON: You leave me no choice now that you've shown such obedience and respect.

CLÉANTE: Father, I promise you I shall remember your goodness until my dying day.

HARPAGON: And I promise that from now on you shall have anything you want from me.

CLÉANTE: Why father, what else could I ask now that you have given me Mariane?

HARPAGON: What's that?

CLÉANTE: I was saying, father, how very grateful I was and that by giving me Mariane you have offered me everything I could wish for.

HARPAGON: Who said anything about giving you Mariane?

CLÉANTE: You did father.

HARPAGON: I did?

CLÉANTE: Of course you did.

HARPAGON: That's not so. It was you who promised to give her up.

CLÉANTE: Me? Give her up?

HARPAGON: Yes.

CLÉANTE: Never!

HARPAGON: So you're not giving her up?

CLÉANTE: On the contrary, I am more set on marrying her than ever.

HARPAGON: What! You're not starting all that again, you scoundrel?

CLÉANTE: Nothing will ever make me change my mind.

HARPAGON: Wait till I get my hands on you, you villain!

CLÉANTE: You can do whatever you like!

HARPAGON: I don't want to see you ever again!

CLÉANTE: Delighted to oblige!

HARPAGON: I'm finished with you!

CLÉANTE: Right! Be finished then!

HARPAGON: I disown you as my son!

CLÉANTE: Very well.

HARPAGON: I hereby disinherit you!

CLÉANTE: As you wish.

HARPAGON: And I give you my curse!

CLÉANTE: Keep your gifts to yourself! (*Harpagon goes out.*)

Scene vi:
LA FLÈCHE, CLÉANTE

LA FLÉche (*entering from the garden with a strong-box*): Oh sir! Here you are! Just in the nick of time! Quick, come with me!

CLÉANTE: What's the matter?

LA FLÈCHE: Come with me I say. We're in luck.

CLÉANTE: How do you mean?

LA FLÈCHE: Here's your answer.

CLÉANTE: Where?

LA FLÈCHE: I've had my eye on it all day.

CLÉANTE: What is it?

LA FLÈCHE: Your father's strong-box. I've pinched it!

CLÉANTE: How did you manage that?

LA FLÈCHE: I'll tell you the whole story. But let's go now, I can hear him yelling. (*They go out.*)

Scene vii:
HARPAGON

HARPAGON (*shouting 'stop thief' in the garden, he enters hatless*): Stop thief! Stop thief! Murderers! Assassins! Justice, merciful heaven! I'm done for, done to death. They've cut my throat! They've stolen my money! Who could have done it? Where's he gone to? Where's he now? Where's he hiding? What'll I do to find him? Which way shall I go? Or not go? Is he there? Is he here? Who can he be? Who's that? Stop! (*He grabs his own arm.*) Villain, give me back my money! Oh, it's me! I'm losing my mind, I don't know where I am, who I am or what I'm doing. Aah! my poor, dear money, my lovely money, my friend, they've taken you from me! And now you've gone, I've lost my prop, my comfort, my joy. I'm finished. There's nothing for me now. I can't live without you. It's the end, I can't go on, I'm as good as dead and buried. Won't somebody bring me back to life by returning my money or telling me who took it? Eh? What did you say? Oh, there's nobody there. Whoever did it must have been watching very carefully for his chance and chose the very moment

I was talking to my villain of a son. I must go. I'll fetch the law and have everyone in the house questioned and tortured – maids, footmen, son, daughter, the whole lot of them, myself included! There's so many of them in the house! I look around but I can't see anyone who doesn't make me suspicious. They all look as if they could be the burglar. What are they talking about over there? About the man who robbed me? What's that noise upstairs? Is the thief up there? Please, I implore you, if anyone knows anything about the thief, tell me! Are you sure he's not hiding among you? They're all staring. Now they're laughing. You'll see, they're all in it, oh yes, up to their necks in this burglary! Come on, quick! officers of the law, constables, magistrates, judges, racks, gibbets, executioners! I'll hang every last one of them. And if I don't get my money back, I'll hang myself as well!

Act V

Scene i:

HARPAGON, *an* OFFICER OF THE LAW *and his*
CONSTABLE

OFFICER: Leave it to me, I know my job, thank you very much. This isn't the first time I've had a burglary to get to the bottom of. I wish I had as many bags full of money as I've had people hanged.

HARPAGON: All the magistrates in the city had better make it their business to take up this case. If they don't get me my money back, I'll take the matter to a higher authority.

OFFICER: We must go through the proper procedures. Now, how much did you say was in this chest?

HARPAGON: Ten thousand crowns, in cash.

OFFICER: Ten thousand crowns?

HARPAGON: Ten thousand.

OFFICER: So we're talking of a sizeable theft.

HARPAGON: There's no punishment bad enough for a crime of such enormity. If it goes unpunished, nothing, however sacred, will be safe.

OFFICER: And in what coin of the realm was the money?

HARPAGON: Good louis-d'ors and pistoles of full weight.[12]

OFFICER: Who do you suspect of perpetrating the theft?

HARPAGON: Everybody. I want you to arrest the whole city and the suburbs too.

OFFICER: In my view, you'd be well advised not to go about alarming people unduly. Far better to keep calm, set about collecting evidence and then proceed, leaving no stone unturned, to recover the money that's been stolen from you.

Scene ii:
MAÎTRE JACQUES, HARPAGON, OFFICER, CONSTABLE

MAÎTRE JACQUES (*calling over his shoulder as he comes on*): I'll be back in a moment. Cut his throat now, have his feet singed and then I want him dropped in boiling water. After that you can hang him from the rafters.

HARPAGON: Who do you mean? The man who stole my money?

MAÎTRE JACQUES: I was talking about a sucking-pig your steward's just sent in. I'm going to prepare him for you according to my own recipe.

HARPAGON: We aren't interested in that. There are more important things for you to talk to this gentleman about.

OFFICER: No need to be alarmed. I'm not here to get you into trouble. We'll take it gently.

MAÎTRE JACQUES: Is this gentleman coming to dinner?

OFFICER: In a situation like this, my good man, you must hold nothing back from your master.

MAÎTRE JACQUES: Don't you worry sir, you'll get the very best of what I can do. I'll do you as proud as I can.

HARPAGON: We're not talking about that.

MAÎTRE JACQUES: If I don't put on as good a dinner as I could wish, you can blame your steward who's clipped my wings with the scissors of his economy.

HARPAGON: You oaf! We're talking about something more important than dinner! I want you to tell me what you know about the money that's been stolen from me.

MAÎTRE JACQUES: Someone's stolen your money?

HARPAGON: Yes you rogue! And I'll have you strung up if you don't return it!

OFFICER: Merciful heaven! Don't be so hard on him. I can tell by his face that he's an honest man. He'll tell you what you want to know without putting him behind bars. Oh yes my lad, if you make a clean breast of it you won't come to any harm and you'll be suitably rewarded by your master. His money was stolen sometime today, and you must know something about it.

MAÎTRE JACQUES (*aside*): This is just my chance to get my own back on that steward of ours. Ever since he came here he's been the blue-eyed boy. He's the only one anybody listens to. And I haven't forgotten that beating he gave me either.

HARPAGON: What's going on inside that head of yours?

OFFICER: Let him alone. He's getting ready to tell you what you want to know. I told you he was an honest man.

MAÎTRE JACQUES: Well sir, since you want me to come out with it straight, I think the one who did it was that precious steward of yours.

HARPAGON: Valère?

MAÎTRE JACQUES: Yes.

HARPAGON: Valère? who seems so trustworthy?

MAÎTRE JACQUES: He's your man. I believe he's the one who stole your money.

HARPAGON: And what grounds do you have for suspecting him?

MAÎTRE JACQUES: Grounds?

HARPAGON: Yes.

MAÎTRE JACQUES: I suspect him on the grounds . . . that I suspect him.

OFFICER: But you must say what evidence you have.

HARPAGON: Did you see him hanging about the spot where I'd put my money?

MAÎTRE JACQUES: That I did! Where did you put it?

HARPAGON: In the garden.

MAÎTRE JACQUES: Exactly! He was hanging about in the garden when I saw him. And what was your money in?

HARPAGON: A strong-box.

MAÎTRE JACQUES: That's it! I saw him with a strong-box.

HARPAGON: And what was this strong-box like? I could easily tell if it was mine.

MAÎTRE JACQUES: What was it like?

HARPAGON: Yes

MAÎTRE JACQUES: It was . . . sort of . . . like a strong-box.

OFFICER: Yes, of course, but give a few details, so we can tell –

MAÎTRE JACQUES: It was a large strong-box.

HARPAGON: The one that was stolen was small.

MAÎTRE JACQUES: Oh, if you're going by size, it was a small one. When I said it was big, I was going by what was in it.

OFFICER: And what colour was it?

MAÎTRE JACQUES: What colour?

OFFICER: Yes.

MAÎTRE JACQUES: It was . . . you know . . . that colour . . . what's the word? Can't you help me out?

HARPAGON: Well?

MAÎTRE JACQUES: Was it red?

HARPAGON: No. Grey.

MAÎTRE JACQUES: That's it! Greyish red. That's what I meant.

HARPAGON: There's no doubt in my mind. It's obviously the same one. Write it down sir, take his statement. Oh Lord! Who can I trust after this? There's no relying on anything any more and after this business I'm beginning to think I'm capable of robbing myself!

MAÎTRE JACQUES: Sir, here he is. Don't let on that it was me that told you.

Scene iii:
VALÈRE, HARPAGON, OFFICER, CONSTABLE, MAÎTRE JACQUES

HARPAGON: Come here! Come here and confess to the foulest, most dastardly deed ever committed!

VALÈRE: What can I do for you sir?

HARPAGON: What, you blackguard! Do you feel no shame for your crime?

VALÈRE: What crime do you mean?

HARPAGON: What crime do I mean you wretch? As if you didn't know what I'm talking about! It's no good trying to hide it. The secret's out. I've just learned the whole story. To think that you could take advantage of my good nature to worm your way into my house so you could go behind my back and try something like that!

VALÈRE: Since you know the full story sir, I won't attempt to make excuses or deny it.

MAÎTRE JACQUES (*aside*): Aha! Did I guess the truth without knowing it?

VALÈRE: I've been meaning to have a word with you on the matter. I was only waiting for the right moment, but, given the way things have turned out, I can only ask you not to be angry and be good enough to listen to what I have to say in justification.

HARPAGON: And what possible justification could you have, you thieving wretch?

VALÈRE: Oh sir, I have done nothing to deserve language of that kind! True, I may have put myself in the wrong with you, but, when all's said and done, what I did is very excusable.

HARPAGON: Excusable? A premeditated stab in the back, a death blow like that?

VALÈRE: Please, don't lose your temper. When you've heard me out, you'll see that less harm's been done than you think.

HARPAGON: Less harm done than I think? Why, you villain, it's my life blood, my very existence!

VALÈRE: On the question of blood sir, yours hasn't come off too badly. My rank is such that I shall not disgrace it and there's nothing in all this that I can't put right.

HARPAGON: And that's exactly what I mean you to do – you will return what you stole from me.

VALÈRE: Your honour sir will be fully satisfied.

HARPAGON: Honour doesn't come into it. But tell me, who put you up to it?

VALÈRE: Oh, how can you ask?

HARPAGON: But I am asking you.

VALÈRE: The god who bears the blame for everything he makes people do. I mean Love!

HARPAGON: Love?

VALÈRE: Yes, Love.

HARPAGON: A fine sort of love that is! Love of my gold!

VALÈRE: No sir. It was not your money that tempted me. That was not what dazzled me. I do assure you that I have no aspirations whatever in the matter of your wealth, provided you let me keep the one treasure I already have.

HARPAGON: Never! By all the devils in Hell, I will not let you keep it! The impudence of it! Wanting to keep what he's stolen!

VALÈRE: Would you really call it stealing?

HARPAGON: Would I call it stealing? A treasure like that?

VALÈRE: Yes, a treasure indeed, and beyond question the most precious you possess. But you wouldn't be losing it if you said I could keep it. On my bended knees, I beg you to grant me this most desirable of treasures. By all that's right, you cannot refuse your consent!

HARPAGON: I'll do nothing of the sort! What are you talking about?

VALÈRE: We are promised to each other and have sworn never to be parted.

HARPAGON: Promised? How wonderful! And this commitment to each other is very amusing!

VALÈRE: We are committed to each other for ever!

HARPAGON: I'll put a stop to it, believe me.

VALÈRE: Only death can separate us!

HARPAGON: That's taking love of my money a bit far!

VALÈRE: I've already explained sir, it was not material considerations that led me to do what I did. My reasons for acting were not at all what you think. The motive for my behaviour was far nobler.

HARPAGON: He'll be telling us next that he wanted my money out of Christian charity! But I'll not have it! I'll set the law on you, you scoundrel, and the law will find in my favour.

VALÈRE: You will act as you choose and I am ready to bear whatever cruelty you think fit. But at least please believe that if any wrong has been done it should be laid at my door and no one else's. Your daughter is in no way to blame.

HARPAGON: I should think not indeed! It would be very odd if my daughter were to have had a hand in a crime like this. But I demand restitution! I insist that you tell me the place where you found what you spirited away!

VALÈRE: Spirited away? I haven't spirited anything away. Neither of us has set foot outside your house.

HARPAGON (*aside*): Oh my lovely money-box! (*To Valère*) Not left the house?

VALÈRE: No sir.

HARPAGON: But tell me. You haven't been tampering –

VALÈRE: Me? Tamper? Now there you wrong both of us. What I feel is pure and honourable, and though I am so deeply in love –

HARPAGON (*aside*): Deeply in love with my money-box?

VALÈRE: I would rather die than give any hint that I harboured a single thought unworthy of one so modest and unassuming as –

HARPAGON (*aside*): Modest? My money-box?

VALÈRE: All I ever asked for was the pleasure of seeing her. Nothing base or unworthy has profaned the love such beauty inspires in me.

HARPAGON (*aside*): Beauty? My money-box? He sounds like a lover talking about his mistress!

VALÈRE: Dame Claude knows the truth of the matter sir. And she can testify –

HARPAGON: What? My servant had a hand in this business?

VALÈRE: Yes sir. She was there when we pledged ourselves to one another. It was only when she saw how honourable my intentions were that she helped me to persuade your daughter to give me her promise and accept mine in return.

HARPAGON (*aside*): Fear of what the law might do has completely turned his wits. (*To Valère*) Why are you confusing the issue by dragging my daughter into it?

VALÈRE: What I'm saying sir is that I had the greatest difficulty in overcoming her modesty and persuading her to accept my proposal.

HARPAGON: Whose modesty?

VALÈRE: Your daughter's. It was not until yesterday that she finally agreed to marry me.

HARPAGON: My daughter has promised to marry you?

VALÈRE: Yes sir, just as I have promised to marry her.

HARPAGON: Oh God! Another calamity!

MAÎTRE JACQUES (*to the Officer*): Keep writing sir, don't stop!

HARPAGON: It's one disaster after another! My troubles keep coming in droves! Come sir, do your duty. I want a charge-sheet made out against him. I want him prosecuted as a thief and a seducer as well!

VALÈRE: I have done nothing to warrant being called such names, and when you know who I am . . .

Scene iv:

ÉLISE, MARIANE, FROSINE, HARPAGON, VALÈRE,
MAÎTRE JACQUES, OFFICER, CONSTABLE

HARPAGON: Oh! wretched girl! You don't deserve to have a father like me! Is this how you behave after everything I've taught you? You go and fall in love with a thieving scoundrel and, without my consent, say you'll marry him. But you'll find you've both made a big mistake. (*To Élise*) In future, four solid convent walls will answer for your conduct and (*to Valère*) you shall pay for your infernal audacity on the gallows!

VALÈRE: This is a matter you won't settle by getting angry. I insist on putting my side of it before sentence is passed.

HARPAGON: I was wrong when I said the gallows: you shall be broken alive on the wheel![13]

ÉLISE (*kneeling before her father*): Oh father! please try not to be so hard! Don't insist on taking your rights as a father to extremes! Don't let yourself be carried away in the first rush of anger. Take time to consider what you should do. Take the trouble to find out more about the man you think has offended you, for he isn't what you take him to be. You'll be less surprised that I've promised to marry him when you learn that if it wasn't for him you would have lost me a long time ago. Yes father, he is the man who rescued me from the wreck when, as you know, I nearly drowned. You owe your daughter's life to him and –

HARPAGON: All that's beside the point and I would have been better off if he'd left you to drown than do what he has done.

ÉLISE: Father! I beg you by the love that a father –

HARPAGON: I won't listen to any more of this. The officer here has his duty to do.

MAÎTRE JACQUES (*aside*): Now you'll pay for that beating you gave me.

FROSINE (*aside*): Oh Lord! What a pickle!

Scene v:

ANSELME, HARPAGON, ÉLISE, MARIANE,
FROSINE, VALÈRE, MAÎTRE JACQUES, OFFICER,
CONSTABLE

ANSELME: My dear Harpagon, whatever is wrong? You look dreadfully upset.

HARPAGON: Oh Seigneur Anselme, you see before you the most unfortunate of men. All kinds of trouble and complications have arisen over the contract you have come to sign! I have suffered mortal blows, one to my fortune and one to my honour. This two-faced rogue here has ridden rough-shod over the most sacred obligations. He wormed himself into my house by pretending to be a servant in order to steal my money and seduce my daughter!

VALÈRE: Who gives a damn for this money you keep making such a song and dance about?

HARPAGON: Yes, the pair of them have gone and got themselves engaged. It's an insult to you Seigneur Anselme. You're the one who should have the law on him, sparing no expense, and obtain satisfaction for his impudence by calling for the full rigour of the courts.

ANSELME: I have no intention of forcing anyone to marry me nor will I make any claim on affections which have already been placed elsewhere. But where your own interests are concerned, you can rely on me to take them up as though they were my own.

HARPAGON: This gentleman is a very honest officer who, he tells me, will not fail to do his duty to the letter. (*To the Officer*) Charge him, throw the book at him and make things look as black for him as you can.

VALÈRE: I fail to see how falling in love with your daughter can be considered a crime. As for the punishment you think will be handed down to me for proposing to her, when you know who I am, you'll –

HARPAGON: I am not interested in all your cock-and-bull stories. These days the world is full of self-styled nobility, frauds who capitalize on the fact that they are nobodies by having the nerve to call themselves by the first illustrious name that comes into their heads.

VALÈRE: I'll have you know that I have more pride than to stoop to laying claim to anything that isn't mine. The whole of Naples can testify to my birth and family.

ANSELME: Be careful. Mind what you're saying. There's more at stake here than you think. You are talking to a man who knows everyone in Naples. I shall soon see through any trumped-up story you concoct.

VALÈRE (*proudly putting on his hat*): I'm not the sort who scares easily. If you know Naples, then you must know who Don Thomas d'Alburcy was.

ANSELME: Of course I do. Few men knew him better than I did.

HARPAGON: I don't give a damn about Don Thomas – nor Don Anybodyelse either.

ANSELME: Please, let him speak. We'll see what he's got to say for himself.[14]

VALÈRE: I say that he was my father.

ANSELME: Your father?

VALÈRE: Yes.

ANSELME: Come now, you can't be serious. You'd better try and come up with a better story than that if you want to be believed. Don't think you'll get very far with this one.

VALÈRE: Take care what you say! This is no fabrication. I do not make any claims that I cannot easily substantiate.

ANSELME: What? You dare to claim that you are the son of Don Thomas d'Alburcy?

VALÈRE: Yes, I do and I am prepared to maintain it against anybody.

ANSELME: Such amazing presumption! Let me tell you, on the contrary, that the man you refer to was lost at sea at least sixteen years ago with his wife and children, while running for their lives from the cruel persecution which followed the troubles in Naples when a number of noble families were driven into exile.[15]

VALÈRE: Yes, and let me tell you, on the contrary, that his son, then aged seven, was saved from the wreck by a Spanish vessel, along with one servant. And it is that rescued son who now stands here talking to you. Let me tell you also that the ship's captain, moved by my plight, took pity on me and brought me up as his own son, and that ever since I was old enough I have made my way as a soldier. It was only recently that I learned that my father was not dead, as I had always believed. I set out to look for him and then, as I passed through this city, I saw, by a circumstance inspired by

Heaven, the adorable Élise. From that moment I was a slave to her beauty. Such was the strength of my feelings for her and the intransigence of her father that I decided to become a servant in his house and send someone else in search of my parents.

ANSELME: But what proof can you provide, other than your word, that will satisfy us that this is not just a tale you have embroidered on some foundation of truth?

VALÈRE: The Spanish captain, a ruby signet ring which belonged to my father, an agate bracelet which my mother put on my arm, and old Pedro, the servant who was rescued from the wreck with me.

MARIANE: Ah! I can vouch for your word! I can confirm that you are no impostor! From what you have said it is clear that you are my brother!

VALÈRE: You are my sister?

MARIANE: Yes! My heart missed a beat the moment you opened your mouth to speak. Our mother – oh how happy you will make her! – has told me so many times about our family's misfortunes. It was the will of Heaven that we too should survive that awful shipwreck, but our lives were spared only at the cost of our freedom. The men who picked up my mother and me from the wreckage of our ship were corsairs. After ten years of slavery we regained our freedom by a stroke of good fortune and returned to Naples. There we found that everything we owned had been sold and that there was no news of my father. We moved on to Genoa where my mother went to collect the meagre remnants of a legacy of which she had been cheated. From there, to escape the barbarous persecution of her relations, she came here and has since not so much lived as languished.

ANSELME: Oh Lord! How wonderful are the ways in which Thy power is made manifest! How true it is that Heaven alone can accomplish miracles! Embrace me my children, and join with me in rejoicing, for I am your father.

VALÈRE: You are our father?

MARIANE: It was for you that my mother has shed so many tears?

ANSELME: Yes, my daughter. Yes, my son. I am Don Thomas d'Alburcy. By the will of Heaven I was saved from the waves with all the money I had with me. For more than sixteen years I have believed that you were all dead. After many wanderings I was ready to begin again and look for the consolation of family life by marrying a good and sweet-natured woman. Uncertain of my safety if I returned to Naples, I renounced my country for ever and, having managed to sell up everything I owned there, I settled here and, calling myself Anselme, hoped to forget the sorrows associated with my real name, one that had brought me nothing but grief.

HARPAGON: Is he your son?

ANSELME: Yes.

HARPAGON: Then I sue you for the ten thousand crowns he stole from me.

ANSELME: He stole from you?

HARPAGON: Yes.

VALÈRE: Who told you that?

HARPAGON: Maître Jacques.

VALÈRE: Did you say that?

MAÎTRE JACQUES: Look, I never said anything.

HARPAGON: Oh yes he did, and the Officer here took down his statement.

VALÈRE: Do you really think I am capable of such villainy?

HARPAGON: Capable or incapable, I want my money!

Scene vi:

CLÉANTE, VALÈRE, MARIANE, ÉLISE, FROSINE, HARPAGON, ANSELME, MAÎTRE JACQUES, LA FLÈCHE, OFFICER, CONSTABLE

CLÉANTE: Stop worrying father, you can drop all your accusations. I have news of your money and am here to tell you that you will get it back – on condition that you let me marry Mariane.

HARPAGON: Where is it?

CLÉANTE: Don't you worry. I guarantee it is in a safe place and only I know where that place is. But you're going to have to tell me what you decide to do. You can choose either to give me Mariane or never see your money-box again.

HARPAGON: Is it still all there?

CLÉANTE: Every last penny. Make up you mind, decide if you agree to the marriage and add your consent to her mother's. She left it entirely up to her daughter to choose between us: you – or me.

MARIANE: But you are forgetting that my mother's consent is now not enough. Heaven has given me back a brother whom you see here but also a father. You must ask for his consent too.

ANSELME: Heaven has not restored me to you, my dear children, to stand in the way of what you wish. Seigneur Harpagon, you must be aware that a young girl is more likely to choose a son than his father. Come now, don't force me to say what I should not have to say. Join me in giving your consent to this double marriage.

HARPAGON: I'll need to see my money-box again before I can make up my mind.

CLÉANTE: You shall see it – all present and correct.

HARPAGON: I have no money to give my children if they marry.

ANSELME: Well, I have enough for both so that needn't worry you.

HARPAGON: Will you undertake to meet the costs of both weddings?

ANSELME: Yes, I agree. Are you satisfied?

HARPAGON: Yes, provided you pay for a new suit of clothes for me for the weddings.

ANSELME: Agreed. Come, let us enjoy the pleasures of this happy day.

OFFICER: One moment gentlemen, one moment. Now hold on, if you don't mind. Who is going to pay me for the statement I've drawn up?

HARPAGON: We're not interested in your statement.

OFFICER: That may be so. But I have no intention of being left with a statement I haven't been paid for.

HARPAGON (*pointing to Maître Jacques*): See him? I give him to you. You can hang him – that should settle the bill.

MAÎTRE JACQUES: Oh dear, what am I supposed to do? If I tell the truth I get a good hiding. And now they're going to hang me for telling lies!

ANSELME: Seigneur Harpagon, you must forgive him for lying.

HARPAGON: Will you pay the Officer then?

ANSELME: So be it. But now let us go and share our joy with your mother.

HARPAGON: And I'll go and see my lovely money-box again.

The Hypochondriac, a Comedy with Music and Dance

Le Malade imaginaire, Comédie mêlée de musique et de danses

Performed for the first time on 10 February 1673 at the Palais Royal by the King's Players

As the first interlude makes clear, *The Hypochondriac* was originally intended to be performed at the Court of Louis XIV. That it was in fact staged at the Palais Royal was due to the hostile influence of Molière's former collaborator Lully to whom the king had granted the monopoly of staging musical plays. Molière challenged the decision but lost, though what was to prove his last play was duly licensed. The music was written by Charpentier and the production was lavish: in addition to the cast, there were nineteen musicians, twelve dancers and numerous extras. The successful opening night promised a long run, but Molière, who played Argan, was taken ill during the fourth performance and died only hours after the final curtain. His last play has remained one of his most popular and since 1673 has been staged over 2000 times at the Comédie-Française.

If *The Hypochondriac* was designed as a spectacle, it is also a comedy which at times is broad and basic and at others is subtle and sophisticated. For while it draws on the conventional ploys of misunderstanding and farce, it also mocks, at a higher level, the follies of characters whose actions and desires contradict what they say. Béline and Monsieur Bonnefoi are not what they seem, for while they speak honeyed words, they are as ruthlessly self-interested as the pompous doctors who are good only at writing bills and taking the credit for the cures which nature performs. They circle Argan, one of Molière's obsessive monsters, who, though a ridiculous figure, is simultaneously their victim and the oppressor of his own family: his self-absorption is a danger to the happiness of others. If love wins in the end, it requires considerable help from Béralde, Toinette and Louison who are constant reminders that there is no substitute for honesty, affection and common-sense.

Thus while the plot is structured around the problem of whom Angélique is to marry, it is complicated and deepened by the clash of egoisms. *The Hypochondriac* thus carries a charge which is both moral and social, for much of its power derives from Molière's hatred of selfishness in general and the hypocrisy of the blinkered medical profession in particular. He had no reason to respect doctors of whom he had seen far too much in his life. But whatever bitterness he felt never clouds the amused, ironical eye he turns on the eternal follies of human nature against which *The Hypochondriac*, as he intended, remains a healthy warning.

Characters

ARGAN, a hypochondriac
BÉLINE, Argan's second wife
ANGÉLIQUE, Argan's daughter,
    in love with Cléante
LOUISON, Argan's younger
    daughter, sister of Angélique
BÉRALDE, Argan's brother
CLÉANTE, in love with Angélique
MONSIEUR DIAFOIRUS, a doctor
THOMAS DIAFOIRUS, his son, in
    love with Angélique
MONSIEUR FLEURANT, an
    apothecary
MONSIEUR BONNEFOI, a notary
TOINETTE, a servant

The scene is set in Paris.

Prologue

After the glorious exertions and victorious exploits of our August Monarch, it is fitting that all whose concern is with writing should devote themselves to celebrating his fame or to diverting his leisure. This is what we have endeavoured to do here and this prologue is intended as a tribute to our great Prince and an introduction to the comedy of The Hypochondriac, which was devised for his relaxation after his mighty labours.

The setting is a rustic – but nevertheless very pleasant – scene.

ECLOGUE

Music and dance

FLORA, PAN, CLIMÈNE, DAPHNE, TIRCIS,
DORILAS, TWO ZEPHYRS, SHEPHERDS *and*
SHEPHERDESSES

FLORA: Come, leave your flocks,
            Come hither, shepherds, come,
            Foregather here beneath these leafy elms,
            I bring you news propitious to these realms
            And joy to hearths and homes.
            Come, leave your flocks,
            Come hither, shepherds, come,
            Foregather here beneath these leafy elms.

CLIMÈNE *and* DAPHNE: Shepherd, dally no more upon your love,
            For Flora calls us, Flora 'tis who calls.

TIRCIS *and* DORILAS: First, cruel one, tell me whom love enthrals

TIRCIS: If my passion you'll approve . . .

DORILAS: If on deaf ears my pleading falls . . .

CLIMÈNE *and* DAPHNE: 'Tis Flora calls us, Flora 'tis who calls.

TIRCIS *and* DORILAS: One word, 'tis all we ask, for us whom love enthrals.

TIRCIS: Must I forever see my true love slighted?

DORILAS: Dare I hope my love will be requited?

CLIMÈNE *and* DAPHNE: Flora calls us, Flora 'tis who calls.

First Ballet is danced

Shepherds and shepherdesses all moving to time take their places around Flora.

CLIMÈNE: Say, O Goddess, what news
　　　　 You bring for our rejoicing.

DAPHNE: We long to learn from you
　　　　 What are these momentous tidings.

DORILAS: We all yearn to know.

ALL:　　 We all burn to hear
　　　　 The news you bring.

FLORA:　 Silence! I shall give the news for which you yearned!
　　　　 Your prayers are granted: LOUIS is returned,
　　　　 And with him comes the reign of love and pleasure.
　　　　 Ended now are your alarms,
　　　　 The world's submitted to his arms,
　　　　 He'll fight no more
　　　　 For want of foe.

ALL:　　 Oh happy tiding!
　　　　 News so sweet, news beguiling!
　　　　 Oh news so joyful, festive, gladsome
　　　　 That brings a happy, royal outcome,
　　　　 Heaven with our hopes conspiring.
　　　　 Oh happy tiding!
　　　　 News so sweet, news beguiling!

Second Ballet is danced

All the shepherds and shepherdesses express in dance the transports of their joy.

FLORA:　 You shepherds with your reeds
　　　　 Set every glen resounding,
　　　　 With echoes of his deeds

Great LOUIS' fame expounding.
From a hundred battles he
Brings home to us the victory
And on the field the flag he raises.
So come you all and with one voice
With sweeter combats now rejoice:
Laud his fame and sing his praises!

ALL: Let us join together with one voice
Now with sweeter combats to rejoice:
We'll laud his fame and sing his praises!

FLORA: Come fair youth and ready your hand
With flowers that bloom at my command,
Prepare a crown for he
Who sings of palms and victory
And best can make a story
To sing Great LOUIS' glory.

CLIMÈNE: If Tircis should the victor prove . . .

DAPHNE: If Dorilas should win it . . .

CLIMÈNE: I promise he shall have my love.

DAPHNE: He'll be mine for ever from that minute.

TIRCIS: For this joy I yearn!

DORILAS: To this hope I turn!

BOTH: What poet could fail to sing
By such a theme inspired?
What glorious fancies spring
To one by love thus fired?

*The violins play an air to encourage the two shepherds to the contest,
while Flora takes her place as judge at the foot of a tree in the centre of
the stage, accompanied by two zephyrs. The rest range themselves on
either side of the stage as spectators.*

TIRCIS: Just as with icy winter snows
A mighty torrent swelling
Rushes on and all its banks o'erflows,
Bearing all before it and compelling
Dike and manor, town and field
And every obstacle to yield,
So sweeps onward in the cause of France
LOUIS' proud and irresistible advance!

Ballet

Shepherds and shepherdesses on Tircis's side dance around him to a repeated refrain, to express their applause.

DORILAS: The awesome lightning striking,
　　　　　The crashing of the thunderhead,
　　　　　Are not more frightening,
　　　　　Though they make brave hearts dread,
　　　　　Than is an army fighting
　　　　　With LOUIS at its head.

Ballet

The shepherds and shepherdesses on Dorilas's side dance as did the others.

TIRCIS: All the deeds of ancient days
　　　　Handed down in song and story
　　　　Now we see surpassed in glory.
　　　　For all the gods of yore
　　　　Whose exploits went before,
　　　　And many battles fought,
　　　　Great LOUIS sets at nought.

Ballet

The shepherds and shepherdesses on Tircis's side dance as before.

DORILAS: Seeing LOUIS' mighty deeds,
　　　　　We can credit ancient stories.
　　　　　But who shall serve our grandsons' needs
　　　　　To give credence to Great LOUIS' glories?

Ballet

The shepherdesses on Dorilas's side dance as before, and then shepherds and shepherdesses on both sides join together.

PAN (*attended by six fauns*): Vainly shepherds you aspire
　　　　　To ape Apollo and his lyre
　　　　　And seek with rustic strings to frame
　　　　　What his finest songs proclaim.

He soars on golden wings;
Your voice with smaller power sings.
'Tis to fly too near the sun
Thus to tempt comparison;
'Tis to fly with frail and waxen wing
Thus his virtues to portray
With your simple rustic lay.
To depict Great LOUIS' glory,
Of such deeds to tell the story,
Is beyond the greatest pen,
A task beyond the power of men.
So silence and sedateness
Serve best to sing his greatness.
Find then other ways
Than song to give him praise.
Better seek to charm his leisure.
And contribute to his pleasure.

ALL: Let's do our best to charm his leisure
And contribute to his pleasure.

FLORA: To such a theme you could not rise
But still you may receive the prize.
Both of you have proved deserving,
For in such a noble enterprise
Lies reward for him who tries.

Enter dancers. The two zephyrs dance with crowns of flowers which they then present to the two shepherds.

CLIMÈNE *and* DAPHNE (*offering their hands*): In such a noble enterprise
Lies reward for him who tries.

TIRCIS *and* DORILAS: Oh! Sweet reward that we attain!

FLORA *and* PAN: Nothing done in LOUIS' service
Is done in vain.

ALL FOUR: To the service of his pleasures
We give ourselves again.

FLORA *and* PAN: Oh happy those who themselves can give
And in his service live!

ALL: Let us all with one accord
Join our pipes and voices:
Today the world rejoices:

Let us sing with one accord
Until the woodland rings
With praise of LOUIS, mightiest of Kings!
Oh happy those who themselves can give
And in his service live!

Final Ballet, in which all join

Fauns, shepherds, shepherdesses, all combine and dance together, after which they go to prepare for the play.

Alternative Prologue[1]

The scene is set in a forest. The curtain rises to a tuneful overture played by the full orchestra. A shepherdess comes forward and meltingly laments her tribulations and her inability to find a remedy for them. Numerous fauns and satyrs, who have gathered for their own games and festivities, meet the shepherdess, listen to her lament and provide a highly entertaining spectacle.

SHEPHERDESS: Vain and foolish doctors you
Have no balm can cure my ills,
Not your Latin nor your skills
Can ease my heart's pain and grief:
Your art commands no belief.

Alas, alas, how can a maid,
How can a maid uncover
What it is that pains her heart
To her shepherd lover
Who alone can mend it?
You can ne'er presume to end it,
You vain and foolish doctors:
With all your vaunted art and skills
You have no balm to cure my ills.

All the art which simple folk
Believe you have is just a joke:

And for my pain will nought avail.
Your foolish jargon can prevail
Only with *imagined* indispositions
And *hypochondriacal* afflictions.
With all your vaunted art and skills
You have no balm to cure my ills.
Vain and foolish doctors, you
Have no balm can cure my ills.

The scene changes to represent a room.

Act I

Scene i:

ARGAN

ARGAN (*alone in his room, seated at a table, reckoning his apothecary's bill with counters[2] and talking to himself*): Three and two make five, and five make ten, and ten make twenty. Three and two make five. (*Reads*) 'And, on the twenty-fourth, to a small injection, insinuative, preparatory and emollient, to lubricate, loosen and cool the gentleman's bowels.' That's one thing I like about Monsieur Fleurant, my apothecary: his bills are always so polite. 'To the gentleman's bowels – thirty sous.' All the same Monsieur Fleurant, politeness isn't everything, you've got to be reasonable as well and not fleece your patients. Thirty sous for an enema! I'm not having it, I've told you before. You only charged me twenty sous in previous bills, and when an apothecary says twenty, he really means ten, so there you are: ten sous. 'And, on the same day, to a robust detergent injection compounded of double-strength purgative electuary, rhubarb, mel rosatum etc., etc.,[3] according to prescription, to flush, irrigate and cleanse the gentleman's lower intestine – thirty sous.' If you've no objection, say ten. 'And, same date, in the evening, to a hepatic, soporific and somniferous julep,[4] compounded to induce the gentleman to sleep – thirty-five sous.' I've no complaints about that, it made me sleep like a top. Ten, fifteen, sixteen, seventeen and a half a sou. 'And, on the twenty-fifth, to a sound purgative, fortifying draught compounded of fresh cassia mixed with Levantine senna etc., according to Monsieur Purgon's orders, to expel and evacuate the gentleman's bile[5] – four livres.' Come Monsieur Fleurant, you can't be serious! you've got to be able to look your patients in the eye! Monsieur Purgon never told you to charge four livres. Make it, say, three livres, if you don't mind. Twenty sous, thirty sous. 'And, on the same day, to an astringent, analgesic potion to relax the gentleman – thirty sous.' Fair enough, ten and five, fifteen sous. 'And, on the twenty-sixth, a carminative[6] injection to expel the gentleman's wind – thirty sous.' No Monsieur Fleurant: ten. 'And, on the same evening, to a repeat injection administered to the gentleman, as above – thirty sous.' No Monsieur Fleurant, make it ten. 'And, on the twenty-seventh, to a powerful draught compounded to disperse and drive out the gentleman's ill humours – three livres.' Agreed, twenty plus ten equals thirty sous; I'm glad you're so amenable to reason. 'And, on the twenty-eighth, to a preparation of clarified and sweetened whey for purifying, thinning, toning, tempering and reinvigorating the gentleman's blood – twenty sous.' Put down ten. 'And, to a cordial and preventive tonic, compounded of twelve grains of bezoar,[7] syrup of lemon and pomegranate etc., etc., according to prescription – five livres.' Now just a minute, please Monsieur Fleurant! If you carry on like that, nobody will want to be ill, so you can settle for four livres. That's twenty plus twenty, forty sous. Three and two are five, plus five makes ten, plus ten make twenty. Total: sixty-three livres and four and a half sous. That means that in the past month, I've had one . . . two . . . three . . . four . . . five . . . six . . . seven . . . eight lots of medicines, and one . . . two . . . three . . . four . . . five . . . six . . . seven . . . eight . . . nine . . . ten . . . eleven . . . twelve injections. And last month, I had twelve lots of medicine and twenty enemas. I'm not surprised I've not been as well this month as last. I'll have to tell Monsieur Purgon so he can put that right. Come and take all this away somebody. Isn't there anybody about? It's no use telling them, I'm always being left by myself. There's no way of making them stay here. (*He rings a bell to summon his servants.*) They can't hear. My bell's not loud enough. (*He rings again.*) Ting-a-ling, ting-a-ling, ting-a-ling! They must be deaf . . . Toinette! (*He rings again.*) Ting-a-ling, ting-a-ling, ting-a-ling! Same as if I'd never rung at all. Damned chit! Hussy! (*Ringing*) Ting-a-ling, ting-a-ling,

ting-a-ling! It's infuriating! (*He stops ringing and shouts instead.*)
Ting-a-ling, ting-a-ling, ting-a-ling! Devil take the wretched woman!
It's inconceivable, how could anyone leave a poor sick man all alone?
Ting-a-ling, ting-a-ling, ting-a-ling! This is pitiful! Ting-a-ling,
ting-a-ling, ting-a-ling! Oh my God, they'll leave me here to die!
Ting-a-ling, ting-a-ling, ting-a-ling!

Scene ii:
TOINETTE, ARGAN

TOINETTE (*as she enters*): I'm coming.

ARGAN: Ah! Damned hussy, you worthless good-for-nothing –

TOINETTE (*pretending to have bumped her head*): Bother you and your
impatience! You make everybody rush around so much that now
I've gone and banged my head on the corner of a shutter.

ARGAN (*furious*): Oh, you no-good –

TOINETTE (*interrupting to prevent him carrying on, cries out in pain*): Ow!

ARGAN: It's a –

TOINETTE: Ow!

ARGAN: It's a whole hour –

TOINETTE: Ow!

ARGAN: You left me –

TOINETTE: Ow!

ARGAN: Be quiet you wretch, so I can give you a good telling off!

TOINETTE: My word! I like that! After what I've just done to myself?

ARGAN: You've had me bawling myself hoarse, you wicked girl!

TOINETTE: And you've made me bump my head and that's just as bad,
so I reckon we're quits.

ARGAN: What? You cheeky –

TOINETTE: You tell me off and I'll cry.

ARGAN: Leaving me alone like that, you –

TOINETTE: Ow!

ARGAN: You minx, you'd –

TOINETTE: Ow!

ARGAN: What! Aren't I even going to have the pleasure of telling you
off?

TOINETTE: Tell me off as much as you like, it's no odds to me.

ARGAN: But you're stopping me, you hussy, by interrupting all the time.

TOINETTE: If you're going to have the fun of telling me off, I'm going to enjoy having a good cry. Each to his own. It's only fair! Ow!

ARGAN: Oh, I can see I'm going to have to put up with it. Take this away hussy, take it away. (*Argan gives her his papers and counters and gets up out of his chair.*) Did my treatment today work all right?

TOINETTE: Treatment?

ARGAN: My injection. Did I pass much bile?

TOINETTE: Good heavens, I keep well out of that sort of thing. It's up to Monsieur Fleurant to poke his nose into all that. He gets paid for it.

ARGAN: Make sure they've got the hot water ready for the one I'm due to have shortly.

TOINETTE: Your Monsieur Fleurant and that Monsieur Purgon are having a fine time with your carcass. They've got their hooks into you and they'll milk you dry. I'd like to know just what's wrong with you that you need all these medicines.

ARGAN: Hold your tongue you ignoramus! Who are you to question doctor's orders? Tell them to send my daughter Angélique to me. I've something to tell her.

TOINETTE: She's coming of her own accord. She must have guessed what you were thinking.

Scene iii:
ANGÉLIQUE, TOINETTE, ARGAN

ARGAN: Come over here Angélique, you've come at the right moment. I wanted to talk to you.

ANGÉLIQUE: I'm all attention.

ARGAN: Wait. Give me my stick. (*He hurries off to answer a call of nature.*) I'll be back in a minute.

TOINETTE (*teasingly*): Go on sir, hurry. Monsieur Fleurant's keeping us busy.

Scene iv:
ANGÉLIQUE, TOINETTE

ANGÉLIQUE (*with a languishing look and confiding tone*): Toinette!

TOINETTE: What?

ANGÉLIQUE: Look at me.

TOINETTE: Well? I'm looking.

ANGÉLIQUE: Toinette!

TOINETTE: What do you mean, 'Toinette'?

ANGÉLIQUE: Can't you guess what I want to talk about?

TOINETTE: I've a fair idea – it's that young man of yours. For the best part of a week we've talked about nothing else. You're never happy unless you're talking about him morning, noon and night.

ANGÉLIQUE: If you know that, why don't you start first and spare me the bother of bringing you round to the subject?

TOINETTE: You don't give me time. You're so keen on the topic that it's difficult to get in first.

ANGÉLIQUE: I admit I never get tired of talking about him and I'm only too glad of any opportunity to open my heart to you. But tell me Toinette, you don't blame me for feeling about him the way I do?

TOINETTE: Not at all.

ANGÉLIQUE: Is it wrong of me to surrender to such delicate sentiments?

TOINETTE: I'm not saying that it is.

ANGÉLIQUE: Would you want me to be indifferent to his tender protestations of the passionate love he feels for me?

TOINETTE: God forbid!

ANGÉLIQUE: Tell me, do you think, as I do, that there's something providential, something like destiny, in the unexpected way we met?

TOINETTE: Oh yes.

ANGÉLIQUE: Don't you think the way he rushed to my defence, though he'd never set eyes on me before, was the action of a gentleman?

TOINETTE: Yes.

ANGÉLIQUE: That no one else would have acted more chivalrously?

TOINETTE: I do.

ANGÉLIQUE: And that he couldn't have behaved more beautifully?

TOINETTE: Oh certainly.

ANGÉLIQUE: Don't you think Toinette that he's ever so handsome?

TOINETTE: Absolutely.

ANGÉLIQUE: That he has the most attractive way with him?

TOINETTE: No doubt about it.

ANGÉLIQUE: That there's something noble in everything he says and does?

TOINETTE: Unquestionably.

ANGÉLIQUE: And no one could talk more lovingly to me?

TOINETTE: True.

ANGÉLIQUE: And that there's nothing more vexatious than the close watch they keep on me, which prevents any exchange of the true love that Heaven has placed in both our hearts?

TOINETTE: Quite so.

ANGÉLIQUE: But, dear Toinette, do you think he loves me as much as he says?

TOINETTE: Ah! now that's where sometimes you need to tread carefully. Real love and pretending are very hard to tell apart. I've known some pretty good play-actors in that line.

ANGÉLIQUE: Oh Toinette, whatever do you mean? Oh dear, is it possible he can talk the way he does and not be telling me the truth?

TOINETTE: Whichever it is, you'll soon find out. The letter he wrote to you yesterday saying he'd made up his mind to ask for your hand is a quick way of letting you know whether he's sincere or not. It'll be a good test.

ANGÉLIQUE: Oh Toinette! If he deceives me I'll never believe another man as long as I live.

TOINETTE: Here's your father coming back.

Scene v:
ARGAN, ANGÉLIQUE, TOINETTE

ARGAN (*sits in his chair*): Right then my girl, I've got some news for you, something perhaps you weren't expecting. I've received an offer for your hand in marriage. What the . . . ? You're laughing? The word marriage tickles your sense of humour does it? There's nothing makes young women giggle more. Ah Nature, Nature! From what I see my girl, there's no need to ask you if you want to get married.

ANGÉLIQUE: It's my duty father to do whatever you tell me to.

ARGAN: I'm very pleased to have such an obedient daughter. So it's all settled. I've already promised he shall have you.

ANGÉLIQUE: Father, I must follow your wishes unquestioningly.

ARGAN: My wife, I mean your stepmother, wanted me to put you into a convent along with your little sister Louison. She's been set on the idea from the start.

TOINETTE (*aside*): The old cat has her reasons.

ARGAN: She didn't want to agree to the marriage, but I got my way and I've given my word.

ANGÉLIQUE: Oh father, I'm so grateful for all your kindness!

TOINETTE: In all honesty I'm relieved about this. It's the most sensible thing you ever did in your life.

ARGAN: I haven't seen the young man yet, but I've been told I shall be pleased with him, and you too.

ANGÉLIQUE: You can be sure I shall father.

ARGAN: What? Have you met him?

ANGÉLIQUE: Now that your consent permits me to open my heart to you, I won't hesitate to say that we met by chance a week ago, and the fact that you've been asked for my hand is the result of our having fallen in love with each other at first sight.

ARGAN: No one said anything about that, but I'm very pleased. If that's how things stand, so much the better. I was told he's a fine, good-looking young man.

ANGÉLIQUE: Yes father.

ARGAN: Tall.

ANGÉLIQUE: Oh yes.

ARGAN: Pleasant manner.

ANGÉLIQUE: Certainly.

ARGAN: Handsome.

ANGÉLIQUE: Very.

ARGAN: Steady, comes of a good family.

ANGÉLIQUE: Absolutely.

ARGAN: Very trustworthy.

ANGÉLIQUE: As trustworthy as there is.

ARGAN: Speaks good Greek and Latin.

ANGÉLIQUE: I don't know about that.

ARGAN: He's to graduate in medicine three days from now.

ANGÉLIQUE: Is he father?

ARGAN: Yes. Didn't he tell you?

ANGÉLIQUE: No indeed. Who told you that?

ARGAN: Monsieur Purgon.

ANGÉLIQUE: Does Monsieur Purgon know him?

ARGAN: What a question! Of course he knows him. He's his nephew.

ANGÉLIQUE: Cléante is Monsieur Purgon's nephew?

ARGAN: Who's Cléante? Aren't we talking about the young man who wants to marry you?

ANGÉLIQUE: Yes, of course.

ARGAN: Well then! He's Monsieur Purgon's nephew, son of his brother-in-law Monsieur Diafoirus, the doctor. The son's name is Thomas, not Cléante, and we arranged the marriage between us this morning — Monsieur Purgon, Monsieur Fleurant and myself. His father is bringing my future son-in-law to see me tomorrow. What's the matter? You look thunderstruck.

ANGÉLIQUE: Father, it's because I realize that you've been talking about one person and I thought you meant someone else.

TOINETTE: Oh sir! How could you have come up with such a ridiculous plan? With all the money you've got, you aren't going to let your daughter marry a doctor?

ARGAN: Yes I am. And what's it got to do with you, you hussy? The cheek of the woman!

TOINETTE: Heavens! Calm down! You start on the name-calling at the drop of a hat! Can't we talk sensibly without flying off the handle? There now, let's discuss this calmly. What are your reasons, may I ask, for wanting a marriage such as this?

ARGAN: My reason is that, being infirm and unwell, I want a son-in-law and close associates who are all doctors, so I can depend on having proper attention when I'm ill, and a steady supply of the medicines I need within the family, and ditto consultations and treatments.

TOINETTE: Well now, that's certainly a reason and it's nice to be discussing it calmly among ourselves. But sir, put your hand on your heart: are you ill?

ARGAN: What do you mean hussy, am I ill? The impudence! Am I ill indeed!

TOINETTE: All right sir, very well, you're ill. Let's not argue about it. Yes, you are very ill, I agree with you there, and more ill than you think. That's settled. But your daughter ought to be marrying to suit herself, and since she isn't ill, there's no need to provide her with a doctor.

ARGAN: It's for my sake that I'm giving her to a doctor. Any daughter with proper feelings would be only too glad to marry a man who could help look after her father's health.

TOINETTE: Merciful heavens sir, do you want a bit of friendly advice?

ARGAN: What advice?

TOINETTE: Think no more of this marriage.

ARGAN: Why not?

TOINETTE: Because your daughter will never agree to it.

ARGAN: She won't agree?

TOINETTE: No.

ARGAN: My daughter?

TOINETTE: Yes, your daughter. She'll tell you she won't have anything to do with Monsieur Diafoirus, nor his son, Thomas Diafoirus, nor with the whole tribe of Diafoiruses.

ARGAN: But I have a great deal to do with them, besides which, the match is more advantageous than you think. Monsieur Diafoirus's son is his sole heir. Moreover, Monsieur Purgon, who has no wife and no children, will leave his whole estate to the heirs of this marriage – and Monsieur Purgon is a man with over eight thousand a year!

TOINETTE: He must have killed off an awful lot of patients to have made all that money.

ARGAN: Eight thousand's a tidy amount, and that's not counting what his father's got.

TOINETTE: All that's very well sir, but I stick to my point. My advice to you, just between the two of us, is to find her another husband. She's not cut out to be Madame Diafoirus.

ARGAN: Well I'm determined she shall be.

TOINETTE: Oh come, don't say that.

ARGAN: How do you mean, 'don't say that'?

TOINETTE: No, you mustn't.

ARGAN: Why mustn't I say it?

TOINETTE: People will say you don't know what you're talking about.

ARGAN: They can say what they like. But I'm telling you, I want her to keep the word I have given.

TOINETTE: No, I'm sure she won't.

ARGAN: I'll make her.

TOINETTE: She won't do it, I tell you.

ARGAN: She'll do it – or I'll put her in a convent.

TOINETTE: You will?

ARGAN: I will.

TOINETTE: Right then.

ARGAN: What do you mean, 'right then'?

TOINETTE: You'll not put her in any convent.

ARGAN: I'll not put her in a convent?

TOINETTE: No.

ARGAN: Oh no?

TOINETTE: No.

ARGAN: Pshaw! That's a good one! I won't put my daughter in a convent if I want to?

TOINETTE: I'm telling you, you won't.

ARGAN: Who's going to stop me?

TOINETTE: You yourself.

ARGAN: Me?

TOINETTE: Yes, you'll not have the heart to do it.

ARGAN: Oh yes I will.

TOINETTE: You're not serious.

ARGAN: I'm perfectly serious.

TOINETTE: Your own fatherly feelings will take over.

ARGAN: They won't take over.

TOINETTE: A few tears, her arms around your neck, a 'dear kind papa' tenderly whispered, and it'll be enough to melt your heart.

ARGAN: It won't do anything of the sort.

TOINETTE: Oh yes it will.

ARGAN: I tell you I won't back down.

TOINETTE: Fiddlesticks!

ARGAN: Don't you say fiddlesticks to me!

TOINETTE: Good heavens, I know you. You're naturally very kind-hearted.

ARGAN (*losing his temper*): I'm not kind-hearted! I can be very nasty when I want to.

TOINETTE: Keep calm sir, you're forgetting that you're ill.

ARGAN: I absolutely order her to get ready to marry the husband I've chosen.

TOINETTE: And I shall forbid her to do anything of the sort.

ARGAN: What are things coming to? The audacity! An insolent servant talking back to her master like this!

TOINETTE: When a master doesn't stop to think what he's doing, a servant with any sense is entitled to put him right.

ARGAN (*running after her*): Oh, the nerve of the woman! I'll murder you!

TOINETTE (*dodging him*): It's my duty to try and put a stop to anything that'll give you a bad name.

ARGAN (*furious, stick in hand, chasing her round his chair*): Come here! I'll teach you how to talk to me!

TOINETTE (*on the opposite side of the chair from Argan*): I'm only doing my duty, trying to prevent you from making a fool of yourself.

ARGAN: Hussy!

TOINETTE: No, I'll never agree to this marriage.

ARGAN: Vixen!

TOINETTE: I don't want her to marry your Thomas Diafoirus.

ARGAN: Baggage!

TOINETTE: And she'll take more notice of me than of you.

ARGAN: Angélique, won't you stop the minx for me?

ANGÉLIQUE: Oh father, don't make yourself ill.

ARGAN: If you don't stop her, I shall give you a father's curse.

TOINETTE: And if she does what you tell her, I'll disown her.

ARGAN (*collapsing on to his chair, worn out by chasing her*): Ah! I'm done for. This is enough to finish me off altogether.

Scene vi:

BÉLINE, ANGÉLIQUE, TOINETTE, ARGAN

ARGAN: Ah! come in wife, come here.

BÉLINE: Whatever's the matter, my dear?

ARGAN: Come and rescue me.

BÉLINE: What on earth is all this fuss then, sweetheart?

ARGAN: Darling girl!

BÉLINE: Darling boy!

ARGAN: They've been getting me all worked up.

BÉLINE: There there! Poor little hubby! What's been going on, dear heart?

ARGAN: It's that brazen Toinette of yours. She's getting cheekier than ever.

BÉLINE: Don't go upsetting yourself.

ARGAN: She made me lose my temper, sweetheart.

BÉLINE: There there, darling boy.

ARGAN: For the last hour she's been thwarting me in what I want to do.

BÉLINE: Now now, calm down.

ARGAN: She had the cheek to say I'm not ill at all!

BÉLINE: The impudence!

ARGAN: You know, dear heart, how I am.

BÉLINE: Yes, dear heart, she's wrong.

ARGAN: My love, the minx will be the death of me.

BÉLINE: Now then, now then.

ARGAN: She's the cause of all the bile I make.

BÉLINE: Don't upset yourself so.

ARGAN: I don't know how many times I've asked you to get rid of her.

BÉLINE: Good heavens my dear, there aren't any maids and valets who don't have their faults. We are sometimes forced to put up with their bad side because of their good points. She's clever, conscientious, hard-working and, above all, she's honest. You know how careful we have to be nowadays with the servants we employ. Toinette, where are you?

TOINETTE (*leaving Angélique, who now goes out, with whom she has been talking in a corner of Argan's room*): Madame?

BÉLINE: Why have you been making my husband lose his temper?

TOINETTE (*sweetly*): Me Madame? Dear me! I don't know what you mean. I always do my best to please the master in everything.

ARGAN: Oh, the deceitful creature!

TOINETTE: He told us he was intending to let his daughter marry the son of Monsieur Diafoirus. I told him I thought it was a very good match for her, but I reckoned he'd be better off putting her in a convent.

BÉLINE: There's no great harm in that. Actually, I think she's right.

ARGAN: Oh! You believe her my dear? But she's a good-for-nothing. She said no end of insolent things to me.

BÉLINE: Well, of course I believe you my dear. Now pull yourself together. Toinette: if you ever annoy my husband again, I'll turn you out of this house. Now, hand me his fur-lined coat and his pillows and I'll make him comfortable in his chair. (*To Argan*) You're in a terrible state. Pull your night cap down over your ears. There's nothing like letting the air in through your ears for giving you a cold.

ARGAN: Ah, my dear! I'm so grateful to you for taking such good care of me.

BÉLINE (*arranging the pillows around Argan*): Get up so I can put this under you. We'll put this one here for support, and this one at the other side. We'll have this one at your back and this one to keep your head up.

TOINETTE: And this one to keep the dew off you (*jamming a pillow down roughly on his head and running off*).

ARGAN (*jumping up in a rage and throwing the pillows after Toinette*): Ah, you wretch! Are you trying to smother me?

BÉLINE: There there! What's the matter now?

ARGAN (*breathless, collapsing in his chair*): Oh! Ooh! Ooooh! I can't bear it!

BÉLINE: But why are you getting so worked up? She was only trying to help.

ARGAN: My love, you have no idea what a nasty creature the hussy can be. Oh! She's made me feel quite ill. It'll take more than eight doses of medicine and a dozen irrigations to set me to rights again.

BÉLINE: There there, my dear, do try to calm yourself.

ARGAN: My sweet, you're all the consolation I have.

BÉLINE: Poor boy!

ARGAN: I'd like to try to acknowledge the fact that you love me. My dear, I intend, as I was telling you, to make my will.

BÉLINE: Please don't let's talk about that, dear heart. I can't stand the thought of it. The very word 'will' makes me tremble with misery.

ARGAN: But I told you to speak to your lawyer about it.

BÉLINE: He's out there. I brought him back with me.

ARGAN: Well let's have him in, my sweet.

BÉLINE: Oh my dear! When you're in love with your husband, as I am, you're in no fit state to think about that sort of thing.

Scene vii:

NOTARY, BÉLINE, ARGAN

ARGAN: Come in Monsieur de Bonnefoi, do come in. Please sit down. Sir, my wife told me you were a man of probity and enjoyed her entire confidence, so I asked her to speak to you about a will I wish to have drawn up.

BÉLINE: I can't, I just can't talk about such things.

NOTARY: She has explained your intentions sir, and what provision you intend to make for her, but I must advise you that in this matter you cannot leave anything to your wife in your will.

ARGAN: Why ever not?

NOTARY: It's contrary to customary law. If you lived in an area where statutory law prevailed then it could be done. But in Paris and those areas where customary law is in force, it cannot, and any such provision would be null and void. The only arrangement a lawfully married man and wife can make for each other's benefit is by mutual gift during their lifetime, and then only if there is no issue whether of that marriage or of a previous one of either spouse, at the time of the demise of the first spouse.

ARGAN: Well your customary law is an ass if it says a man can't leave anything to a wife who loves him tenderly and takes such good care of him! I'd like to consult my lawyer as to what I can do about it.

NOTARY: It's not lawyers that you should go to see. They usually take a strict view of these matters and consider it a serious crime to dispose of anything to the detriment of the law. They are men who make difficulties and are quite ignorant of the ways that exist to allow us to do whatever we like with a clear conscience. There are other people you can consult who are much more accommodating and have ways of quietly getting round the law, who can obtain authorization for what is not legal, smooth out the wrinkles in a case and find a means of evading customary law through some indirect application. Where should we be if it weren't so? There must be some flexibility, or otherwise we'd never get anything done and our job wouldn't be worth the candle.

ARGAN: My wife was right, sir, when she said you were a very astute and straightforward man. How, pray, should I set about giving my estate to my wife and ensuring that my children get nothing?

NOTARY: How should you set about it? You can choose a close friend of your wife, discreetly mark you, make a will bequeathing whatever you can to him, and subsequently he would transfer it back to her. Alternatively, you can contract a large number of debts, all entirely above board, with sundry creditors who would then allow your wife to obtain money against their names and also provide her with a statement to the effect that in acting thus they were only wishing to be kind. Or again, you could during your lifetime make over to her ready cash and any bearer bonds that you may have to hand.

BÉLINE: Heavens! you mustn't bother your head with all that. If anything happens to you, dearest, I shan't want to go on living.

ARGAN: Sweetheart!

BÉLINE: Yes, my dear, if I were so unfortunate as to lose you . . .

ARGAN: My dear wife!

BÉLINE: Life would have no meaning for me.

ARGAN: My love!

BÉLINE: And I should follow you to the grave to show how much I loved you.

ARGAN: Dearest, you're breaking my heart. Please, don't take on so.

NOTARY: This isn't quite the time for tears. We haven't got to that stage yet.

BÉLINE: Ah sir, you don't know what it is to have a husband you love dearly.

ARGAN: The only regret I'd have, if I did die my dear, is that I have no child by you. Monsieur Purgon told me he could make me able to father one.

NOTARY: There's still time for that.

ARGAN: I must make my will, my love, the way the gentleman says. But, as a precaution, I intend to let you have the twenty thousand livres in gold which I keep behind the panelling in my dressing-room, plus two bearer bills which are due, one from Monsieur Damon and one from Monsieur Géronte.

BÉLINE: No no, I don't want anything to do with this. How much did you say you had in your closet?

ARGAN: Twenty thousand livres, my love.

BÉLINE: Please don't talk to me about money! And how much are the bills for?

ARGAN: One, my sweet, is for four thousand and the other six.

BÉLINE: All the money in the world is nothing to me, dearest, compared with you.

NOTARY: Do you wish us to proceed with drawing up the will?

ARGAN: Yes sir. But we shall be more comfortable in my little study. Help me along there my love.

BÉLINE: Come on, my poor little boy.

Scene viii:
ANGÉLIQUE, TOINETTE

TOINETTE (*entering with Angélique*): They're with a notary and I heard the word 'will' mentioned. Your stepmother isn't letting the grass grow under her feet and I don't doubt she's pushing your father into some plot to undermine your interests.

ANGÉLIQUE: He can give his money to whoever he likes as long as he does not give my heart away. You heard what dreadful plans he has for me Toinette. Please don't abandon me in my hour of need.

TOINETTE: Me, desert you? I'd rather die. Your stepmother has taken me into her confidence as a way of getting me on her side, but it won't do her any good I've never liked her and I've always been behind you. Leave it to me. I'll do everything I can to help. But if I'm to be of any real use I'm going to have to change my tactics, disguise the feelings I have for you and pretend to go along with the wishes of your father and your stepmother.

ANGÉLIQUE: And do try, I beg you, to get word to Cléante about this marriage they've arranged.

TOINETTE: There's only one person I can rely on to do that for me: the old money-lender, Punchinello. I'm walking out with him. It'll cost me a few buttery words but I don't mind spending them on you. It's too late for today, but tomorrow morning, first thing, I'll send for him and he'll be delighted to –

BÉLINE: Toinette!

TOINETTE: She's calling. Good-night. Count on me.

The scene changes to a street.

First Interlude

Enter Punchinello, come to serenade his love under cover of night. He is interrupted first by violins upon which he vents his irritation, and then by the Watch which is made up of musicians and dancers.

PUNCHINELLO: O love, love, love, love. Poor Punchinello, what tomfool idea have you gone and got into your head now? What are you playing at, crazy fool that you are? You leave your business and let your affairs take care of themselves. You've stopped eating, you hardly drink, you can't sleep at night, and all for what? For a she-dragon, an out-and-out she-dragon, a she-devil who puts you in your place and makes fun of everything you can find to say to her. But it's no good trying to understand it. If it's love you want, well you've got to be as mad as the rest of 'em. It's not exactly the best thing at my time of life, but what can I do about that? You can't always be sensible when you want to and old heads can be turned as easily as young ones.

I'm here to see if I can't melt my tigress with a serenade. There are times when there's nothing so affecting as a lover singing his tale of woe at the hinges and bolts of his mistress's door. (*Picking up his lute*) Here's what I'll use to accompany my voice. O night, lovely night! waft my plaintive cry to the pillow of my unyielding mistress. (*He sings.*)

Notte e dì v'amo e v'adoro,	*Night and day I love and adore you,*
Cerco un sì per mio ristoro.	*I await your 'yes' and do implore you.*
Ma se voi dite di nò,	*But if a 'no' is your reply,*
Bell' ingrata, io morirò.	*Fair tormentor, I shall die.*
Fra la speranza	*Though by hope sustained*
S'afflige il cuore,	*A heart continues pained,*
In lontananza	*For when you're far away*
Consuma l'hore.	*The hours slowly pass each day.*
Si dolce inganno	*The sweetest dream or reverie*
Che mi figura	*That seems to promise me*

Breve l'affanno	*A rapid end to my suffering*
Ahi! troppo dura,	*Is too long enduring,*
Cosi per tropp'amar languisco e muoro.	*For, too much loving, I pine, I'm dying.*

Notte e dì v'amo e v'adoro,	*Night and day I love and adore you,*
Cerco un sì per mio ristoro.	*I await your 'yes' and do implore you.*

Ma se voi dite di nò,	*But if a 'no' is your reply,*
Bell' ingrata, io morirò.	*Fair tormentor, I shall die.*

Se non dormite	*If you cannot sleep and find repose*
Almen pensate	*Then give some thought to all my woes*
Alle ferite	*And to the wounding dart*
Ch'al cuor mi fate.	*You've shot quite through my heart.*

Deh! almen fingete	*Ah! but at least please feign*
Per mio conforto;	*To ease my pain;*
Se m'uccidete,	*If to kill me you are set,*
D'haver il torto:	*Please feel some small regret:*
Vostra pietà mi scemerà il martoro.	*Your pity will a martyr comfort yet.*

Notte e dì v'amo e v'adoro,	*Night and day I love and adore you,*
Cerco un sì per mio ristoro.	*I await your 'yes' and do implore you.*

Ma se voi dite di nò,	*But if a 'no' is your reply,*
Bell' ingrata, io morirò.	*Fair tormentor, I shall die.*

An old woman appears at the window and ridicules Punchinello, replying as follows:

Zerbinetti, ch' ogn' hor con finti sguardi	*Gallants all, who ever look with cheating eye*

Mentiti desiri	*With desires that lie*
Fallaci sospiri	*And deceitfully sigh*
Accenti buggiardi,	*And false words cry,*
Di fede vi pregiate.	*You say your love is true.*
Ah! che non m'ingannate	*Ah! deceive me? That you shall*
	not do
Che già so per prova	*For I already know of old*
Ch'in voi non si trova	*There is in your heart so cold*
Costanza nè fede,	*Neither faithful love nor true,*
Oh! quanto è pazza colei che vi	*And foolish she who would trust*
crede!	*in you!*
Quei sguardi languidi	*Those looks so languishing*
Non m'innamorano,	*No spark of love inspire,*
Quei sospir fervidi	*Those sighs so burning*
Più non m'infiammano;	*Will not light my fire;*
Vel giuro a fè.	*This I swear and do confess.*
Zerbino misero:	*Worthless that you be:*
Del vostro piangere	*Whatever your distress*
Il mio cor libero	*My heart flies free*
Vuol sempre ridere.	*And mocks what you profess.*
Credet' a me	*Believe me now, be told*
Che già so per prova	*That I already know of old*
Ch'in voi non si trova	*There is in your heart so cold*
Costanza nè fede,	*Neither faithful love nor true,*
Oh! quanto è pazza colei che vi	*And foolish she who would trust*
crede!	*in you!*

Violins strike up.

PUNCHINELLO: What damned music is that? It's interrupting me.
   The violins continue playing.

PUNCHINELLO: Be quiet there! Stop those fiddles! Leave me to lament
   the cruelty of my unbending mistress in peace!
   The violins continue playing.

PUNCHINELLO: Be quiet, I tell you. I want to sing.
   The violins continue playing.

PUNCHINELLO: Will you be quiet!
   The violins continue playing.

PUNCHINELLO: Oho!

The violins continue playing.

PUNCHINELLO: Aha!

The violins continue playing.

PUNCHINELLO: Is this a joke?

The violins continue playing.

PUNCHINELLO: Oh, what a din!

The violins continue playing.

PUNCHINELLO: To the devil with you!

The violins continue playing.

PUNCHINELLO: I'm starting to lose my temper!

The violins continue playing.

PUNCHINELLO: Will you be quiet? (*The music stops.*) Ah! Heaven be praised for that.

The violins start up again.

PUNCHINELLO: Not again!

The violins continue playing.

PUNCHINELLO: Damn those fiddles!

The violins continue playing.

PUNCHINELLO: What idiotic music this is!

The violins continue playing.

PUNCHINELLO (*singing along derisively with the violins*): Tra la la, tra la la.

The violins continue playing.

PUNCHINELLO: Tra la la, tra la la.

The violins continue playing.

PUNCHINELLO: Tra la la, tra la la, tra la la.

The violins continue playing.

PUNCHINELLO: Tra la la, tra la la, tra la la.

The violins continue playing.

PUNCHINELLO: Tra la la, tra la la, tra la la.

The violins continue playing.

PUNCHINELLO (*continues mocking with a lute which he only pretends to play, mouthing 'plink, plonk' etc.*): By Jove, this is fun! Please carry on fiddling. I'm enjoying this – it's the best way of shutting them up. Carry on, scrape away! (*The music stops.*) Music never does what you want it to. Now then, let's get down to it. But before I sing I'd better have a little warm-up and play something just to get the tone right. Plink, plonk, plunk. This is no weather for tuning lutes. Plink, plonk, plunk. Plink, plonk, plonk. The strings won't hold in this weather. Plink, plonk, plunk. I can hear something. I'll put the lute down by the door.

ARCHERS OF THE WATCH (*patrolling the street, hurrying to the noise they can hear and singing throughout*): Who goes there? who goes there?

PUNCHINELLO (*aside*): Who the devil's that? Is that the fashion nowadays – talking to music?

ARCHERS: Who goes there? who goes there? who goes there?

PUNCHINELLO (*afraid*): Me, me, me.

ARCHERS: Who goes there? Say, who goes there?

PUNCHINELLO: Me I say, it's me.

ARCHERS: Who is me? Who is me?

PUNCHINELLO: Me, me, me, me, me!

ARCHERS: Your name, your name, your name without delay.

PUNCHINELLO (*pretending to be brave*): My name is – go hang yourselves.

ARCHERS: This way, comrades, and do or die:
Seize whoever gave that rude reply!

All the archers come on and while they look for Punchinello there is dancing to the music of violins.

Ballet

PUNCHINELLO: Who goes there? (*Violins and dancing.*)

PUNCHINELLO: Who are these rogues I can hear? (*Violins and dancing.*)

PUNCHINELLO: Ayee! (*Violins and dancing.*)

PUNCHINELLO: Hello! Where are my footmen and my servants? (*Violins and dancing.*)

PUNCHINELLO: S'death! (*Violins and dancing.*)

PUNCHINELLO: S'blood! (*Violins and dancing.*)

PUNCHINELLO: I'll flatten them! (*Violins and dancing.*)

PUNCHINELLO (*calling his servants*): Champagne, Poitevin, Picard, Basque, Breton! (*Violins and dancing.*)

PUNCHINELLO: Bring me my musketoon. (*Violins and dancing.*)

PUNCHINELLO (*pretends to fire a shot with a pistol*): Bang!
They all fall down then take to their heels.

PUNCHINELLO (*derisively*): Ha ha ha ha! I scared them. They must be a silly lot to be as afraid of me as I am of others! My word, cheek is all you need in this world. If I hadn't come on as strong as a lord, if I hadn't outfaced them, they'd have got me for sure! Ha ha ha!

The archers return and, hearing what he says, seize him by the collar.

ARCHERS (*singing*): We have got him, hold him tight,

Bring a lantern for some light.

Ballet

All the archers come on with lanterns.

ARCHERS (*singing*): Traitor, scoundrel, so it's you,

Villain, gaol-bird, rogue audacious

Varlet, thief and fraud mendacious,

You dared to scare us through and through!

PUNCHINELLO: Good sirs, it was because I'd taken drink.

ARCHERS: No, no, no, we'll hear no reason,

We will teach you what to think.

Seize him, march him off to prison.

PUNCHINELLO: Gentlemen, I'm no thief.

ARCHERS: Off to prison.

PUNCHINELLO: I'm a citizen of this town.

ARCHERS: Off to prison.

PUNCHINELLO: What have I done?

ARCHERS: Seize him, march him off to prison.

PUNCHINELLO: Gentleman, let me go.

ARCHERS: No.

PUNCHINELLO: I implore you.

ARCHERS: No.

PUNCHINELLO: I beg you.

ARCHERS: No.

PUNCHINELLO: Please!

ARCHERS: No, no.

PUNCHINELLO: Gentlemen . . .

ARCHERS: No, no no.

PUNCHINELLO: If you please.

ARCHERS: No, no.

PUNCHINELLO: For pity's sake?

ARCHERS: No, no.

PUNCHINELLO: For heaven's sake?

ARCHERS: No, no.

PUNCHINELLO: Mercy, mercy!

ARCHERS: No, no, no, we'll hear no reason,
           We will teach you what to think.
           Seize him, march him off to prison.

PUNCHINELLO: Is there no way, gentleman, of touching your hearts?

ARCHERS: There's an easy way for those who know,
           We're less inhuman than you think,
           Give us money for a drink
           And then we'll let you go, yes go.

PUNCHINELLO: Alas, good sirs, I assure you I haven't got a penny on me.

ARCHERS: If you've got no cash to hand us,
           You must choose, and please be quick,
           Twixt thirty good backhanders
           And a dozen lashes with a stick.

PUNCHINELLO: If it's absolutely necessary for me to have the one or the other, I'll choose the backhanders.

ARCHERS: Come, make ready – and no stalling:
           Count the blows as they are falling.

Ballet

The archers dance and strike him in time to the music.

PUNCHINELLO: One, and two, three and four, five and six, seven and eight, nine and ten, eleven and twelve and thirteen and fourteen and fifteen.

ARCHERS: Aha! he tried to dodge one then,
           The forfeit is – begin again!

PUNCHINELLO: Oh sirs, my poor head has taken as much as it can stand – you've made it swell up like a baked apple. I'd rather have the stick than begin again at the beginning.

ARCHERS: Agreed, if a stick will make you happy
           You shall have it, pretty snappy.

Ballet

The archers dance and beat him in time to the music.

PUNCHINELLO: One, two, three, four, five, six, ouch! ouch! ow! — I can't take any more. Gentlemen, here take the money.

ARCHERS: Oh, what a noble, generous fellow:
      Farewell, farewell, good Punchinello!

PUNCHINELLO: Gentlemen, I give you a very good night.

ARCHERS: Good night, goodnight, good Punchinello!

PUNCHINELLO: Your servant, sirs.

ARCHERS: Good night, goodnight, good Punchinello!

PUNCHINELLO: Your most humble valet.

ARCHERS: Good night, goodnight, good Punchinello!

PUNCHINELLO: Until we meet again.

Ballet

They all dance with delight at the money they have received. The scene changes back to Argan's room.

Act II

Scene i:
TOINETTE, CLÉANTE

TOINETTE: What do you want sir?

CLÉANTE: What do I want?

TOINETTE: Ah! It's you! What a surprise. What have you come here for?

CLÉANTE: To know my destiny, to speak to my lovely Angélique, learn what her feelings are and ask her what she has decided about this disastrous marriage I've just heard about.

TOINETTE: Yes, but you can't come straight out with it like that to Angélique: you've got to be more subtle. You've been told how she's kept under strict guard, not allowed to go out or talk to anyone, and how it was only through the connivance of her old aunt that we were

permitted to go to the theatre where you first fell in love with her
– and we took very good care to say nothing about that little adventure.

CLÉANTE: Yes, and that's why I haven't come as Cléante, openly, as
the man who loves her, but as the friend of her music-master, who
gave me permission to say that he's sent me to replace him.

TOINETTE: Here's her father. Go and wait over there and let me tell
him you're here.

Scene ii:
ARGAN, TOINETTE, CLÉANTE

ARGAN: Monsieur Purgon said I was to walk up and down in my room
every morning, twelve steps this way and twelve steps that way, but
I forgot to ask him if he meant crosswise or lengthways.

TOINETTE: Sir, there's a gentleman –

ARGAN: Not so loud, you good-for-nothing! Your voice goes right
through my head. You just will not remember that you should never
bellow like that at people who are ill.

TOINETTE: Sir, I wanted to tell you –

ARGAN: Not so loud I said.

TOINETTE (*whispers inaudibly*): Sir . . .

ARGAN: What?

TOINETTE (*as before*): I was saying . . .

ARGAN: What are you mumbling?

TOINETTE (*aloud*): I was saying there's a man here wants to speak to
you.

ARGAN: Show him in. (*Toinette beckons to Cléante to come forward.*)

CLÉANTE: Sir . . .

TOINETTE (*sarcastically*): Not so loud, otherwise your voice will go
right through the master's head.

CLÉANTE: Sir, I am delighted to find you up and about and see that
you're feeling better.

TOINETTE (*pretending to be angry*): What do you mean, 'feeling better'?
It's not true – the master's still poorly.

CLÉANTE: I heard he was better and I think he's looking well.

TOINETTE: What do you mean, 'looking well'? The master's looking terrible and whoever told you he's feeling better doesn't know what they're talking about. He's never been worse.

ARGAN: She's right.

TOINETTE: He can get about, sleep, eat and drink like anybody else. But that doesn't mean to say he's not very ill.

ARGAN: That's true.

CLÉANTE: Sir, I'm very sorry to hear it. I was asked to come here by your daughter's singing teacher. He's had to go out of town for a few days and, as I'm a close friend of his, he's sent me as his replacement to continue her lessons in case the interruption makes her forget what she's already learned.

ARGAN: Very well. Call Angélique.

TOINETTE: I think sir it would be better if I showed this gentleman to her room.

ARGAN: No, have her brought here.

TOINETTE: He can't give her a proper lesson unless they're on their own.

ARGAN: Of course he can.

TOINETTE: Sir, it'll only make your ears ring and you mustn't have anything to upset you in the state your in. It'll go right through your head.

ARGAN: Not at all, I like music. I shall enjoy . . . Ah! here she is (*To Toinette*) Go and see if my wife's finished dressing. (*Toinette goes out.*)

Scene iii:

ARGAN, ANGÉLIQUE, CLÉANTE

ARGAN: Come in my girl. Your music-master has gone to the country and this is someone he's sent to give you your lesson instead.

ANGÉLIQUE: Heavens!

ARGAN: What's the matter? What are you so surprised about?

ANGÉLIQUE: It's just . . .

ARGAN: Just what? What's upsetting you like this?

ANGÉLIQUE: It's such a strange coincidence father.

ARGAN: Coincidence?

ANGÉLIQUE: Last night I dreamt I was in a most dreadful predicament and someone who looked exactly like this gentleman came up to me. I asked him to help and he saved me from the danger I was in. So it was surprising to come in here and meet, when I was least expecting it, the very person who'd been in my thoughts all night.

CLÉANTE: It doesn't make me the least unhappy to occupy your thoughts whether waking or dreaming, and I should certainly count myself fortunate indeed if you were really in trouble and considered me worthy of helping you out. There's nothing I wouldn't do to . . .

Scene iv:
TOINETTE, CLÉANTE, ANGÉLIQUE, ARGAN

TOINETTE (*ironically*): My goodness sir, I'm on your side now. I take back everything I said yesterday. Monsieur Diafoirus the Elder and Monsieur Diafoirus the Younger are here; they've come to see you. My, you're going to get a fine son-in-law there! You'll see, he's such a handsome lad, and clever too. He hasn't said more than a couple of words but I'm amazed. Your daughter will be delighted with him.

ARGAN (*to Cléante, who makes as if to go*): Don't go sir. The fact is I'm arranging my daughter's marriage and they've brought her intended along. She's never seen him before.

CLÉANTE: You are extremely kind sir in wishing me to witness such an agreeable meeting.

ARGAN: He's the son of a brilliant doctor and the marriage is to take place in four days.

CLÉANTE: Indeed.

ARGAN: Pass the word on to her music-master so that he can come to the wedding.

CLÉANTE: I won't fail to do so.

ARGAN: I hope you will be able to come too.

CLÉANTE: You really are most kind.

TOINETTE: Come along, make room – here they come.

Scene v:

MONSIEUR DIAFOIRUS, THOMAS DIAFOIRUS,
ARGAN, ANGÉLIQUE, CLÉANTE, TOINETTE

ARGAN (*raising his hand to his hat but not removing it*): Sir, Monsieur Purgon has forbidden me to take my hat off. Being a member of the profession yourself, you'll understand why.

M. DIAFOIRUS: The purpose of all our visits is to bring relief to patients, not to inconvenience them.

ARGAN: Sir, I receive — (*They both speak at the same time, interrupting each other and getting confused.*)

M. DIAFOIRUS: Sir, we've come —

ARGAN: With the greatest pleasure —

M. DIAFOIRUS: My son Thomas and I —

ARGAN: The honour you do me —

M. DIAFOIRUS: To express to you, sir —

ARGAN: And I wish I could —

M. DIAFOIRUS: Our pleasure in —

ARGAN: Have called on you —

M. DIAFOIRUS: The kindness you have shown —

ARGAN: And assured you —

M. DIAFOIRUS: In receiving us —

ARGAN: But you know, sir —

M. DIAFOIRUS: Into the honour, sir —

ARGAN: That a poor invalid —

M. DIAFOIRUS: Of becoming connected by marriage —

ARGAN: Who has no alternative —

M. DIAFOIRUS: And to assure you —

ARGAN: But to tell you here and now —

M. DIAFOIRUS: That in all matters relating to our profession —

ARGAN: That he will take every opportunity —

M. DIAFOIRUS: As, indeed, in all others —

ARGAN: Of showing you, sir —

M. DIAFOIRUS: We are always ready, sir —

ARGAN: That he is at your service —

M. DIAFOIRUS: To demonstrate our zeal. (*Turning to his son*) Come Thomas, step forward and pay your respects.

THOMAS (*a great booby, fresh out of medical school, who does everything clumsily and at the wrong moment*): Is it the correct thing to start with the father?

M. DIAFOIRUS: Yes.

THOMAS: Sir, in you I come to salute, acknowledge, cherish and revere a second father – but a second father to whom I make bold to say I am more indebted than to my founding father. He begot me, but you have chosen me. He took me to his bosom out of necessity, but you have accepted me out of kindness. My kinship with him is a product of the body, but with you it is the result of a deliberate act of your will. And so, inasmuch as the faculties mental are superior to the faculties corporeal, so am I more deeply in your debt and likewise esteem the more precious our future affiliation, in the matter of which I come today to offer you in advance my most humble and most submissive respects.

TOINETTE: Thank God for universities which turn out such clever young men!

THOMAS: Was that all right papa?

M. DIAFOIRUS: *Optime.*

ARGAN (*to Angélique*): Come along, greet this gentleman.

THOMAS: Do I kiss her?

M. DIAFOIRUS: Yes, yes.

THOMAS (*to Angélique*): Madame, it was meet and right that Heaven should have bestowed on you the name of stepmother, since –

ARGAN: She's not my wife. That's my daughter you're talking to.

THOMAS: Then where's your wife?

ARGAN: She's coming.

THOMAS: Do I wait until she gets here papa?

M. DIAFOIRUS: You can pay your compliments to the young lady in the meantime.

THOMAS: Mademoiselle, even as the statue of Memnon[8] once emitted a harmonious sound when illumined by the first rays of each new sun, so do I find myself moved by sweetest joy when the sun of your beauty rises. Even as the naturalists observe that the flower named heliotrope turns ever to face the star of day, so shall my heart turn ever, from this day forth, towards the resplendent luminaries which are your lovely eyes, as if towards its own Pole star. Permit me then, Mademoiselle, to offer today upon the altar of your charms a heart which draws breath only, and seeks no other glory than, to be, Mademoiselle, for life, your most humble, most obedient and most faithful servant and spouse.

TOINETTE (*mocking him*): That's where book-learning gets you – it teaches you how to make a fine speech.

ARGAN (*to Cléante*): What do you say to that?

CLÉANTE: The gentleman is doing splendidly. If he's as good a doctor as he is an orator, it would be a pleasure to be one of his patients.

TOINETTE: It would indeed. It would be marvellous if his cures turn out to be as good as his speeches.

ARGAN: Quickly now, bring my chair and seats for everybody. You sit there daughter. As you see, sir, everyone admires your son. I think you're very lucky to have a boy like that.

M. DIAFOIRUS: Sir, it's not because I'm his father, but I can say I have good reason to be pleased with him. Everyone who knows him says he is a most blameless young man. He has never shown the sprightly imagination or the quickness of wit that may be observed in some young men, but it is precisely their absence that I have always taken to augur well for his judgement, a quality indispensable in those who would practise our healing art. When he was a little boy he was never what is termed impish or lively but ever gentle, mild and quiet, never saying anything at all nor playing the games that children play. We had the greatest difficulty in teaching him to read: he was nine before he even knew his letters. 'Never mind,' said I to myself, 'the tree that blossoms late is the tree that gives the best fruit. It is harder to write on marble than on sand, but what is inscribed thereon lasts infinitely longer, and this slowness of understanding, this sluggishness of the imagination are the marks of sound judgement yet to come.' When I sent him to college he found the going hard, but he bore up against every difficulty and his tutors spoke to me warmly of his diligence and hard work. At length, by dint of sheer, dogged persistence, he succeeded splendidly in passing all his examinations, and I can say without boasting that in the two years since taking his bachelor's degree no other student has made his presence more felt than he in the disputations of our Faculty. He has acquired a formidable reputation, and there is no proposition put forward but he'll argue the very opposite to the last ditch. Solid in debate, a very Turk in defence of his principles, he never changes his views and pursues his opinion to the outer limits of logic. But what pleases me most about him, and in this he follows my own example, is his blind attachment to the opinions of ancient authorities and his refusal ever to try to understand or even listen to the arguments in favour of such so-called discoveries of our own age as the circulation of the blood[9] and other notions of similar ilk.

THOMAS (*taking a great scroll from his pocket and presenting it to Angélique*): I have written a thesis against the Circulationists which, with your permission sir, I venture to offer to the young lady as a tribute laid before her of the first fruits of my genius.

ANGÉLIQUE: Sir, it is an article which would be of no use to me. I know nothing of such matters.

TOINETTE: Give it anyway. It's worth having for the picture on the front. It'll look nice in the bedroom.

THOMAS: And with your further permission, sir, I should like to invite her to come one of these days and observe a woman being dissected[10] and hear the dissertation which I am to give on the subject.

TOINETTE: Highly entertaining, I'm sure. Some young men take their young ladies to the theatre. But taking a young lady to a dissection is much more original.

M. DIAFOIRUS: But to continue. As far as the qualities required for marriage and propagation are concerned, I can assure you that, by our medical standards, he is everything that could be desired. He possesses to a praiseworthy degree the proliferating stock and the proper temper suitable for the begetting and procreation of well-constituted infants.

ARGAN: Is it not your intention sir, to promote his career at Court and procure him a post of physician there?

M. DIAFOIRUS: To be quite frank, I have never found practising our profession among people of consequence very congenial. My experience has been that it's better for us to confine our dealings to the general public. They are far less demanding. You don't have to answer to anybody for your actions and, provided you stick to the broad principles of professional practice, you needn't worry about what happens. What's so irritating about persons of consequence is that when they're ill they absolutely insist that their doctor should make them better!

TOINETTE: That's rich. They've got a nerve, expecting you gentlemen to cure them. That's not what you're there for. You're there to collect your fees and prescribe remedies. It's up to them to get better, if they can.

M. DIAFOIRUS: That's quite true. We've no obligation beyond giving people the usual treatment.

ARGAN (*to Cléante*): Sir, let my daughter sing a little something for the company.

CLÉANTE: I was waiting for the order sir. It occurs to me that the young lady and I might entertain your guests by singing a passage from a little opera written quite recently. (*Giving Angélique a sheet of paper*) Here's your part.

ANGÉLIQUE: Mine?

CLÉANTE (*aside to Angélique*): Please don't say no. Let me explain to you about this scene that we have to sing. (*Aloud*) I haven't much of a singing voice myself but we'll get by if I just growl away. Perhaps you would be kind enough to make allowances for me since I shall need to direct the young lady as she sings.

ARGAN: Are the words interesting?

CLÉANTE: Properly speaking, it's a little improvised opera and what you are going to hear is no more than rhythmical prose, or a sort of free verse, such as their feelings and the occasion might suggest to two people talking naturally together and expressing themselves spontaneously.

ARGAN: Very well. Let's hear it.

CLÉANTE (*assuming a shepherd's name, he explains to his mistress how he has continued loving her since they first met; then they both express their thoughts to each other in song*): The substance of the scene is as follows. A certain shepherd is intent upon the attractions of a play that has just begun, when his attention is caught by a disturbance which he hears right next to him. He turns and sees a loud-mouthed, boorish man behaving rudely to a shepherdess. He promptly springs to the defence of a sex to whom all men should defer and, after chastising the bully for his insolence, approaches the shepherdess and sees a young lady with the most lustrous eyes he has ever seen. She sheds tears which he thinks the loveliest in the whole world. 'Ah!' says he to himself, 'how could anyone ever offend such a beautiful creature? What man is there, be he ne'er so barbarous, who could not be moved by such tears?' He wastes no time but dries those tears which he finds so exquisite, and the lovely shepherdess is at equal pains to thank him for the trifling service he has rendered, but in a manner so charming, so tender, so heartfelt that the shepherd finds it quite irresistible. Every word, every glance is a shaft of fire which pierces his very heart. 'How could any deed', says he, 'merit such gratitude so charmingly expressed? And what would a man not do, what service would he not perform or dangers gladly run, to earn, however fleetingly, the sweet, soul-stirring notice of one so grateful?' The play runs its course but he pays no attention, though he regrets it is so short since the final curtain will separate him from his lovely shepherdess. From that first glimpse, from that first moment, he carries away a love as strong as any that takes many years to reach full ripeness. At once he begins to suffer the pangs of absence, the torments of being deprived of what he has so briefly seen. He tries by every means to catch another glimpse of the vision of which he retains, sleeping and waking, so clear an image. But the strict watch kept on his shepherdess means that all his efforts came to nought. Yet so strong is his love that he resolves to ask for the hand in marriage of the adorable creature without whom he cannot live, and he obtains her permission to do so by means of a letter which he cleverly manages to have conveyed to her. But at this very moment he learns that the father of the wondrous girl has arranged for her to wed another and that everything is in train for the celebration of the marriage. Imagine the cruel blow to the affections of the unhappy shepherd! Behold him stricken with mortal sorrow! He cannot bear the frightful thought of seeing the woman he loves in the arms of another man. With the desperation of love, he finds a way of entering his shepherdess's house to discover her feelings and hear from her own lips the fate to which he must resign himself. There he discovers all is made ready and his worst fears realized. There he is witness to the coming of the unworthy rival whom the whim of a father sets up against the tender feelings of his own heart. He observes this man stand, ridiculous but triumphant, beside the lovely shepherdess, like one who knows that he has conquered. The sight fills him with a rage which he can hardly control. He casts despairing glances at the woman he adores, but respect for her father there present prevents him from speaking except with his eyes. At last, casting aside all constraint, his love will not be denied and he addresses her as follows (*singing*):

> Fair Phyllis, in pain and woe I languish.
> Break this cruel silence, end my anguish.
> Tell me, tell me: what is my fate?
> Is it life or death I must now await?

ANGÉLIQUE: Ah, Tircis, sad at heart am I,
> For I'm to wed another, a prospect you deplore.
> I raise my eyes to Heaven and I sigh:
> Do I need do any more?

ARGAN: By Jove, I never knew that girl of mine was clever enough to sing like that, at sight and without hesitating.

CLÉANTE: Alas, fair Phyllis,
> How happy were your Tircis' part
> Could he but claim as his
> A place within your heart!

ANGÉLIQUE: In this fearful plight I'll tell you true:
> The one I love, Tircis, is you.

CLÉANTE: Oh wondrous words, oh farewell pain!
> To hear them I am fain.
> Repeat them, Phyllis, say them once again.

ANGÉLIQUE: 'Tis you, O Tircis, you I love.

CLÉANTE: O Phyllis say that word again.

ANGÉLIQUE: 'Tis you I love.

CLÉANTE: Repeat once more that blithe refrain!

ANGÉLIQUE: 'Tis you, O Tircis, you I love,
> Tircis is the one I love.

CLÉANTE: You gods and kings that look down from on high,
> Can you say you are more blest than I?
> Yet Phyllis there is one thought
> That comes to trouble this transport:
> Is this a rival here they've brought?

ANGÉLIQUE: Oh! I hate him worse than death!
> To me, as to you, his presence is a breath
> Of cruel torment and wretchedness.

CLÉANTE: Yet a father to his suit would make you give assent.

ANGÉLIQUE: I'd sooner die, yes die,
> Than to such a fate consent:
> I'd rather die, yes die!

ARGAN: And what's the father got to say to that?

CLÉANTE: He doesn't say anything.

ARGAN: He must be a fool of a father to let all this nonsense go on and not say anything!

CLÉANTE (*singing*): Oh dearest love –

ARGAN: No no, that's enough of that. Plays like this set a very bad example. This shepherd Tircis is a rogue and Phyllis the shepherdess is a brazen hussy talking like that in front of her father. Show me that paper. Eh? Where are the words you sang? There's only notes written down here.

CLÉANTE: Didn't you know sir that they've recently come up with a method of writing notes and words all in one?

ARGAN: I see. Your servant, sir, I bid you good day. We could have done without your damned opera.

CLÉANTE: I had hoped you'd find it entertaining.

ARGAN: There's nothing entertaining in such silly nonsense. Ah! here comes my wife.

Scene vi:

BÉLINE, ARGAN, TOINETTE, ANGÉLIQUE,
MONSIEUR DIAFOIRUS, THOMAS DIAFOIRUS

ARGAN: My love, this is the son of Monsieur Diafoirus.

THOMAS (*starts to give the speech he has learnt by heart, but his memory fails and he falters*): Madame, it was meet and right that Heaven should have bestowed on you the name of stepmother, since you tread with a step so . . .

BÉLINE: I am delighted, sir, that I came in time to have the honour of meeting you.

THOMAS: Since you tread with a step so . . . tread with a step so . . . Madame, you've interrupted me in the middle of my sentence and now I can't remember . . .

M. DIAFOIRUS: Thomas, keep it for another time.

ARGAN: I wish you'd been here earlier my dear.

TOINETTE: Oh Madame! You've missed a treat not being here for 'the second father', 'the statue of Memnon' and 'the flower called heliotrope'.

ARGAN (*to Angelique*): Now come along my girl, give the gentleman your hand and pledge him your troth as your future husband.

ANGÉLIQUE: Father!

ARGAN: Why 'father'? What's that mean?

ANGÉLIQUE: I beg you, don't be in such a hurry. At least give us the time to get to know each other and see if there grows between us the mutual inclination which is so necessary to make a perfect marriage.

THOMAS: For my own part, Mademoiselle, the inclination is fully grown in my bosom and I need to wait no longer.

ANGÉLIQUE: You may be quick in these matters sir, but I am not, and I will confess that your virtues haven't made all that much impression on me.

ARGAN: Oh well, there'll be plenty of time for that to take care of itself once you're married.

ANGÉLIQUE: Oh father, please give me time. Marriage is a bond which should never be imposed by force. And if this gentleman is a gentleman, he cannot want to have a wife who's been thrust upon him.

THOMAS: *Nego consequentiam*, young lady: I deny your conclusion. I can be a gentleman and still accept you from your father.

ANGÉLIQUE: Forcing yourself on someone against her will is a poor way of making her love you.

THOMAS: We read the ancient writers, Mademoiselle, and learn that it was the custom for young men to carry off by force, from beneath the paternal roof, the maidens who were to be married, so that it would not appear that they were rushing into the arms of a man of their own volition.

ANGÉLIQUE: The ancients, sir, lived in ancient days, but we live in modern times. In this day and age, there is no need for that kind of play-acting. When marriage is congenial to us, we know exactly how to reach out for it and don't need to be dragged to the altar. Be patient. If you love me sir, my wishes should be yours.

THOMAS: They are, Mademoiselle – except where my love is concerned.

ANGÉLIQUE: But the greatest mark of love is the willingness to give way to the wishes of the person you love.

THOMAS: *Distinguo*, Mademoiselle: I make a distinction. Where love is not involved, *concedo*, I concede the point. But where love is concerned, *nego*, I demur.

TOINETTE (*to Angélique*): It's no good arguing. The young gentleman is fresh out of college and he'll always get the better of you. What's the point of resisting and saying no to the honour of being attached to the Faculty?

BÉLINE: Maybe she's got someone else in mind.

ANGÉLIQUE: If I did Madame, it would be one such as reason and propriety would approve.

ARGAN: Dear me! What sort of fool does all this make me look?

BÉLINE: If I were you my dear, I wouldn't force her to marry, but I know what I would do.

ANGÉLIQUE: I know what you mean Madame, and I am quite aware of what excellent plans you have for me. But unfortunately it may turn out that your advice will not be followed.

BÉLINE: That's because sweet, well-brought-up daughters like you scoff at the idea of being obedient and respectful of their father's wishes – which was the way things used to be once upon a time.

ANGÉLIQUE: There are limits to a daughter's duty, Madame. Neither in reason nor in justice can it be made to apply to every circumstance.

BÉLINE: What you mean is that your mind is set on marriage but you want to choose a husband to suit your own fanciful ideas.

ANGÉLIQUE: If my father won't find me a husband I like, then I beg him at least not to force me to marry one I could never love.

ARGAN: Gentleman, I'm very sorry about all this.

ANGÉLIQUE: Everybody has a purpose when they marry. Since I myself am determined to marry for love and intend to regard my husband as a life-long companion, I will admit that I approach marriage with caution. There are women who take a husband as a way of escaping the control of their parents and of acquiring the freedom to do whatever they want. There are others, Madame, for whom marriage is a matter of material interest. They marry with an eye to a settlement, to becoming rich by the death of their husbands, and run callously through a succession of them so that they can get their hands on their estates. Such women don't, of course, stand on ceremony and care very little about the men they marry.

BÉLINE: I see you're very eloquent today. But I'd like to know what you meant by all that.

ANGÉLIQUE: What I meant, Madame, by what I said?

BÉLINE: You are being very silly my girl, and I don't think I can put up with it any longer.

ANGÉLIQUE: What you'd like Madame is to provoke me into being rude to you, but I warn you, I do not intend to give you that satisfaction.

BÉLINE: I never heard such insolence.

ANGÉLIQUE: No Madame, you can say what you like, but it won't work.

BÉLINE: Wherever you go, people raise their eyebrows at your silly pride and brazen effrontery.

ANGÉLIQUE: None of this will do you any good, Madame. I will not let you provoke me, and to remove any hope you might have of succeeding in doing so I shall now remove myself from your sight.

ARGAN: Listen, there's no middle way through this. Either you decide to marry this young man four days from now, or else it's a convent for you. (*To Béline*) Don't be upset, I'll make her comply.

BÉLINE: I'm sorry, but I must go too dear — there's some business in town that I absolutely must attend to. I'll be back soon.

ARGAN: Run along my sweet, and call in at your notary's so that he can press on with, ahem, you know . . .

BÉLINE: Goodbye, dear heart.

ARGAN: Goodbye, my love. (*Béline goes out.*) How that woman loves me — I can hardly believe it.

M. DIAFOIRUS: We must also take our leave of you sir.

ARGAN: Pray sir, won't you tell me how I am?

M. DIAFOIRUS (*feels his pulse*): Now Thomas, take the gentleman's other hand to show him you can take a pulse properly. *Quid dicis?* What do you say?

THOMAS: *Dico*, I say, that the gentleman's pulse is the pulse of a man who is not at all well.

M. DIAFOIRUS: Good.

THOMAS: That it's strongish, though not strong.

M. DIAFOIRUS: Very good.

THOMAS: Falling off a little now.

M. DIAFOIRUS: *Bene.*

THOMAS: Even a touch erratic.

M. DIAFOIRUS: *Optime.*

THOMAS: Which suggests an imbalance in the splenic parenchyma, in other words the spleen.

M. DIAFOIRUS: Excellent.

ARGAN: No. Monsieur Purgon says it's my liver that's not right.

M. DIAFOIRUS: Quite so. When one says parenchyma it covers both because of the sympathetic proximity which links them through the *vas breve*, the *pylorus*, and often the *meatus cholodici*. I expect he's recommended that you eat plenty of roast meats?

ARGAN: No, only boiled.

M. DIAFOIRUS: Quite so. Roast or boiled – same thing. Very prudent prescribing on his part. You couldn't be in better hands.

ARGAN: Tell me sir, how many grains of salt should you put on your egg?

M. DIAFOIRUS: Six, eight, ten and so forth, always even numbers, just as with pills you take odd numbers.

ARGAN: Until we meet again sir.

Scene vii:
BÉLINE, ARGAN

BÉLINE: I've just looked in my love before going out, to let you know that there's something you should keep an eye on. As I was passing the door to Angélique's room, I saw a young man with her. He made himself scarce the moment he saw me.

ARGAN: A young man with my daughter!

BÉLINE: That's right. Your little Louison was with them. She'll be able to tell you more.

ARGAN: Send her in here my love, send her in here. Oh! the baggage. No wonder she was so wilful.

Scene viii:
LOUISON, ARGAN

LOUISON: What do you want papa? Stepmother said you were asking for me.

ARGAN: Yes. Come here. A bit nearer. Turn round. Head up. Look at me. Well?

LOUISON: Well what papa?

ARGAN: So?

LOUISON: What?

ARGAN: Isn't there something you want to tell me?

LOUISON: If you're bored and you'd like me to, I'll tell you the story of the 'Ass's Skin' or 'The Fox and the Crow'. I've just had to learn them.[11]

ARGAN: That's not what I want you to tell me.

LOUISON: What is it then?

ARGAN: Ah slyboots, you know very well what I mean.

LOUISON: Excuse me papa, but I don't.

ARGAN: Is this how you obey me?

LOUISON: What do you mean?

ARGAN: Didn't I say that you were to come and tell me straightaway if you saw anything?

LOUISON: Yes papa.

ARGAN: And have you done so?

LOUISON: Yes papa. I've come and told you everything I've seen.

ARGAN: And have you seen anything today?

LOUISON: No papa.

ARGAN: Nothing?

LOUISON: No papa.

ARGAN: You're sure?

LOUISON: I'm sure.

ARGAN: In that case, I've got something to show *you*. (*He reaches for a cane.*)

LOUISON: Oh papa!

ARGAN: Ah! you little witch! You didn't tell me you'd seen a man in your sister's room!

LOUISON: Papa!

ARGAN: This will teach you to tell lies!

LOUISON (*falling to her knees*): Oh, forgive me papa! It was because my sister said I wasn't to tell you . . . but I will, I'll tell you everything.

ARGAN: You must be beaten first for telling lies. Then we'll see about the rest.

LOUISON: Forgive me papa.

ARGAN: No!

LOUISON: Dear papa, don't beat me!

ARGAN: I will.

LOUISON: For pity's sake, don't beat me papa!

ARGAN (*holding her so he can give her the cane*): Come on now.

LOUISON: Oh papa! You've hurt me. Stop . . . I'm dying. (*She pretends to be dead.*)

ARGAN: Come now, whatever's up? Louison, Louison! Oh, good Lord! Louison. Oh, my little girl! Oh wretch that I am, my poor Louison is dead! Oh villain, what have you done? Damn this cane! Damn all canes! Oh, my poor child! My poor little Louison!

LOUISON: There there papa. Don't cry like that. I'm not quite dead.

ARGAN: Oh! you little minx! Oh very well, I forgive you this time – provided you tell me absolutely everything.

LOUISON: I will papa, I will.

ARGAN: Mind you do, because I know a little bird that can see everything and he'll tell me if you're telling lies.

LOUISON: But you mustn't tell my sister I told you.

ARGAN: I won't.

LOUISON: Well papa, the fact is a man came into her room while I was there.

ARGAN: And?

LOUISON: I asked him what he wanted and he said he was her singing teacher.

ARGAN: Aha! So that's their little game! And?

LOUISON: Then my sister came in.

ARGAN: And?

LOUISON: She said: 'Go, go away, get out! For heaven's sake, you'll drive me to despair!'

ARGAN: And?

LOUISON: He didn't want to go.

ARGAN: What did he say to her?

LOUISON: He said . . . oh all sorts of things.

ARGAN: And then what?

LOUISON: He said this and that and how he loved her and how she was the most beautiful girl in all the world.

ARGAN: And after that?

LOUISON: After that, he went down on his knees in front of her.

ARGAN: And after that?

LOUISON: After that, he kissed her hands.

ARGAN: And after that?

LOUISON: After that, stepmother came to the door and he ran away.

ARGAN: Anything else?

LOUISON: Oh no papa.

ARGAN: But I can hear that little bird whispering something. Wait. (*Listening*) Eh? Aha! Yes? Oho! That little bird is telling me there's something you saw that you're not telling me.

LOUISON: Then that little bird is a fibber.

ARGAN: Be careful.

LOUISON: No papa, don't believe it. It's telling fibs. Honest.

ARGAN: Well, we'll see about that. Run along now and keep your eyes open. Off with you. (*She goes out.*) Children aren't children any more. Oh, the troubles I have! I don't even have a minute's peace to give a thought to being ill. To tell the truth, I feel done in. (*He sits in his chair.*)

Scene ix:
BÉRALDE, ARGAN

BÉRALDE: Now brother, what's the matter? How are you?

ARGAN: Ah brother, I'm very ill.

BÉRALDE: Ill? In what way?

ARGAN: Yes, I feel so worn out you wouldn't believe it.

BÉRALDE: That's a pity.

ARGAN: I've hardly the strength to speak.

BÉRALDE: I came brother to put to you an offer of marriage for my niece Angélique.

ARGAN (*vehemently, getting out of his chair*): Don't talk to me about that wretched girl, brother! She's a brazen-faced, impudent baggage, and I'll have her inside a convent two days from now.

BÉRALDE: Now that's better. I'm very glad to see you're beginning to get your strength back. My visit's clearly doing you good. But look, we can talk about that business later. I've brought along for you a musical entertainment I've just happened across. It'll drive away your troubles and put you in a better frame of mind for what we've got to talk about. There are gypsies dressed up like Moors to dance and sing for us. I'm sure you'll like it. It'll do you as much good as one of Monsieur Purgon's prescriptions. Now come along.

Second Interlude

Argan's brother brings, for his entertainment, a company of gypsy men and girls in Moorish costume, who perform dances interspersed with songs.

FIRST GIRL: Rejoice, rejoice in the spring,
The springtime of your years,
While youth has its day;
Rejoice, rejoice in the spring,
The springtime of your years,
And love while you may.
For love is the only true pleasure:
Without it you'll find
No peace for the mind
Nor comparable charms to treasure.
Rejoice, rejoice in the spring,
The springtime of your years,
While youth has its day;
Rejoice, rejoice in the spring,
The springtime of your years,
And love while you may.
Waste not these moments that hasten away,
For Beauty's bold grace
Time will efface
And old Age deface
And youth will replace,
And all love's joy shall be dust and decay.
Rejoice, rejoice in the spring,
The springtime of your years,
While youth has its day;
Rejoice, rejoice in the spring,
The springtime of your years,
And love while you may.
SECOND GIRL: When to love you are pressed,
With what thoughts are you blest?
Young hearts! yearn and ache
And eagerly make
All speed for love's sake!

    Cupid deploys such infinite art
    That for all our alarms
    We lay down our arms
    When he shoots his first dart.
    Yet all that is said
    Of love's sorrows so tragic
    And the tears that are shed,
    All leads us to dread
    The lure of its magic.

THIRD GIRL: It is sweet in youth when we discover
    How to languish
    With a lover
    Who loves us truly!
    But should he fickle be,
    Oh the pain! Ah! the anguish!

FOURTH GIRL: But if our lover should prove a rover,
    The worst is not that all is over:
    The pain that starts,
    The rage that stays,
    Are born of knowing that with deceiving ways
    He has stolen away our hearts.

SECOND GIRL: When we are young and tender,
    Which path should we follow?

FOURTH GIRL: Should we to love's joys surrender
    And defy the pain and all the sorrow?

ALL TOGETHER: It's love we will follow however it starts:
    Though its joys be capricious,
    Its charms are delicious.
    Despite the pain of its darts,
    Its delights are delicious
    And gladden all hearts.

Ballet

The entire company of Moors dance together and put the performing monkeys they bring with them through their paces.

Act III

Scene i:
BÉRALDE, ARGAN, TOINETTE

BÉRALDE: Well now brother, what did you make of that? Better than a good dose of salts wasn't it?

TOINETTE: Humph! There's nothing wrong with a good dose of salts.

BÉRALDE: Well now, shall we have that little chat?

ARGAN: Have some patience brother. I'll be back soon.

TOINETTE: Just a minute sir, you're forgetting you can't walk without your stick.

ARGAN: You're right.

Scene ii:
BÉRALDE, TOINETTE

TOINETTE: Please sir, you mustn't give up defending your niece's interests.

BÉRALDE: I will do anything I can to get her what she wants.

TOINETTE: We must at all costs prevent this crazy marriage he's got his head so ridiculously set on. I've been thinking it would be a good plan to bring in a doctor of our own to put him off Monsieur Purgon and ridicule his methods. But since we don't have a suitable person to do this, I've decided to put on a little performance of my own.

BÉRALDE: What do you mean?

TOINETTE: It's a fantastic idea, but it might come off better than a sensible one. Leave it all to me. You do what you can from your end. Here he is. (*She goes out.*)

Scene iii:
ARGAN, BÉRALDE

BÉRALDE: Brother, will you allow me to ask you at the outset not to get worked up while we talk?

ARGAN: Agreed.

BÉRALDE: And to react to what I might say without getting tetchy?

ARGAN: Yes.

BÉRALDE: And to discuss the matters we need to talk about in a spirit of calm detachment?

ARGAN: Lord, yes! What a preamble!

BÉRALDE: Then why is it brother, that with all the money you have and only one daughter – for I'm not counting little Louison – why, I ask, are you thinking of putting her in a convent?

ARGAN: Why? Because brother I am master in my own house and can do whatever I think fit.

BÉRALDE: Your wife won't fail to advise you to dispose of both your daughters that way. I have no doubt that in the goodness of her heart she would be delighted to see both of them become nuns.

ARGAN: Ah! Now we're getting to the point. My poor wife's dragged straight into it. She's the cause of all the trouble and everyone is against her.

BÉRALDE: Not at all brother, let's leave her out of it. She's a woman who has the very best of intentions towards your family and is utterly disinterested, extraordinarily attached to you, and she shows your children unimaginable affection and kindness – all that goes without saying. Let's say no more about her and come to your daughter. What's your idea brother in wanting her to marry the son of a doctor?

ARGAN: The idea is, brother, for me to have the kind of son-in-law I need.

BÉRALDE: But that's got nothing to do with your daughter, and now a second candidate has come forward who would suit her better.

ARGAN: Yes, but the first one suits me better.

BÉRALDE: But is she to take a husband for her own sake or for yours?

ARGAN: For both, brother, hers and mine. I want to have people in the family who will be useful to me.

BÉRALDE: I suppose on the same principle that if your other daughter were old enough, you'd marry her off to an apothecary.

ARGAN: Why not?

BÉRALDE: How can you possibly go on being eternally besotted with apothecaries and doctors? Have you made up your mind to be ill despite everything these people and nature can do for you?

ARGAN: What do you mean by that brother?

BÉRALDE: What I mean brother is that I don't know any other man who is less ill than you are. I couldn't ask for a better constitution than yours. One obvious sign that you are fit and well and in perfect shape is that, despite all the good care you've taken of yourself, you haven't yet managed to undermine your health or succumbed to all the medicines they've made you take.

ARGAN: But don't you see that's what has kept me going? Monsieur Purgon says I shouldn't survive if he went three days without looking in on me.

BÉRALDE: If you're not careful, he'll take such good care of you that he'll see you off into the next world.

ARGAN: Let's pursue this matter a little further. So you don't believe in medicine?

BÉRALDE: No, and I don't see that it's necessary to my salvation that I should.

ARGAN: What? You don't accept the truth of what is universally accepted and has been revered down all the centuries?

BÉRALDE: Far from accepting it as true, I regard it, between ourselves, as one of the greatest follies of mankind. Looking at it philosophically, I can't think of any piece of mummery that's more absurd. I don't know anything more ridiculous than the idea that one man should make it his business to cure another.

ARGAN: And why won't you accept that one man may cure another?

BÉRALDE: Because brother the workings of the human mechanism are still a mystery which we do not understand, because nature has placed a veil over our eyes too thick for us to see anything through it.

ARGAN: So according to your reckoning doctors don't know anything?

BÉRALDE: Not at all. Most of them know their classics, speak fluent Latin, have learnt the Greek names for all the ailments and can define and classify them. But when it comes to curing them, that's something they know nothing about.

ARGAN: But you must surely agree that doctors know more about these matters than ordinary people?

BÉRALDE: Brother, they know what I've told you, which doesn't amount to much when it comes to curing people. The so-called excellence of their art comes out in pretentious mumbo-jumbo, a farrago of gibberish, which gives you words instead of explanations and promises not results.

ARGAN: But there are plenty of people about who are as wise and as clever as you are. Yet when they're ill, we observe that they all send for a doctor.

BÉRALDE: That's a sign of human frailty, not proof of the skills of doctors.

ARGAN: But doctors must believe in the value of their art, since they use it to treat themselves.

BÉRALDE: That's because some of them honestly share the common mistaken beliefs which they exploit for their own ends, and others who don't believe any of it but still take the money. Your Monsieur Purgon, for instance, makes no bones about it. He's a doctor to the soles of his boots, a man who has more faith in his medical principles than in anything capable of mathematical proof. He'd consider it criminal even to question them. Medicine has no mysteries for him, no uncertainties, no difficulties. Impelled by galloping prejudice, unshakeable self-confidence and no more common-sense or intelligence than a brute beast, he goes on his way purging and bleeding right and left with never a second thought. You mustn't hold all the things he does to you against him – he'll pack you off into the next world with the best of intentions and in killing you off treat you no differently than he would his wife and children and, if needs be, himself.

ARGAN: The fact is brother, you've got it in for him. But let's get to the point. What are you supposed to do then, when you're ill?

BÉRALDE: Nothing.

ARGAN: Nothing?

BÉRALDE: Nothing. Rest – that's all you need do. Nature, when left to itself, will quietly find its own way out of the sickness it has succumbed to. It's our anxiety, our impatience, that spoils everything. Most people die of the cure, not the disease.

ARGAN: But you must agree brother that there are ways and means of giving nature a helping hand.

BÉRALDE: Good heavens brother, that's exactly the sort of empty idea we're only too ready to swallow! Since the beginning of time men have always been given to extravagant notions which we all come to believe in because we find them reassuring and would like them to be true. When a doctor talks to you about assisting or helping or relieving nature, or removing what's obstructing it or giving it what it lacks, of setting it to rights and restoring the full operation of its functions, when he talks of rectifying the blood, settling the bowels or cooling the brain, reducing the spleen, reconditioning the lungs, cleansing the liver, strengthening the heart, re-establishing or maintaining the body's natural heat, and of possessing the secret of prolonging life for many, many years, he's just giving you the usual guff about medicine. But when you get down to the truth of the matter and the test of experience, you find there's nothing in what he says, and it all turns out like those marvellous dreams you have that leave you when you wake up feeling annoyed for having believed them.

ARGAN: What you mean is that all the scientific knowledge in the world is contained in your head and that you claim to know more about these things than the greatest doctors of our times.

BÉRALDE: All your great doctors are two quite distinct sorts of people, depending on whether they're talking or doing. Listen to them speak and they're the cleverest men in the whole world. But see them at work, they are the most ignorant of men.

ARGAN: Oh yes, I can see you're a great doctor. I only wish one of those fine men was here to answer your arguments and cut your cackle.

BÉRALDE: Brother, I have no wish to take it on myself to combat medicine. People are entitled to run the risk and believe whatever they like. What I'm saying is just between ourselves. I only wish I could have made you see something of the error of your ways and taken you, for your amusement, to see one of Molière's plays on this topic.

ARGAN: I've no patience with your Molière and his plays, he's an impertinent jackanapes. It's all very amusing I must say, poking fun at worthy men like doctors.

BÉRALDE: He doesn't poke fun at doctors but at the absurdities of medicine.

ARGAN: And who is he to think he can lay down the law about medicine? Some imbecile he must be, with an exaggerated opinion of himself, to make mock of consultations and treatments, set himself up against the whole Faculty and put highly respectable people like doctors into his plays.

BÉRALDE: What else would you like him to put into them if not men of all professions? Kings and princes are put on stage every day, and they aren't any less respectable than doctors.

ARGAN: By God, if I were a doctor I'd get my own back on him for his insolence. When he was ill I'd leave him to die without lifting a finger. He could say or do what he liked, but I wouldn't prescribe any treatment, no bleeding, no enemas, and I'd say to him: 'Die and be damned, that'll teach you to make fun of the Faculty of Medicine!'

BÉRALDE: You're very cross with him.

ARGAN: Yes, he's an ignorant clown, and if doctors have got any sense, they'll all do what I say.

BÉRALDE: He'll have more sense than the doctors and not ask for their help.

ARGAN: Too bad for him if he refuses treatment.

BÉRALDE: He's got good reasons for not wanting anything to do with them. He maintains that it's only the vigorous and healthy who have the strength to cope with illness and treatment at the same time and, as far as he's concerned, he's only got enough strength to put up with being ill.

ARGAN: What a ridiculous thing to say! Look brother, let's not talk about that man any more. It heats my bile and you'll bring on my trouble.

BÉRALDE: Willingly. And to change the subject, let me say that just because your daughter has shown some small reluctance to follow your wishes, you shouldn't take any extreme decision to pack her off to a convent. And as for choosing a son-in-law, you mustn't let yourself be carried away blindly by your anger but try to make some concession to your daughter's feelings in this matter, since marriage is for life and her happiness depends on it.

Scene iv:

MONSIEUR FLEURANT *holding a syringe*, ARGAN,
BÉRALDE

ARGAN: Ah brother, do you mind?

BÉRALDE: Mind? What are you going to do?

ARGAN: I need to have a little injection. It won't take long.

BÉRALDE: You're mad! Can't you go for one minute without having an injection or taking more medicine? Put it off until another time and enjoy a moment's peace.

ARGAN: This evening, Monsieur Fleurant, or tomorrow morning then.

M. FLEURANT (*to Béralde*): What do you mean by interfering with the doctor's orders and preventing this gentleman from having his injection? Who do you think you are? The nerve!

BÉRALDE: Come sir, it's obvious you're not used to looking people in the face in your dealings with them.

M. FLEURANT: You've no business to be mocking medicine and wasting my time. The only reason I came here was to effect a specific treatment and I shall tell Monsieur Purgon that I have been prevented from carrying out his instructions and performing my duty. You'll see, you'll see . . .

ARGAN: Brother, it'll be your fault if something dreadful happens.

BÉRALDE: Dreadful? To miss one of Monsieur Purgon's injections? Again I ask brother, is there no way of curing you of the doctoritis you suffer from? Are you going to be swamped by their remedies for the rest of your life?

ARGAN: By God brother, you talk like a man who's fit and well. But if you were in my shoes, you'd change your tune. It's easy to be rude about medicine when you're in good health.

BÉRALDE: What exactly is wrong with you?

ARGAN: You'll get me all worked up. I only wish you had what I've got. Then we'd see if you still talked as much nonsense. Ah! Here's Monsieur Purgon.

Scene v:

MONSIEUR PURGON, ARGAN, BÉRALDE, TOINETTE

M. PURGON: Fine news I've been hearing downstairs as I walked through the door! So, someone has been making mock of my instructions and refusing to have the treatment I prescribed.

ARGAN: Sir, it's not –

M. PURGON: The audacity! A patient who rebels against his doctor! Unnatural!

TOINETTE: Shocking!

M. PURGON: An enema I had taken the trouble to make up myself!

ARGAN: It wasn't me!

M. PURGON: Compounded and prepared in strict accordance with the principles of medicine –

TOINETTE: He did wrong!

M. PURGON: And which would have produced a startling effect on the bowels.

ARGAN: Brother!

M. PURGON: To dismiss it so contemptuously –

ARGAN: He's the one who –

M. PURGON: What outrageous behaviour!

TOINETTE: True enough.

M. PURGON: An enormity, a crime against medicine!

ARGAN: He's the cause –

M. PURGON: An act of treason against the Faculty, for which no punishment can be strong enough.

TOINETTE: You're right.

M. PURGON: I declare I shall have nothing more to do with you.

ARGAN: It was my brother –

M. PURGON: That I no longer wish to be connected with you.

TOINETTE: You do well.

M. PURGON: And to put an end to all my links with you, here is the deed of gift containing the settlement I was about to give my nephew on his marriage. (*He angrily tears it up.*)

ARGAN: It was my brother who caused all the trouble.

M. PURGON: Despising my enema, indeed!

ARGAN: Bring it back again. I'll take it at once.

M. PURGON: Just when I was about to cure you!

TOINETTE: He doesn't deserve to be cured.

M. PURGON: I was about to give your system a thorough clean and flush out all the bad humours.

ARGAN: Oh brother!

M. PURGON: All I needed was another dozen treatments and I'd have got to the bottom of it.

TOINETTE: He's not worthy of your care.

M. PURGON: But since you don't want to be cured by me –

ARGAN: It's not my fault.

M. PURGON: Since you've failed to observe the obedience a patient owes his doctor –

TOINETTE: It cries out for vengeance!

M. PURGON: Since you have openly rebelled against the treatment I prescribed –

ARGAN: Ah! I never did.

M. PURGON: I must inform you that I abandon you to your sickly constitution, to the perturbations of your bowels, the corruption of your blood, the bitterness of your bile and the turgidness of your humours.

TOINETTE: Quite right.

ARGAN: Oh God!

M. PURGON: And I predict that within four days you'll be beyond all help.

ARGAN: Oh, mercy!

M. PURGON: You will fall into a state of bradypepsia –

ARGAN: Monsieur Purgon!

M. PURGON: From bradypepsia into dyspepsia –

ARGAN: Monsieur Purgon!

M. PURGON: From dyspepsia into apepsia –

ARGAN: Monsieur Purgon!

M. PURGON: From apepsia into lientery –

ARGAN: Monsieur Purgon!

M. PURGON: From lientery into dysentery –

ARGAN: Monsieur Purgon!

M. PURGON: From dysentery into dropsy –

ARGAN: Monsieur Purgon!

M. PURGON: And from dropsy to the autopsy that you will have brought on yourself through your own folly. (*He goes out.*)

Scene vi:

ARGAN, BÉRALDE

ARGAN: Oh my God! I'm as good as dead. Brother, you've done for me!

BÉRALDE: Why? What's the matter?

ARGAN: I'm finished. Already I can feel that medicine is taking its revenge on me.

BÉRALDE: Great heavens brother, you're mad. I'd give anything to prevent other people seeing you in the state you are now. Please, get a grip, pull yourself together and don't give so much rein to your imagination.

ARGAN: Brother, did you hear all the hideous diseases he threatened me with?

BÉRALDE: How naïve can you be!

ARGAN: He said I'd be beyond help within four days.

BÉRALDE: Just because he says so can't affect the outcome. Has the oracle spoken? To hear you carry on, anyone would think that Monsieur Purgon holds your life by a thread which he has absolute authority to lengthen or shorten as he fancies. Just remember this: the living principle is within you and the wrath of Monsieur Purgon is as powerless to kill you as his remedies are to keep you alive. If you choose, this business can be your chance to rid yourself of all doctors. Or if you're really so constituted that you can't manage without them, you can easily find another one who wouldn't expose you to such risks.

ARGAN: Ah, but brother, he understands my natural temper and knows the best way of treating me.

BÉRALDE: I must say, you are a terribly obstinate man and you have a very peculiar way of looking at things.

Scene vii:

TOINETTE, ARGAN, BÉRALDE

TOINETTE: Sir, there's a doctor asking to see you.

ARGAN: What doctor?

TOINETTE: A doctor who does doctoring.

ARGAN: I asked you who he was.

TOINETTE: I don't know who he is, but he and I are as alike as two peas. If I didn't know my mother was an honest woman, I'd say he was a younger brother she'd produced for me since my father died.

ARGAN: Show him up. (*Toinette goes out.*)

BÉRALDE: This is the very thing you needed! One doctor leaves you and another turns up.

ARGAN: I'm very afraid that you're letting me in for a lot of trouble.

BÉRALDE: Not bringing that up again are you?

ARGAN: Listen, I'm very worried about all those diseases I never heard of before, all the . . .

Scene viii:

TOINETTE *disguised as a doctor*, ARGAN, BÉRALDE

TOINETTE: Sir, permit me to call on you and offer my humble services for any bleedings and purgings you may be in need of.

ARGAN: I'm greatly obliged to you sir. (*Aside*) Good God! He's the image of Toinette!

TOINETTE: Sir, please excuse me one moment. I've forgotten to give instructions to my servant. I'll not be long. (*She goes out.*)

ARGAN: Wouldn't you say that was really Toinette?

BÉRALDE: It's true there's certainly a remarkably close resemblance, but I've come across similar cases before and you often read about such freaks of nature.

ARGAN: Well I must say I'm astonished, and . . .

Scene ix:

TOINETTE, ARGAN, BÉRALDE

TOINETTE (*she has changed out of her medical robes so quickly it is hard to believe it was she who had come in as a doctor*): Did you want something sir?

ARGAN: What?

TOINETTE: Didn't you call?

ARGAN: Me? Certainly not.

TOINETTE: It must have been my ears burning.

ARGAN: Stay a minute and see how much this doctor looks like you.

TOINETTE (*as she goes out*): Me, stay? I've got far too much to do downstairs, and I've seen all I want of that man.

ARGAN: If I hadn't seen both of them, I would have believed they were one and the same.

BÉRALDE: I've read some amazing accounts of resemblances of this kind. There have been cases in our own day and age where everybody has been confused.

ARGAN: I'd have been confused myself by these two. I could have sworn they were the same person.

Scene x:
TOINETTE *disguised as a doctor*, ARGAN, BÉRALDE

TOINETTE: I am most sincerely sorry sir.

ARGAN: It's amazing!

TOINETTE: I hope you will forgive my curiosity, sir, in wishing to see so celebrated an invalid as yourself. Your reputation, which spreads far and wide, will excuse the liberty I have taken.

ARGAN: Only too glad to be of use, sir.

TOINETTE: I observe, sir, that you are staring at me. How old do you think I am?

ARGAN: I should think you can't be more than twenty-six or seven.

TOINETTE: Ha, ha ha! I'm ninety.

ARGAN: Ninety?

TOINETTE: Yes. You see before you the effect of the secrets of my art, which have kept me young and vigorous.

ARGAN: By God, you're a young-looking ninety.

TOINETTE: I am a travelling doctor, I go from town to town, from province to province and from one kingdom to another seeking out signal opportunities to exercise my talents, looking for patients worthy of my ministrations, cases which require the application of the profound discoveries that I have made in the field of medicine. I do not condescend to pass the time with the ordinary run of minor ailments, trifles like rheumatism, assorted swellings, fevers, vapours and headaches. I want serious illnesses – solid, long-lasting fevers with spells of delirium, interesting scarlet fevers, savage plagues, deliciously advanced cases of dropsy, serious pleurisies with inflammation of the lungs. That's where I feel at home and that's where I triumph! Sir, I only wish you had every malady I've just mentioned, that you'd been given up for dead by all the doctors, despaired of, at death's door, so that I could demonstrate both the effectiveness of my treatments and my desire to be of service to you.

ARGAN: I am obliged to you sir for your kind consideration.

TOINETTE: Let me take your pulse. Come on, let's have you beating properly. Oh, I'll soon have you ticking away the way you should. Aha! what a cheeky little pulse! I can see you don't yet know who I am. Who's your doctor?

ARGAN: Monsieur Purgon.

TOINETTE: He's not on my list of great physicians. What does he reckon is wrong with you?

ARGAN: He says it's my liver, others think it's my spleen.

TOINETTE: They're all ignoramuses. Your trouble is lungs.

ARGAN: My lungs?

TOINETTE: Yes. What are your symptoms?

ARGAN: I get headaches from time to time.

TOINETTE: Quite. That's the lungs.

ARGAN: Sometimes it seems as if I've got this mist before my eyes.

TOINETTE: Lungs.

ARGAN: At other times I get queasy.

TOINETTE: Lungs.

ARGAN: On occasion I feel weary in every limb.

TOINETTE: Lungs.

ARGAN: Then I get pains in my stomach, as if I had colic.

TOINETTE: Lungs. Is your appetite for your food all right?

ARGAN: Yes doctor.

TOINETTE: Lungs. Fond of a glass of wine?

ARGAN: Yes doctor.

TOINETTE: Lungs. Do you come over all sleepy after meals? Feel you want a nap?

ARGAN: Yes doctor.

TOINETTE: Lungs, lungs, I assure you. What diet has your own doctor prescribed?

ARGAN: He says I must have soup.

TOINETTE: Ignoramus!

ARGAN: Chicken.

TOINETTE: Ignoramus!

ARGAN: Veal.

TOINETTE: Ignoramus!

ARGAN: Lots of broth.

TOINETTE: Ignoramus!

ARGAN: New-laid eggs.

TOINETTE: Ignoramus!

ARGAN: And before retiring, a few prunes to keep the bowels open.

TOINETTE: Ignoramus!

ARGAN: And above all, to take plenty of water with my wine.

TOINETTE: Ignorantus, ignoranta, ignorantum! You must always drink your wine neat. Then, and to strengthen your blood which is too thin, you need to eat good prime beef, fat pork, plenty of good Dutch cheese, cornflour custards and rice puddings and chestnuts and waffles, to thicken and conglutinate it. Your doctor is a fool. I'll choose one for you and send him along. I'll look in on you myself from time to time when I'm in town.

ARGAN: I'd be most grateful.

TOINETTE: What the devil are you doing about this arm?

ARGAN: What?

TOINETTE: I should have that arm off at once if I were you.

ARGAN: Why?

TOINETTE: Can't you see, it's drawing in all the goodness and preventing the other one getting its share?

ARGAN: Yes, but I need that arm.

TOINETTE: I should have that right eye out too if I were in your shoes.

ARGAN: Have an eye out?

TOINETTE: Don't you see how it encroaches on the other one and takes all the nourishment? Take it from me: have that eye out at once. You'll be able see a lot better with the left.

ARGAN: Surely there's no hurry for that?

TOINETTE: Goodbye. I'm sorry I must leave so soon, but I have to be present at an important consultation on a man who died yesterday.

ARGAN: On a man who died yesterday?

TOINETTE: Yes — to consider and ponder what should have been done to cure him. Till we meet again.

ARGAN: As you know, invalids aren't expected to show people to the door. (*Toinette goes out.*)

BÉRALDE: He seems a very smart sort of doctor.

ARGAN: Yes, but he's in a bit too much of a hurry for me.

BÉRALDE: All great physicians are like that.

ARGAN: Wanting to cut one arm off and take an eye out so the others would get along better! I'd much rather they went on not doing so well. Some operation that would be, to leave me one-eyed and one-armed!

Scene xi:
TOINETTE, ARGAN, BÉRALDE

TOINETTE (*offstage*): I'll thank you to clear off! I don't think it's at all funny.

ARGAN (*as Toinette enters*): What's the matter?

TOINETTE: That doctor of yours, why, he wanted to feel my pulse.

ARGAN: Amazing! He's ninety!

BÉRALDE: Well now brother, since your Monsieur Purgon has fallen out with you, won't you let me tell you about the young man who has asked for my niece's hand?

ARGAN: No brother. I mean to put her into a convent since she won't do what I want. It's clear to me there's some sort of romantic nonsense behind it. I've found out about a certain secret meeting and Angélique thinks I don't know.

BÉRALDE: Come brother, even if she is a little bit fond of someone, is that so very wrong? Why should it upset you if the intention is for it all to end honourably in marriage?

ARGAN: That's as may be, but, brother, a nun she shall be. I've made up my mind.

BÉRALDE: So you intend to make one person happy.

ARGAN: I know what you mean. You keep coming back to it. It's my wife you've got in mind.

BÉRALDE: Well yes brother, to be quite frank, I do mean your wife. I can no more stand to see you infatuated by her than besotted with doctors. I can't bear to see you walk straight into every trap she lays for you.

TOINETTE: Oh sir, don't talk like that about the mistress! There's not a word to be said against her. She's a woman without guile and she loves the master – really loves him! There's no telling how much she loves him.

ARGAN (*to Béralde*): Ask her to tell you about the way she's forever hugging me.

TOINETTE: That's true.

ARGAN: How worried she gets about my health.

TOINETTE: No doubt about it.

ARGAN: And all the care she takes of me and the trouble she goes to.

TOINETTE: Unquestionably. (*To Béralde*) Would you like me to prove to you, with a practical demonstration I shall put on in a moment or two, exactly how much the mistress loves the master? (*To Argan*) Please sir, won't you let me show him how little he knows and make him see how wrong he is?

ARGAN: How?

TOINETTE: The mistress will be back in a moment. Stretch out in your chair and pretend to be dead. You'll see how grief-stricken she'll be when I tell her the news.

ARGAN: All right.

TOINETTE: Good. But don't keep her in despair for too long. It might be the death of her.

ARGAN: Leave it to me.

TOINETTE (*to Béralde*): You hide yourself over there.

ARGAN: I suppose pretending to be dead isn't dangerous?

TOINETTE: Of course not. How could it be dangerous? Just stretch out. (*Aside, to Argan*) It'll be a pleasure to show your brother how wrong he is. Here's the mistress. Keep still.

Scene xii:
BÉLINE, TOINETTE, ARGAN, BÉRALDE

TOINETTE (*crying out*): Oh heavens! It's terrible! What a dreadful thing to happen!

BÉLINE: What's the matter Toinette?

TOINETTE: Oh Madame!

BÉLINE: What is it?

TOINETTE: Your husband is dead!

BÉLINE: My husband, dead?

TOINETTE: Alas, yes! The poor departed is deceased.

BÉLINE: Are you sure?

TOINETTE: Quite sure, Nobody knows it's happened yet. I was here all
by myself. He just faded away in my arms. See, there he is, stretched
out in his chair.

BÉLINE: Heaven be praised! That's a great weight off my back. Don't
be so silly Toinette. You're not crying just because he's dead are
you?

TOINETTE: I thought you were supposed to Madame.

BÉLINE: Go on with you. I shouldn't bother. He's not much of a loss.
What use was he when he was alive? He was a nuisance to everybody,
dirty, disgusting, always wanting an enema or cramming more medicine into himself, forever snivelling, coughing and spitting, dull,
boring, cantankerous, wearing everybody out and grumbling at the
servants day and night.

TOINETTE (*aside*): Some funeral oration I must say!

BÉLINE: Toinette, you must help me carry out my plan. You can rely
on me, if you serve me well, to see that you are rewarded. Luckily
no one knows what has happened, so we'll transfer him to his bed
and keep his death quiet until I've completed my business. There
are papers and money I want to get hold of. I've given him the best
years of my life and it's only fair I should get something out of it.
Come on Toinette. First we'll get his keys.

ARGAN (*sitting up suddenly*): Not so fast.

BÉLINE (*surprised and dismayed*): Aah!

ARGAN: So, Madame! So, wife! Is this how you love me?

TOINETTE: Oh! The deceased isn't defunct!

ARGAN (*to Béline who runs out*): I was very pleased to learn how much
you loved me and hear the splendid eulogy you pronounced over
me. It was a useful warning and it will make me wiser in future and
stop me doing all sorts of silly things.

BÉRALDE (*emerging from his hiding-place*): Well brother, you see how
it is?

TOINETTE: Goodness! I'd never have believed it. But I can hear your
daughter coming. Get back the way you were both of you and let's
see how she'll take the news of your death. It's something that's not

a bad idea to put to the test, and while you're at it you might as well find out what the rest of the family thinks about you too.

Scene xiii:
ANGÉLIQUE, ARGAN, TOINETTE, BÉRALDE

TOINETTE (*crying out*): Merciful heaven! Ooh! What a terrible thing to happen! Oh, unhappy day!

ANGÉLIQUE: What's the matter Toinette? Why are you crying?

TOINETTE: Alas, I have some sad news for you.

ANGÉLIQUE: What is it?

TOINETTE: Your father is dead!

ANGÉLIQUE: My father is dead Toinette?

TOINETTE: Yes. He's over there. He had a sudden attack and has only just this minute passed on.

ANGÉLIQUE: Oh heavens! This is terrible! Such a cruel blow! Alas, to lose my father who meant all the world to me, and, to make it even more dreadful, to lose him at a time when he was angry with me! What will become of me, unhappy daughter that I am, and where shall I find consolation for such a loss?

Scene xiv:
CLÉANTE, ANGÉLIQUE, ARGAN, TOINETTE,
BÉRALDE

CLÉANTE: Whatever is the matter dear Angélique? Why are you crying?

ANGÉLIQUE: Alas, I weep for the dearest, the most precious of all the things in my life that I could have lost. I weep for my father's death.

CLÉANTE: My God! How awful! And so unexpected! Alas, after I'd begged your uncle to speak to him on my behalf, I decided to come myself, see him and try pleading with him, and ask him respectfully to change his mind and give me your hand.

ANGÉLIQUE: Oh Cléante, let's not say any more of that! Let's abandon all thought of marriage. Now that I've lost my father I feel I have lost the world and no longer want to be part of it – I renounce it for ever. Yes father, I opposed your wishes before, but now I will at least comply with one of your intentions and in so doing make amends for the sorrow which I reproach myself for having caused you. Let me give you my word now father, and may this kiss be the mark of my grief and my affection.

ARGAN (*sits up*): Oh, my dear girl!

ANGÉLIQUE (*startled*): Oh!

ARGAN: Come, don't be afraid, I'm not dead. Oh yes, you are my own flesh and blood, my own true daughter, and I'm overjoyed to have seen your kind and loving nature.

ANGÉLIQUE: Oh father, what a relief! Since Heaven by this great happiness has restored you to me and made my wishes come true, let me now throw myself at your feet and beg one favour of you. If you are not disposed to grant what my heart desires, if you refuse to let me have Cléante as my husband, I beg you, at least don't make me marry someone else. This is the only favour I ask of you.

CLÉANTE (*on his knees*): Sir, won't you be moved by her prayers and mine? Do not oppose the mutual feelings of a love that is so pure!

BÉRALDE: Brother, can you resist such an appeal?

TOINETTE: Sir, how can you remain unmoved by love like this?

ARGAN: If he agrees to become a doctor, I'll give my consent for the marriage. That's it, become a doctor and I'll let you have my daughter.

CLÉANTE: Willingly sir. If that's all I need do to become your son-in-law, I'll become a doctor, even an apothecary if that's what you want. It's no great matter and I'd do far more than that to win my lovely Angélique.

BÉRALDE: An idea occurs to me brother. Why don't you become a doctor yourself? It would be even more convenient if you could yourself provide all the ministrations you need.

TOINETTE: That's true. It's the best and quickest way of curing yourself. Why, there isn't an ailment brazen enough to take on a doctor in person.

ARGAN: I think brother you're having a little joke at my expense. Aren't I a bit old to start studying?

BÉRALDE: Study? That's a good one! You know enough already. There are lots of doctors who're no wiser than you are.

ARGAN: But you have to be able to speak Latin, recognize the various complaints and know the treatments for them.

BÉRALDE: Once you put on a doctor's cap and gown, all that will come to you by itself. Thereafter, you'll find you have all the skills you need.

ARGAN: You mean anyone can hold forth about illness once they've put a gown on?

BÉRALDE: Certainly. All you need do is open your mouth. When you're wearing your cap and gown, any nonsense you spout becomes wisdom and all the mumbo-jumbo, good sense.

TOINETTE: Listen sir, your beard alone goes a long way. A beard accounts for more than half of a doctor's dignity.

CLÉANTE: Well I'm ready for anything.

BÉRALDE: Would you like this business to be arranged straightaway?

ARGAN: What do you mean, straightaway?

BÉRALDE: Here and now. In your own house.

ARGAN: In my house?

BÉRALDE: Yes. One of my friends is in the Faculty and he'll come round at once and have the ceremony performed here, in your own room. And it won't cost you a penny.

ARGAN: Yes, but what'll I have to say? What answers will I give?

BÉRALDE: They'll tell you in a couple of words what you have to do, and they'll write down what you're supposed to say. Go and put on some suitable clothes while I send for them.

ARGAN: All right then. Let's do it. (*He goes out.*)

CLÉANTE: What did you mean? What's all this about having a friend in the Faculty?

TOINETTE: What are you up to?

BÉRALDE: Just a little something to amuse us this evening. The actors have devised a short interlude around the ceremony for conferring a doctor's degree, with music and dance. I want us all to take part in the entertainment and my brother shall have the leading role.

ANGÉLIQUE: But uncle, it seems to me that you're making rather too much fun of father.

BÉRALDE: No, it's not so much making fun of him as playing along with his fads and fancies. And it'll just take place among ourselves. We can all have a role and that way we'll be performing the play for each other's amusement. After all, it is carnival time. Come along, let's go and get everything ready.

CLÉANTE (*to Angélique*): Do you agree?

ANGÉLIQUE: Yes, since it's all my uncle's idea.

Finale

*A burlesque ceremony, in words, song and dance, of the conferment of a
doctor's degree.*

Ballet

*Attendants come on, prepare the room and position the benches in time
to music. After this the whole company, made up of eight syringe-bearers,
six apothecaries, twenty-two doctors and the graduand, with eight surgeons
dancing and two singing, enter and take their places according to their
rank.*

PRESIDENT:[12]   Savantissimi doctores,
             Medicinae professores,
             Quid hic assembled estis,
             Et vos, other messiores
             Sententiarum Facultatis
             Fideles executores,
             Surgeons and apothecaries,
             Atque tota compania also,
             Salus, honor et argentum,
             Atque bonum appetitum.
             Non possum, docti confreri,
             In me satis admirari
             Qualis bona inventio
             Is medici professio,
             Quam bella chosa est et bene trovata,
             Medicina illa benedicta,
             Quae, suo nomine solo,
             Marveloso miraculo,
             Since si longo tempore,
             Has made in clover vivere
             So many people omni genere.
             Per totam terram videmus
             The great reknown ubi sumus,
             Et quod grandes et petiti
             Sunt de nobis infatuti:

Totus mundus, currens ad nostros remedios,
Nos regardat sicut deos,
Et nostris ordonnanciis
Principes et reges soumissos videtis.

'Tis therefore nostrae sapentiae
Boni sensus atque prudentiae,
Jolly hard to travaillare,
A nos bene conservare
In tali credito, voga et honore,
And take good care to non recevere
In nostro docto corpore
Only personas capabiles,
Et totas dignas to fill
These places honorabiles.

That's why nunc convocati estis,
Et credo quod trovabitis
Dignam materiam medici
In savanti homine that here you see,
Whom in things omnibus,
Dono ad interrogandum
And very thoroughly examinandum
Your capacitaties.

FIRST DOCTOR: Si mihi licentiam dat dominus praeses,
Et tanti docti doctores,
Et assistantes illustrious,
Learnedissimo bacheliero,
Quem estimo and honoro,
Domandabo causam est rationem why
Does opium facit dormire.

ARGAN: Mihi a docto doctore
Domandatur causam et rationem why
Does opium facit dormire?
To which I respondeo:
Because est in eo
Virtus dormitiva,
Cujus est natura
Sensus assoupire.[13]

CHORUS: Bene, bene, bene, bene respondere:
    Dignus, dignus est intrare
    In nostro docto corpore.
    Bene, bene respondere.

SECOND DOCTOR: Cum permissione domini praesidis,
    Doctissimae Facultatis,
    Et totius his nostris actis
    Companiae assistantis,
    Domandabo tibi, docte bacheliere:
    Quae sunt remedia,
    Quae, in maladia
    Called hydropisia,
    Convenit facere?

ARGAN: Clysterium donare,
    Postea bleedare,
    After that purgare.

CHORUS: Bene, bene, bene, bene respondere:
    Dignus, dignus est intrare
    In nostro docto corpore.

THIRD DOCTOR: Si bonum semblatur domino praesidi,
    Doctissimae Facultati
    Et companiae praesenti,
    Domandabo tibi, docte bacheliere:
    Quae remediae eticis
    Pulmonicis atque asmaticis,
    Do you think it suitable to facere.

ARGAN: Clysterium donare,
    Postea bleedare,
    After that purgare.

CHORUS: Bene, bene, bene, bene respondere:
    Dignus, dignus est intrare
    In nostro docto corpore.

FOURTH DOCTOR: Super illas maladias,
    Doctor bachelerius dixit maravillas,
    But at the risk of boring dominum praesidi,
    Doctissimam Facultatem,
    Et totam honorabilem
    Companiam giving heedem,

Faciam illi unam questionem:
De hiero maladus unus
Tombavit in meas manus;
Habet grandam fievram cum redoublamentis,
Grandam dolorem capitis,
Et grandum malum in the ribs,
Cum granda difficultate
Et pena de respirare.
Would you tell mihi,
Docte bacheliere,
Quid illi facere?

ARGAN: Clysterium donare,
Postea bleedare,
After that purgare.

FIFTH DOCTOR: But if said maladia,
Opiniatra,
Non vult get betterare,
Quid illi facere?

ARGAN: Clysterium donare,
Postea bleedare,
After that purgare,
Rebleedare, repurgare and reclysterare.

CHORUS: Bene, bene, bene, bene respondere:
Dignus, dignus est intrare
In nostro docto corpore.

PRESIDENT: Juras gardare statuta
Per Facultatem praescripta,
Cum sensu and jugeamento?

ARGAN: Juro.

PRESIDENT: Essere in omnibus
Consultationibus
Ancieni aviso,
Aut bono,
Aut baddo?

ARGAN: Juro.

PRESIDENT: That you'll never ever te servire
De remedis aucunis,
Excepting only those of doctae Facultatis;

Even if your maladus should croako
Et mori de suo malo?

ARGAN: Juro.

PRESIDENT: Ego, cum isto boneto
Venerabili et docto,
Dono tibi et concedo
Virtutem and power
Medicandi,
Purgandi,
Bleedandi,
Prickandi,
Cutandi,
Carvandi,
Et killandi,
Impune per totam terram.

Ballet

All the surgeons and apothecaries step forward and bow respectfully to him in time to the music.

ARGAN: Grandes doctores doctrinae,
Of rhubarb and of senna,
It would doubtless be in me a cosa foolish,
Inepta et ridicula,
If I should commit myself
Your praises donare,
And undertakeabam to addare
Sunbeams to the sun,
And stars to the cielo,
Waves to the oceano,
And roses to the printempo.
So please accept cum deep emotio,
Pro toto remercimento,
Rendam gratiam corpori tam docto.
Vobis, vobis debeo
More than to nature or to my own pater:
Natura et pater meus
Hominem me habent factum.

But vos, which is more important,
Avetis factum medicum,
Honor, favor, et gratia.
Qui in hoc corde here present,
Imprimant ressentimenta
Which will endure in saecula.

CHORUS: Vivat, vivat, vivat, for ever vivat,
Novius doctor, qui tam bene speakat!
Mille, mille annis, et manget et bibat,
Bleedat and killat!

Ballet

All the surgeons and apothecaries dance to the sound of the instruments and voices and the noise of clapping hands and apothecaries' pestles on mortars.

FIRST SURGEON: May he see doctas
Suas prescriptiones
Omnium surgeonarum
Et apothiquarum
Fill up all the pharmacias!

CHORUS: Vivat, vivat, vivat, for ever vivat,
Novius doctor, qui tam bene speakat!
Mille, mille annis, et manget et bibat,
Bleedat and killat!

SECOND SURGEON: May all his anni
Be to him boni
And favorabiles,
And never habere at all
Quam plaguas, poxas
Fievras, pluresias,
Apoplexias et dissenterias!

CHORUS: Vivat, vivat, vivat, for ever vivat,
Novius doctor, qui tam bene speakat!
Mille, mille annis, et manget et bibat,
Bleedat and killat!

Final ballet

Doctors, surgeons and apothecaries all go out, as they came in, according to their ceremonial rank.

EXPLANATORY NOTES

The School for Wives

1. *Pantagruel to Panurge*: in Rabelais's *Gargantua et Pantagruel* (Book III, ch. 5), Pantagruel gives this answer to Panurge who has spoken in praise of debts.
2. *their mother's ear*: in accordance with Church doctrine, painters traditionally showed Christ entering the Virgin's ear at the same time as the message delivered by the angel at the Annunciation. Agnès confuses the Virgin Birth with the dogma of the Conception *per aurem*.
3. *Arnolphe*: although Saint Arnulphius separated from his wife Scariberge by mutual consent, he had been known since the Middle Ages as the patron saint of deceived husbands.
4. *examples of that sort*. Arnolphe includes himself in the comparison, for he is as ridiculous as Gros-Pierre who is lord of his little island (*île*); *souche* means 'the stump of a tree'. Molière also includes a joke at the expense of Thomas Corneille, younger brother of Pierre, who was known as Monsieur de l'Isle.
5. *A certain Greek once said . . .*: the anecdote appears in the *Opera moralis* of Plutarch (*c.* 46–*c.* 120).
6. *full weight*: loss of weight meant loss of value and could occur by use and, more particularly, by the practice of clipping coins.

The School for Wives Criticized

1. *Place Maubert*: a square east of what would become the 'Latin Quarter', long associated with popular unrest and its unruly student population.
2. *Place Royale*: now the Place des Vosges.
3. *de bon oeil*: 'glad to see you'. Bonneuil is near Charenton.
4. *Damon*: by tradition he is identified as Molière himself.
5. *Palais Royal*: a palace, completed in 1636, built by Cardinal de Richelieu who made a gift of it to Louis XIII in 1639, after which date it gradually ceased to be known as the 'Palais-Cardinal' and became the Palais Royal. Molière's company had been based in its theatre since 1660. It was there that *The School for Wives* was first staged on 26 December 1662.
6. *Attic salt*: elegant, delicately turned wit in the manner of the ancient Athenians. The use of such abstruse expressions, like the taste for images (*craving, insipid, fare, peppered*), was a feature of the preciosity which Molière mocks.
7. *has taken?*: *The School for Wives*, II.v.
8. *sitting down or standing up*: seats on the stage (where men of fashion sat to

be seen) cost half a louis, and boxes more. Fifteen sous was the price of admission to standing room in the pit, filled by a varied crowd (public officials, members of the liberal professions, students, artisans, servants) which could decide the success or failure of a play. Molière preferred the rowdy honesty of the pit to the snobbish reactions of the more fashionable theatre-goers

9. *Marquis de Mascarille*: a pretentious character satirized in *Les Précieuses ridicules* (1659)

10. *syllables indecent*: in precious circles war was waged on certain prefixes and suffixes which were considered unseemly or vulgar. A near-equivalent in English is the reaction of the staider Victorians to words such as titillate, elements of which they found shocking and offensive.

11. *Lysidas, the author*: contemporaries identified Lysidas with a number of authors who had criticized *The School for Wives*. Nowadays the leading contenders are Thomas Corneille (see note 4 to *School for Wives*) and Donneau de Visé, author of a number of published attacks on Molière's play.

12. *quite unprejudiced*: in 1663 Molière was on good terms with the actors of the Théâtre du Marais. Professional rivalry, however, placed a considerable strain on his relations with the players based at the Hôtel de Bourgogne.

13. *serpents*: *The School for Wives*, V.iv.

14. *Cuisinier français*: published in 1659 by La Varenne, the king's chef.

15. *through the ear*: *The School for Wives*, V.iv.

16. *the scene . . . inside the house*: ibid., I.ii

17. *too readily*: ibid., I.iv.

18. *the maxims*: ibid., III.ii.

19. *in the fifth act*: ibid., V.iv.

Don Juan

1. *tobacco*: smoked in pipes or taken as snuff, tobacco had been in use for medicinal and recreational purposes for a century. In 1561 Jean Nicot presented to Catherine de Medici samples of the plant which was first known as Nicotiana. Louis XIII had forbidden its sale but under Colbert it became a state monopoly in 1674. Much had been written for and against the 'stinking habit', though more frequently in England than in France. Similar in spirit to Sganarelle's eulogy is the claim made by Bobadill in Ben Jonson's *Every Man in his Humour* (c. 1598): while in the Indies, he had received 'no other nutriment in the world for the space of one and twenty weeks but the fume of this simple only. Therefore it cannot be but 'tis most divine' (III.v).

2. *swinish Epicurean*: an echo of Horace's self-deprecating description of himself (*Epistles*, 1.4.16) as 'Epicuri de grege porcum'.

3. *Sardanapalus*: a legendary prince of Assyria, remembered for his debauched life.

4. *fuss . . . about antimony*: the use of an emetic based on antimony (a metallic element used in hardening alloys) had been controversial since the early sixteenth century. After considerable opposition from doctors, its use was approved by the Faculty of Medicine and the *Parlement* of Paris in 1666, just a year after the first performance of *Don Juan*.

5. *go to the stake for it*: the passage concerning the Bogey Man ('le Moine bourru'), which in some quarters was thought sacrilegious, was cut after the first performance.

6. *starve to death*: this and the seven preceding exchanges, known as the 'scene with the poor man', were cut after the first performance. At first judged blasphemous, they were restored in the first printed edition of the play in 1682.

7. *an arm-chair*: according to social etiquette, precedence was indicated by seating arrangements. For a tradesman to move from a stool to an arm-chair was honour indeed.

The Miser

1. *limping cur*: Louis Béjart, who played La Flèche, walked with a limp.

2. *eight per cent . . . per annum*: this would not have been lost on contemporary audiences since the legal limit for interest rates was 5%.

3. *her money coming to me*: Harpagon holds his dead wife's estate in trust and is bound by law to account for it to both his children.

4. *Gombaud and Macaea*: a shepherd and shepherdess whose love had for a century been a popular theme for tapestries. Such pastoral subjects had become unfashionable and the sample being offered is clearly worthless.

5. *Pigeon-Holes*: also known in England as Troll-Madam and Nine Holes, a game in which players rolled thirteen balls towards as many holes marked 'win' or 'lose'. 'Snakes and ladders' in the list of games is the nearest English equivalent of the *jeu de l'oie*.

6. *your seedcorn*: Rabelais, *Gargantua et Pantagruel*, Book III, ch. 2.

7. *Grand Turk . . . Venice*: for centuries, the Republic of Venice had been the major opponent of Turkish expansion in the Mediterranean.

8. *the fair*: one of the two great Paris fairs: Saint-Germain (3 February to Palm Sunday) was south of the river, and the Foire Saint-Laurent (28 June–30 September) north of the river.

9. *barley concoctions*: barley was an ingredient in a range of dishes and preparations used by ladies to maintain a fresh complexion and was said to 'fill out the figure'.

10. *Adonis . . . Anchises*: Adonis was the god of spring; Cephalus was the husband of Phocris; Paris, son of Priam, kidnapped Helen and thus began the Trojan Wars; Apollo was the sun God. Saturn, son of Jove, was always represented as an old man; Priam was king of Troy; Nestor, a general in the

Trojan War, was respected for his age and wisdom; Anchises was rescued from the ruins of Troy by his son Aeneas. These heroes from classical mythology were familiar reference points in seventeenth-century literature and art.

11. *main courses*: the following three exchanges, added to the 1682 edition of the play, are still sometimes included in modern performances.

12. *full weight*: see note 6 to *School for Wives*.

13. *the wheel*: a traditional punishment for serious crimes. The criminal was attached to a horizontally hung cartwheel and was literally broken alive by an iron bar wielded by the executioner.

14. *for himself*: here starts a traditional piece of stage-business by which Harpagon snuffs out candles which Maître Jacques, regardless of expense, manages to keep relighting.

15. *driven into exile*: in 1647 a popular revolt against Spanish rule in Naples had been led by a fisherman named Masaniello. It failed, but in the aftermath many aristocratic families fled the city.

The Hypochondriac

1. *Alternative Prologue*: in 1673, the text of the Prologue and the musical interludes was printed. When it was republished the following year, it contained only this shorter Prologue. Both were included in the first, defective edition of *The Hypochondriac* in 1674 and in the version, overseen by La Grange in 1682, which is now accepted as the definitive text.

2. *with counters*: by the widespread system of accounting, tokens representing graduated amounts (demi-sou, i.e. 6 deniers, 1 sou, 10 sous, 1 livre, 5 livres, etc.) were displayed in separate rows so that the running total was visible. Thus, in checking the cost of the julep, Argan first halves the charge of 35 sous, then puts counters in their respective piles as follows: $10 - 5 - 1 - 1 - \frac{1}{2}$, making $17\frac{1}{2}$ sous in all. The remainder of his calculations follow this model.

3. *rosatum, etc., etc.*: the 'detergent injection' (a rectal enema intended to cleanse and clear) consisted of an 'electuary', a preparation of medicinal powders, rose honey (*mel rosatum*) and various kinds of vegetable matter.

4. *julep*: that is, a liver-friendly, tranquillizing, sleep inducing potion, taken orally and prepared from distilled water and a varity of sweet syrups.

5. *bile*: according to the theory of humours, an excess of bile accounted for the choleric temper. The preparation contains cassia (the sweet pulp of the fruit pods of *Cassia fistula*) and senna, also a purgative, prepared from the leaves of several species of cassia: Argan seems to refer to Mecca senna (*Cassia angustifolia*), so called because it was exported through Mecca, in the Levant. Dr Purgon is ironically named, as is the apothecary: *fleurant* is a poetic word meaning 'sweet-smelling'.

6. *carminative*: having anti-flatulent properties.

7. *bezoar*: perhaps animal bezoar made of concretions found in the stomach and intestines of certain animals and accepted by medical opinion as an antidote to poison; or possibly mineral bezoar, derived from antimony, used as an emetic. See note 4 to *Don Juan*.

8. *statue of Memnon*: Memnon, son of Aurora, was killed by Achilles in the Trojan War. After his death a statue was raised to him which emitted a melodious sound at each sunrise when Memnon greeted his mother. The sound was said to resemble the snapping of a harp-string. When the sun set the sound was lugubrious.

9. *circulation of the blood*: William Harvey (1578–1657), discoverer of the circulation of the blood, published *Exercitatio Anatomica de Motu Cordis et Sanguinis* in 1628. His ideas did not find immediate acceptance and were still widely contested when *The Hypochondriac* was performed in 1673. In 1670 and 1672 'anti-circulation' theses were defended in the Faculty of Medicine in Paris.

10. *a woman being dissected*: the bodies of executed criminals had begun to be used for dissection, though the practice was still rare. In 1667 a semi-public dissection performed on the corpse of a woman in the Academy of Sciences in Paris caused an outcry.

11. *learn them*: the first was a nursery rhyme and the second is from La Fontaine's *Fables* (1668), Book I.ii.

12. PRESIDENT: the speeches which follow are written in the kind of burlesque dog-Latin used notably by the Théâtre Italien. Molière injects enough French, Italian and Spanish to make it comprehensible to contemporary audiences. It follows the traditional structure of such speeches: a greeting, praise of medicine, a eulogy of the Faculty of Medicine in Paris, an outline of the purpose of the examination and a peroration on the duties of doctors.

13. *assoupire*: the answer (that opium makes people sleep because it has soporific qualities) is a reflection of authentic responses which claimed that the stomach digests because its has digestive properties, etc.